LOST
VOICES
OF THE
NILE

LOST VOICES
OF THE
NILE

EVERYDAY LIFE IN
ANCIENT EGYPT

CHARLOTTE BOOTH

AMBERLEY

This edition published 2016
First published 2015

Amberley Publishing
The Hill, Stroud
Gloucestershire, GL5 4EP

www.amberley-books.com

British Library Cataloguing in Publication Data.
A catalogue record for this book is available
from the British Library.

ISBN 978 1 4456 6027 1 (paperback)
ISBN 978 1 4456 4298 7 (ebook)

Typesetting and Origination by Amberley
Publishing.
Printed in the UK

All photographs and drawings are by the author
unless otherwise stated.

Dedicated to my mum, who encouraged my love of Egyptology
from a young age.
Margaret Dorothy Hanna
22 April 1939 – 23 May 2014

CONTENTS

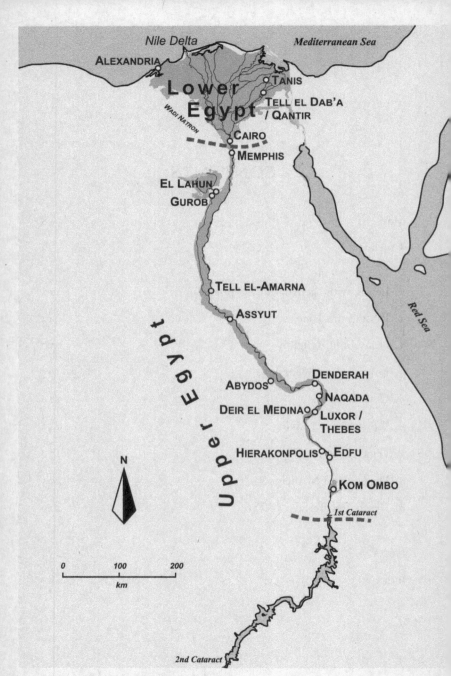

Map of Egypt courtesy of Peter Robinson.

TIMELINE

Pre-Dynastic Period

Before 3150 BCE

Early Dynastic Period

Dynasty 0: 3150–3050 BCE
Dynasty 1: 3050–2890 BCE
Dynasty 2: 2890–2686 BCE

Old Kingdom

Dynasty 3: 2686–2613 BCE
Dynasty 4: 2613–2500 BCE
Dynasty 5: 2498–2345 BCE
Dynasty 6: 2345–2181 BCE

First Intermediate Period

Dynasty 7 and 8: 2180–2160 BCE
Dynasty 9 and 10: 2160–2040 BCE

Middle Kingdom

Dynasty 11: 2134–1991 BCE
Dynasty 12: 1991–1782 BCE

Second Intermediate Period

Dynasty 13: 1782–1650 BCE
Dynasty 14: exact dates unknown
Dynasty 15: 1663–1555 BCE
Dynasty 16: 1663–1555 BCE
Dynasty 17: 1663–1570 BCE

New Kingdom

Dynasty 18: 1570–1293 BCE
Dynasty 19: 1293–1185 BCE
Dynasty 20: 1185–1070 BCE

Third Intermediate period

High Priests (Thebes): 1080–945 BCE
Dynasty 21 (Tanis): 1069–945 BCE
Dynasty 22 (Tanis): 945–715 BCE
Dynasty 23 (Leontopolis): 818–715 BCE
Dynasty 24 (Sais): 727–715 BCE
Dynasty 25 (Nubians): 747–656 BCE
Dynasty 26 (Sais): 664–525 BCE

Late Period

Dynasty 27 (Persian): 525–404 BCE
Dynasty 28: 404–399 BCE
Dynasty 29: 399–380 BCE
Dynasty 30: 380–343 BCE
Dynasty 31: 343–332 BCE

Graeco-Roman Period

Macedonian Kings: 332–305 BCE
Ptolemaic Period: 305–30 BCE

I.

LIVING WITH THE ANCIENT EGYPTIANS

'Seven houses, forty-nine cats, 343 mice.'[1]

In a book of this type, which investigates the everyday lives of the Egyptians, it is easy to present the ancient Egyptians as a homogenous society who were easily categorised into particular behaviours, beliefs and practices. The ancient Egyptian society was as diverse as any modern one, and making generalisations about them is as misleading as making generalisations about a society or nation today. A statement like 'the British eat fish and chips every day' or 'the Spanish enjoy bullfighting' will be followed by a barrage of questions and comments: 'What about the vegetarians?', 'In modern Britain we are more conscious of our health and avoid fried food,' and 'There are many Spaniards who are against animal cruelty.' Any ancient Egyptian reading an average book (including this one) about their 'everyday lives' would no doubt make similar comments and objections. All humans, ancient and modern, are comprised of conflicting emotions and characteristics, and cannot be categorised so simply. We are only able to unravel some of these contradictions of personalities from the evidence available, showing that people in ancient Egypt really were not much different from those in the modern world.

When approaching a book like this we are limited by the available evidence, although with ancient Egypt we are extremely lucky as a great deal of information has been drawn from archaeology, human remains and the written record. However, the majority of evidence only provides information about the top 10 per cent of society: the middle classes, elite and royalty. The majority of ancient Egyptian society, the farmers, peasants and thousands of lower-class women and children, is simply anonymous. Rarely, the name of a servant will be preserved in the tomb of their employer, ensuring they will be available to the tomb owner in the afterlife. One such servant was Ptahsankh, who tended land belonging to the scribe Ramose from Deir el-Medina. In one of Ramose's tomb chapel paintings he is depicted ploughing with West and Beautiful Flood, Ramose's cows. Ptahsankh states, 'The fields are in a good state and their grain will be excellent.'[2]

Most of these anonymous ancient Egyptians lived a pastiche of the life discussed in the following pages, or at best aspired to live such a life. Unfortunately, until the evidence of the lives of the anonymous 90 per cent is found, there is little that can be done to address this imbalance.

In order to truly understand the scale of this imbalance it is essential to understand the structure of ancient Egyptian society. There was a very strict hierarchy, like a pyramid, with the king at the top, followed by a small number of officials, then the middle classes and finally the peasants forming the base of the pyramid. Most of the evidence we have comes from royalty, the elite and the middle classes.

Although there are numerous written texts from ancient Egypt, these refer to an even smaller proportion of the Egyptian society as estimates for literacy range between 1 and 4 per cent.[3] Even for someone holding an elite position in society, such as a vizier or an entrepreneur running a large estate, literacy was not considered essential as any written records could be produced by a professional scribe. Therefore, the number of elite, administrative positions skews the perceived level of literacy in Egypt. It should also be considered that, for the most part, girls were not educated and therefore literate women were unusual, although not unheard of. In some instances where female literacy is discussed, the prejudices of the Egyptologists themselves influence the interpretation of the evidence. For example, in the tomb of Menna (TT69), in Luxor, a scribal kit is depicted under the chair of Menna's wife. If this was under Menna's chair it would automatically be interpreted as evidence of his literacy. However, as it is under his wife's chair some suggest it does not show literacy but is simply a sign of revered status. Even in the case of four Middle Kingdom women who held the title of scribe it is suggested the titles were honorary.[4] However, why this should be the case is never adequately explained.

Whereas illiterate elites could employ the services of a scribe should they need to record something, this may be beyond the financial means of an illiterate labourer. However, such workers were still able to communicate in written form, as is demonstrated by New Kingdom laundry lists. The laundry men at Deir el-Medina each collected clothes from approximately eight households daily to wash along the Nile edge. In order to record what they had collected they drew the items (e.g. loincloths, fringed shawls and tunics), and marked each with a dot corresponding to the number which had been collected.[5] This raises a further issue of a scale of literacy. Does a laundry list constitute literacy or merely communication? Either way, it is just as important to Egyptologists reconstructing the lives of the lower classes and provides an insight into their daily activities.

The most valuable information we have about the day-to-day lives of the ancient Egyptian community can be found in their villages, and excavations have uncovered a number of villages, including (but not limited to) the Middle Kingdom town of El-Lahun (Kahun), the Second Intermediate Period city of Tell el-Dab'a and the New Kingdom towns of Deir el-Medina and Tell el-Amarna.

There are two types of village structure: the organic and the purpose built. Deir el-Medina is an example of a purpose-built village, constructed to house the workmen who built the Valley of the Kings. It was constructed as a single project within a non-expandable village wall, and the only adjustments made were within the designated footprint of each of the houses within the wall. On the other hand, Tell el-Dab'a was an organic town which was first inhabited in the Middle Kingdom and expanded until it was elevated to capital city during the Second Intermediate Period, and again during the reign of Ramses II (1279–1212 BCE) when it was known as Pi-Ramses.

El-Lahun was originally built to house the workmen who constructed the pyramid of Senusret II (1897–1878 BCE) in the Middle Kingdom, and is the largest known settlement from this period. It was originally called Hetep-Senusret ('Senusret is Satisfied') and had an approximate ground-plan of 260 x 260 metres square. Initially it housed the workmen and their families, and once the pyramid was complete it housed the priests who maintained Senusret II's funerary cult.

The village was surrounded by an enclosure wall, and the streets and houses were laid out in regular lines and arranged so the western block, which was on higher ground, could be guarded by a single watchman. This western area was divided from the eastern block by a large mud-brick wall, and there is some discussion as to whether the two sides of the settlement were able to communicate with each other.

The western block was comprised of back-to-back terraced houses.[6] Although they were unable to deviate from the basic footprint of their home, the inhabitants renovated their houses within the basic external walls to accommodate their family needs, to the extent that they sometimes bought the house next door and knocked through.

The streets were wide in El-Lahun, some as much as five metres across and the side streets between three and four metres wide.[7] Evidence of channels between the houses was discovered by Petrie, which were used to drain water from flash floods and household waste. This is the earliest known drainage system of this type and Petrie assumed all settlements had such systems.

To the west end of the northern extreme of the town was an elevated platform which Petrie called the acropolis, or 'high city'.[8] This platform accommodated a large, palatial house, which he thought may have housed the guards when the king visited; others believe it to be an administrative centre, religious building or even the home of the mayor. There were also a number of large, palatial buildings (42 by 60 metres) to the east of this palace and it seems that some of the highest officials in the land lived here. This could have included the vizier, treasurer and secretary of royal documents. It is suggested that these large houses are better described as urban estates, which acted as administrative and economic hubs in the city, accommodating the needs of the family as well as serving a business function.[9] There also seems to have been a prison in the city, although this is thought to be situated in the part of the settlement now lost.[10]

During the New Kingdom reign of Amenhotep III (1386–1349 BCE), El-Lahun was re-inhabited, although only the western workman's village was reoccupied and there were many abandoned buildings. At this time the temple of Senusret II was being dismantled in order to reuse the blocks, and the reoccupation may have been related to this project. In the Roman Period, when the area was dug for limestone, the town was once more temporarily occupied.[11]

The village of Deir el-Medina has provided most of the information we have about New Kingdom daily life. It was called 'The Place of Truth' and was built to house the workmen who carved and decorated the Valley of the Kings. Situated on the west bank of the Nile, at Luxor, away from Theban life, it comprised a village, temples, chapels and an extensive cemetery with more than 400 tombs. The inhabitants here were therefore socially isolated and reliant on the government for staples (food and water), which were transported to the village on a daily basis. However, they were not prisoners, and moved freely to the markets on the east bank and visited relatives in other parts of the country.

They were kept informed of what was happening in the wider world by messengers coming to the village. For example, in 'year one, first month of winter, day sixteen, the scribe Paser came with good news, saying "Sety II has arisen as ruler"'.[12] Although many of these messengers were anonymous, one, Amenemheb, was the father of Ramose, who was to become the scribe at Deir el-Medina during the reign of Ramses II (we learnt about his cows above). Amenemheb was responsible for carrying messages and reports between the officials of Thebes[13] and clearly educated his son in administration, enabling him to rise to such an important position.

Of course, such a message system meant the villagers were reliant on the government and scribes for accurate information, and there was always the danger of information being censored or spun.

The village which now stands was initially constructed during the reign of Thutmose I (1524–1518 BCE), although most of the surviving evidence is from the nineteenth and twentieth dynasties, when the village was at its prime. Although Deir el-Medina was built as a single project, over the centuries houses were extended, knocked through or remodelled, all within the non-expanding enclosure wall. The absentee record shows that workmen took days off work in order to construct or decorate their houses. One entry claims Paneb paid the draftsman one sack of an unknown produce 'for the construction work he did in my house; a workroom and another wall'.[14]

Deir el-Medina remained inhabited for over 400 years, with only a brief abandonment during the reign of Akhenaten, when the capital city moved to Tell el-Amarna (see below). The village comprised approximately sixty-eight houses and housed only the tomb workmen and their families. Workmen included sculptors, engravers, coppersmiths, carpenters, plaster-makers and masons.[15] Auxiliary staff serving the village, such as wood cutters, fishermen, carriers of vegetables and gardeners, lived outside the walls. The original village had one main street running north to south, with smaller narrow alleys running between the houses. These alleys may have been covered with reeds, providing shade from the sun. Each house had its own water jar, and records show each family received between 96 and 115 litres per day. It is likely that water carriers delivered the water to a centralised water storage point and the families collected it from here.

Both Ramses III (1182–1151 BCE) and later Ramses VI (1141–1133 BCE) tried unsuccessfully to dig a well on the northern edge of Deir el-Medina. The hole that remains is 52 metres deep, and when it was clear they were not going to reach water it was slowly filled up with rubbish and ostraca (fragments of limestone or pottery used as notepaper). These ostraca have proved essential to our understanding of New Kingdom daily life, as they include information on economic transactions, letters, administrative records, humour and literary texts. The written evidence coupled with the archaeological evidence of the houses, tombs and household items means we are often able to recreate the life of named individuals, know where they lived and where they were buried and are able to hold their possessions.

An extremely fragmentary papyrus from the village, currently in the Turin Museum, lists the occupancy of thirteen houses. It is surprising that none of the houses list more than five people living in them and there are seven houses occupied by single men. It is not clear why such a census was compiled, although it has been suggested it was connected with ration distribution or a wider monitoring of the village inhabitants. This list has proven interesting, as it outlines some of the social dynamics within the town. For example, Thutmosis, son of Khaemhedje, lived only two doors away from his sister Tenetpaip and her husband Amennakhte. More interesting is Tarekhan, who lived in her husband's house and then moved to the house of her son and his wife,[16] perhaps following her husband's death or maybe even their divorce.

The cemetery serving Deir el-Medina was situated in the western cliffs and is particularly interesting. The tombs were constructed by the craftsmen who cut and decorated the royal tombs, but less rigidity in the artwork means scenes of daily life dominate over religious imagery.

The men residing at Deir el-Medina all had a role to play in the construction of the royal tomb, so during the week all except the elderly and very young were absent from the village, working in the Valley of the Kings on the other side of mountain. The working week was eight days long and the men were absent from the village for this duration,[17] before coming home for a two-day weekend. The workmen were divided into two gangs, the left side and the right side, although how this connected to their placement in the tomb is uncertain. It is assumed the right side gang was responsible for working on the right side of the tomb, and the left side gang on the left side of the tomb.[18] There was one foreman on each side, and like most occupations in Egypt it was hereditary, meaning it was common for one family to hold the position for many generations.

The foreman and the chief scribe acted as intermediaries between the workmen and the government, as well as keeping extremely detailed records of the workmen and their movements. From these records we learn that some roles were worked in shifts, such as doorkeeper, and one of the records states, 'There was no doorkeeper here [today] except Psarpot, for Sanehem slept and the doorkeeper Sunero came only at noon.'[19]

Roles were sometimes filled by newcomers to the village, and conversely there were often more children than jobs. As only one son could take the role of his father, the other sons no doubt left the village to gain employment elsewhere.

While the workmen were away from the village, working in the Valley of the Kings, they constructed a small village of workmen's huts near the tomb within which they were working. These huts were not houses, as they were only 1.5 metres by 1.7 metres and were made of stone without mortar. There is evidence of cooking and the remains of fish bones, as well as the bones of two domestic cats, indicating this was where the workmen rested, ate, prepared tools and completed portable work for the tomb.[20]

There were also a number of small guard huts, where the guards sat and kept watch on the entrances and paths into the Valley of the Kings twenty-four hours a day. The tombs were always at threat from tomb robbers, as were the storage huts that housed the tools needed by the workmen, as these were a valuable commodity.[21]

From this small, temporary village in the Valley of the Kings there were hundreds of ostraca fragments, including workmen's lists and letters, as well as images of tomb art to be rendered within the tomb. Evidence suggests the workmen were also making limestone jewellery moulds at the site, which were then sent to the jewellery workshops.[22] Whether this was official work or a way to while away a lunch break is unknown.

One of these small huts belonged to the village scribe, who was on the same level as the foreman and was responsible for tomb administration: recording absences from work, the number of tools distributed (and returned) and general work progression, which he passed to the vizier and ultimately to the king. This role was also hereditary. The scribe and the foreman were the highest-paid positions in the village.

With no monetary system in Egypt, wages came in the form of rations, which included fish, vegetables, water, wood for fuel, pottery for household use and sometimes clothing. On festival days the workmen received extra rations, including sesame oil, blocks of salt, natron (a natural salt from the Wadi Natron) and even oxen. Rations provided enough food to feed a large family, plus a little extra to use as currency. Marketplaces worked on a barter system, where items of clothing, food, animals, shoes, beer and even services were swapped for other items. Each item had a relative market value, which varied depending on demand. As long as the seller and the buyer were happy with the exchange it did not matter if the items were not equal in market value. As people did not necessarily visit the marketplace with all the items a seller may require, credit was often given between friends, relatives and neighbours, although from the legal records it seems these credit notes were not always paid.

There was no word in ancient Egyptian for 'market' and it was not a major aspect of the Egyptian economy, but they were essential for local economy and, in particular, social interaction. An experimental archaeology project carried out in 2009 demonstrated that the most successful people in the reconstructed marketplace were those who were more sociable, happy to converse and willing to argue over a price. Shy people were easily sold items at inflated prices, or were unable to persuade others to buy their goods, essentially rendering them worthless.[23]

The main village of Deir el-Medina also housed a number of small, homemade chapels to the north of the site. These were financed, built, decorated, maintained and serviced by the people in the village for the worship of local deities as well as acting as social clubs and meeting areas.[24]

Deir el-Medina was abandoned as a village at the end of the

twenty-first dynasty, primarily because of security concerns after attacks by Libyans from the western desert. The villagers left Deir el-Medina for the security of the temple complex at Medinet Habu, meaning the village houses were then only used for storage.

The eighteenth-dynasty city of Tell el-Amarna, or Akhetaten as it was then known, was built during the reign of Akhenaten (1350–1334 BCE), who decided he wanted a new city to dedicate to his favoured god, the Aten, on a site which had not been used previously to worship any other deity. 'Behold, it is Pharaoh who found it – but being the property of a god, not being the property of a goddess, not being the property of a male ruler, not being the property of a female ruler, and not being the property of any people.'²⁵ This city, although built as a singular project, is different from Deir el-Medina or El-Lahun, as the palace forms the centre of the main settlement. This centre also included temples and military barracks, but no evidence has been found of shops, taverns or schools, so these activities may instead have taken place within the homes or open spaces. The houses expanded to the north and south from this centre, each forming a small village-like area centred on a large official house. The cemetery was built on the periphery of the town.

The elite tombs in this cemetery are different from others in Egypt, as the religious imagery is replaced with images of Akhenaten and the royal family. It is the only time in Egyptian history where the tomb owner is not the dominant figure in the tomb. Instead, he is always presented as a small figure in relation to the king, who is seen favouring him with golden jewellery from the Window of Appearances.

The city boundaries were marked by sixteen boundary stelae carved in years five, six and eight of Akhenaten's reign. They outlined the outer limits of the city and were a method unique to Amarna. The texts on the stelae discuss the founding of the city and the intended buildings as well as describing some of the problems

Akhenaten may have faced in Thebes. Akhenaten does not specify what these problems were but states he no longer wanted to listen to the 'evil words', which was his reason for moving the capital. The inscription is believed to be a verbatim record of one of the king's speeches:

> It was worse than those things I heard in regnal year four,
> It was worse than those things I heard in regnal year three,
> It was worse than those things I heard in regnal year two,
> It was worse than those things I heard in regnal year one,
> It was worse than those things Nebmaatre (Amenhotep III) heard,
> It was worse than those things which ... heard,
> It was worse than those things Menkheperure (Thutmosis III) heard,
> And it was worse than those things I heard by any kings who had
> ever assumed the White Crown (ruler of the south).[26]

The city was divided into quarters, or suburbs, and communal wells were placed in public squares or were shared between several houses. There was also a sculptors' quarter and a workman village, similar to Deir el-Medina, with seventy-two houses placed in the desert to the east of the city in six orderly, parallel rows.

The houses at the workman village all appear to have an upper storey and, although they were unable to change the footprint of the house, should the occupants need it they were able to expand upwards or downwards. The upstairs of these houses were used for the bedrooms, and the front room of the house served as an area of 'cottage industry', with food preparation, weaving, metalworking and stone bowl production carried out here.[27] Outside the walls of the workman village at Amarna were subsidiary buildings for their use, including chapels, animal pens and a central square.[28] It was to this square that the rations and weekly supplies were delivered, and in other villages such squares may have been important for public activities such as celebrations, information gathering or public trials and executions (see chapter seven). Unfortunately these activities, as well as the spaces themselves, are not easily identified in the archaeological record.

The workman village at Tell el-Amarna was cramped, dirty and unhygienic. Evidence of rats, fleas and bed bugs has been identified and such living conditions were a breeding ground for tuberculosis and parasitic infections. It is thought that fleas travelling on the Nile rats were responsible for the European bubonic plague, and evidence suggests that near the end of the reign of Akhenaten Amarna suffered an epidemic, killing many members of the royal family in a short space of time.

Rats were not just a problem at Amarna, as at the village of El-Lahun Petrie discovered the earliest rat trap. It is a pottery box with slits in the side and a slideable end that can be raised in order to allow the rat to enter and lowered to prevent it escaping. Petrie commented that 'nearly every room has its corners tunnelled by the rats, and the holes are stuffed up with stones and rubbish to keep them back'.[29] It is quite likely that with the large number of rats at Lahun there were numerous cats at the village as well.

Evidence indicates that pigs were kept in the workman village at Amarna, as well as at Elephantine, Tell el-Dab'a and Memphis.[30] It is often stated that the Egyptians did not eat pork, but such evidence suggests they were either farmed or domestically raised. They may have been kept for waste disposal, although evidence of parasitic worms in mummies contracted through eating undercooked, infected pork indicates that pork was eaten (see chapter eight).

Between 50,000 and 100,000 people lived in the main city at Tell el-Amarna during the height of Akhenaten's reign, 10 per cent of which were elite. The wealth of the homeowners was reflected in the size and grandeur of the houses. The two main residential areas were the north and south suburbs, which housed up to 90 per cent of the total population.

The southern suburb contained approximately 2,000 houses – as well as workshops, which highlight the area as one of industry and manufacture – and housed 50 per cent of the population of Amarna.[31] It seemed to be comprised of various residential areas for different social groups, as there were rich, palatial homes alongside the small houses of the poorer classes. The most famous workshop located here was that of the sculptor Thutmose, in whose workshop the famous bust of Nefertiti was discovered. This suburb also housed High Priests of Aten and Viziers, and was therefore primarily an area for the rich and influential.

The northern suburb was made up of approximately 600 houses and seemed to be divided into industry quarters, with one section being associated with fishing – as indicated by the number of hooks and fish-related products discovered there – and others associated with carpentry and clerical work. The houses were smaller than in the southern suburb and there were not as many palatial homes.[32]

The third suburb was the royal suburb, in the northern part of the city, which housed the North Palace, the North Riverside Palace and the administrative buildings.

This grandiose city of Tel el Amarna was short lived and was quickly abandoned following Akhenaten's death. Tutankhamun (1334–1325 BCE) returned the capital city to Thebes and the majority of people left Amarna, leaving only a couple of faience factories still in use. By the end of the reign of Horemheb (1321–1293 BCE) these were also abandoned and the stone blocks reused elsewhere, leaving the city to the sands.

Although there were variations between settlements, the house layout and size was similar across the different villages. In the modern world, we are used to, and even expect, a certain amount of space, with rooms for designated activities (e.g. bedroom, kitchen, bathroom or office), and in the West most people expect a separate bedroom for every individual or couple living in the home. In ancient Egypt this was unheard of and the houses were often small and, to the modern mind, cramped.

The houses at Deir el-Medina were very similar to the workman houses at other villages. They were only one storey high, with a staircase at the rear leading to a flat roof used for storage, a sleeping area or a place to dry meat or hang washing. Poorer families used the roofs more often than richer families, who had more square metres within the house itself. One house at Amarna even had an oven on the roof, showing this area was utilised as a cooking space. As the streets and alleys at ground level at Deir el-Medina were narrow, cramped and no doubt crowded with people, animals and overspill from the houses, it may have been possible to navigate across the village using some of these roofs.[33]

Houses at Amarna are thought to have had an upper floor instead of simply a flat roof, although as only the foundations survive it is difficult to ascertain the likelihood of this. However, examination of the walls at Deir el-Medina proves them to be too thin to support a second storey,[34] whereas at Tell el-Amarna it was possible. On the flat roofs, simple, temporary reed structures may have been placed to provide extra sleeping or work space, as can still be seen in modern Egypt.

Across all settlements the majority of the houses had cellars, which were used for valuable storage space, and in some instances the burial of young children. The lack of storage space at Tell el-Amarna encouraged the inhabitants to encroach into the street, and some homes had brick mangers, water pots and awnings outside their homes.[35]

Egyptian houses were constructed of mud-brick on stone-rubble foundations. Mud-bricks were made by mixing Nile mud with water, which was poured into wooden brick moulds and left in the sun to dry. This method is still used in Egypt today. The outside of the house was whitewashed and the front door painted red, which was seen as a colour of divine protection and therefore protected the house from potentially dangerous forces.[36] The wooden door frames bore the names of the inhabitants in red ink, identifying who lived there in the absence of street names. This did not prevent letters and notes from going astray, and one villager tried to defend himself against the accusations of a woman by claiming he never received her note:

> As for the matters of illness about which you write me, what have I done against you? As for the medication which you mentioned, did you write me about them, and did I fail to give them to you? As Ptah endures, and as Thoth endures, I have not heard from anyone: it was not told to me.

Many of the smaller houses only had four rooms, the first opening onto the street and the rest laid out as one long corridor. To enter the first room there were a couple of steps leading down from the street level.

The dominant feature in the first room was often an enclosed box-bed built onto one of the walls. Some believe they may have been used as a marital bed and many clay models of women emphasising fertility were discovered in these structures. Bernard Bruyère, who excavated at Deir el-Medina (1922–1951), believes the box-beds and feminine figurines emphasise the important cult of the family in the home and in this room in particular. The box-beds were approximately 1.7 metres long, 80 centimetres wide and 75 centimetres tall. This has led to the suggestion that this structure was like a play pen, providing somewhere safe to put the babies and toddlers while the mother pottered around the house.[37] Their size, coupled with the fact that some were decorated with images of Bes and Taweret (see chapter three), indicates they were more than likely used as shrines to these deities. Furthermore, the shrine housing statues of deities and ancestors was also located in this room in the home.

In eight houses from Deir el-Medina images of Bes were discovered in this first room, in addition to painted scenes of women breastfeeding, and this has led some scholars to believe this was the room used for giving birth[38] with the box-bed functioning as a birthing bed. However, evidence shows women in ancient Egypt gave birth squatting on two bricks, which would not have been possible in such a cramped space. Additionally, as this room was reached directly from the street it seems too public for something so personal and potentially life-threatening. There can be little doubt, however, that the decoration in these rooms had a feminine theme, indicating this was a room closely associated with women. For example, in the house of Nebamun, at Deir el-Medina, on the wall of his first room was painted a nude musician playing a double lute surrounded by Convolvulus leaves, a plant steeped in erotic overtones. These images were obvious to anyone entering the house, indicating that sexuality was considered a legitimate, public and acceptable element of daily life.

The decoration of the second room was far more masculine than the first room. This room led off the first and was reached by steps leading upwards, once more making the floor level with the street outside. The room was dominated by a large platform used as a seating area during the day and a bed at night. This divan was painted white and had armrests that were flared at the top, like a column capital, and painted yellow, red and white. Nearby was a small hearth. It is believed this divan was where the men of the house conducted business and met with visitors.[39]

In houses built on bedrock, beneath this divan a cellar was dug for extra storage space. A false door stela, painted or carved onto one of the walls, dedicated to a favourite deity or ancestor, allowed the spirits to enter the house and participate in daily activities. There was often a wooden pillar on a stone base in this room and the ceiling was higher than both the third and the first rooms, leading some to suggest this was to accommodate window grills at the top of the walls which provided light and fresh air.[40]

Leading from this room was the third room, which served as a work-area, storeroom and sleeping area for female members of the household. Often craftsmen used this room to work on private commissions, which they sold to increase their household income. This room was therefore a transient room which was able to accommodate the needs of the family, who utilised it as they needed to.

The kitchen was at the rear of the house in a walled but open area with a clay oven and occasionally a silo for storing grain. There was no ceiling but shade was provided by reed matting laid over the walls. Although the kitchen was outside, beams in the Amarnan houses were black with smoke from lamps, indicating that the houses in general were poorly ventilated; this led to a condition called anthracosis where soot settles in the lungs, causing breathing difficulties. Further cellar space was dug beneath the perimeter walls of these kitchens, where food could be stored in a relatively cool environment.

Although the workman houses were compact, with some of the smallest houses at El-Lahun measuring only 8 by 7.5 metres – which was enough for two main rooms and two smaller rooms with a corridor between them – there were at times three generations living in them. Families on average had ten children, and unmarried female relatives and ill or elderly relatives may have lived together in the family home. A study of the population at Deir el-Medina has shown that in a thirty-house sample between 42 and 43 per cent of the population were children.[41]

In addition to the human inhabitants, many households also had cats for rodent control, a guard or hunting dog, some ducks or geese (for eggs and meat) and goats (for milk). The stela of Wah-Ankh Intef II (eleventh dynasty) lists and names five of his dogs, immortalising them for eternity. Although it is not clear exactly when the Egyptians domesticated the hunting dog, they appear in graves with humans from the Pre-Dynastic Period; the first dynasty queen Herneith had her pet dog buried at the entrance to her tomb, protecting her for eternity.[42] Royalty continued to have dogs throughout the pharaonic period and a mummified dog found in the Valley of the Kings is thought to have belonged to Amenhotep II. Tutankhamun is also depicted hunting with his hounds on the side of the painted chest discovered in his tomb.

Furthermore, dogs were the pet of choice for many officials in the New Kingdom. Maiheperi, the Nubian solider buried in the Valley of the Kings, had numerous decorated dog collars in his tomb, one inscribed with the name Taentniwet (She of the Town (Thebes)). The chief of police under Akhenaten, Mahu, is depicted in his tomb next to his pet dog. The discovery of a veterinary papyrus from El-Lahun shows just how common dogs were in the households of ancient Egyptian villages.[43] While hunting was the main purpose of having a dog, they were also used to guard flocks and crops from wild animals.[44] In total the names of seventy-seven dogs are known, and sometimes their name gives a clue about their role. A twelfth dynasty dog from Asyut was called He Is a Shepherd, and others were called The Good Watcher, The Little Woofer,[45] Ebony and Brave One.[46]

The domestic cat was equally common in ancient Egypt and the ancient Egyptian word for cat was *miw*, in reference to the noise they make. Egyptians were possibly the first nation to domesticate cats, and this could be why Egypt is often synonymous with them. The earliest evidence of a cat being buried with a human is from the Badarian Period (4000 BCE), although it is thought it was a tame wildcat rather than a fully domesticated pet.[47] However, more compelling evidence was discovered at Hierakonpolis, where two adults and four kittens were buried together in a pit dated 3800–3600 BCE.[48] Investigations of the mandible and cranium size have led scholars to believe they were domestic cats. Additionally, the kittens were not from the same litter, and the adult female cat was not old enough to have given birth, indicating they were not a family unit. However, the relationship of the male adult cat to the rest is unknown, and his being the father of the kittens cannot be eliminated. In order for all six of them to be sacrificed at the same time, at least four captures were made – adult male and female and two lots of kittens – in a short space of time, indicating they were more than likely already in captivity. Furthermore, the pit where the cats were buried was near other, contemporary pits containing a juvenile baboon and nine dogs, both adult and sub-adult, indicating they were all domesticated or at least living in captivity.

The first evidence in a tomb painting of a fully domesticated cat is from the eleventh dynasty. A twelfth-dynasty burial has the skeletons of seventeen cats and a number of jars which may have contained milk offerings for them, indicating they were expected to survive the afterlife. They were no doubt attracted to the villages and then tolerated in the home as rat- and mouse-catchers; in the Rhind Mathematical Papyrus a problem starts with 'seven houses, forty-nine cats, 343 mice'.[49] There is also the suggestion that cats were trained to help their master hunt in the marshes by fetching the birds that he had felled with his throw-stick. However, this is pure conjecture and anyone who has tried to train a cat to fetch knows it would be easier to fetch the birds yourself.

Most of the cat owners, identified in the tombs by a cat seated beneath their chair, nibbling a fish, eating fruit or sleeping, were women. The tomb of Ipuy (TT17), however, shows a young kitten seated on the tomb owner's lap, pawing at the sleeve of his tunic, while its mother is beneath the chair of his wife. Unlike dogs, most cats do not seem to have had proper names, although perhaps this is down the archaeological record rather than social practice. There is only one New Kingdom incident where the cat's name, The Pleasant One, is known.

Early evidence at Deir el-Medina shows cattle also lived within the village enclosure wall. Even in the palatial houses at El-Lahun, enclosed areas and feeding troughs indicate livestock were housed near the large, central courtyards. Rich houses, therefore, no doubt smelt as bad as the poorer ones. Large cattle, or oxen, were primarily kept for milk; small cattle, sheep and goats were kept for their milk and fleece. When they became too old, they were slaughtered for meat.

Palatial houses were not present at Deir el-Medina but can be found at all other villages. These houses were often north-facing to take advantage of the cooling northern winds. However, if this was not possible a corridor led from the less-than-ideal entrance to a second, north-facing entrance. The interiors of these houses were often complicated, with numerous rooms and corridors designed to confuse visitors and therefore impress them by the size and complexity of the house. The house of Nakht, the overseer of public works at Tell el-Amarna, for example, had thirty rooms, a large columned reception hall and a garden with an offering table to make open-air offerings to the Aten. Columns were a sign of wealth and villas at Tell el-Amarna and El-Lahun had large, columned rooms designed to impress. Even in small workman houses they often had a wooden column painted to look like stone in the second room.

Large houses were divided into suites, often comprising small, three-roomed apartments with a reception room, bedroom and side-room, perhaps used as a dressing room or storeroom. These suites housed the women, guests and administrative staff. All the suites were centred round an open courtyard with a southern, covered colonnade. It is possible these courtyards may also have had trees or a central pool for bathing and may have contained fish and ducks. Some New Kingdom tomb images show the tomb owner seated by one of these pools with a small fishing rod, passing the time in a relaxing manner. It is even thought that fruit trees and vegetables may have been grown in planters and pots in this area, providing fresh food for the family that they could consume or sell. It is near these courtyards that animal pens have been discovered.

At Tell el-Amarna the main difference between a worker's house and an elite villa, other than size, was the inclusion of specific rooms designated as bedrooms, some with ensuite bathrooms. In Deir el-Medina the living spaces were used as sleeping spaces at night, and people washed in the Nile or with a bowl of water. Large houses at Tell el-Amarna, however, had purpose-built beds, whereas smaller homes used bedrolls to sleep on. As beds were expensive and a sign of status it was perhaps unheard of to share one, and indeed only single beds have been discovered.[50] Most people used headrests made of wood, stone or clay in place of pillows or cushions. These were T-shaped structures with a slightly curved edge on the T-bar, into which the neck was placed. They were often decorated with images of Bes and Taweret, who protected the sleeper throughout the night. In ancient Egypt, sleeping was considered a dangerous time when individuals were vulnerable and open to attack from demons and the restless dead, so the protection of household deities was considered essential.

Dreams were considered important as they were believed to be messages from the gods. The Dream Interpretation Book by the scribe Kenherkhopshef from Deir el-Medina gives a wonderful insight into the concerns of the ancient Egyptian villagers. Their dreams covered a number of activities: seeing something or eating and drinking (either too much or not enough) were the most common dreams; others dreamt of everyday activities, from weaving, brewing and pickling to copulation.[51] Gain and loss was a particular theme, such as receiving a house, wealth or a wife, or losing something through robbery, taxation or the calamity of being an orphan.[52] The Egyptians were also concerned with starvation or violent deaths, indicating this was perhaps something that was a distinct possibility in their world. On the other hand, other dreams reflected aspects of life which were thought to be pleasant, such as 'sitting with the villagers' or having 'gossip about you cease', something almost everyone can relate to.

Villas and palaces sometimes had ensuite, stone-lined shower rooms comprising a stone slab where the bather stood as a servant poured water over him. The water drained away through stone channels. Two examples can be seen at the palace of Ramses III at Medinet Habu. Nakht's house at Amarna also had a separate WC with whitewashed walls, one of which may have contained the earliest lavatory stool – a U-shaped stone seat, beneath which a bowl filled with sand was placed. Several tombs have also yielded stools with large holes carved in the seat, which could have been used in the same way.[53] Those not lucky enough to have an inside lavatory went outside. This no doubt attracted flies to the villages.

Many houses, regardless of size, had a doorkeeper's room, ensuring all visitors were vetted and announced. In the smaller houses it is likely that a child or elder sat here, rather than a paid member of staff, and instead of a designated room it may have simply been a low stool. This would have stood as the first line of home security. Door bolts and keys have been found at El-Lahun, suggesting it was possible to lock your home, but security was still clearly a concern. A letter from a woman at Deir el-Medina requests her friend house-sit while she is away: 'Please have Amenemwia dwell in my house so he can keep an eye on it.'[54]

For the majority of people, the home was the central place in their lives, and not just somewhere where they slept at the end of the day. Although in Deir el-Medina the workmen were away for days at a time, for the women, children, elderly and infirm the home was essentially their world. These homes were places for food preparation, dining, sleeping, workshop production, cottage farming and worship. The houses were busy hubs, with people coming and going. A woman spent the majority of the time in the rear of the house producing food for the family and for market, and it is possible that for laborious jobs like grinding grain friends got together and worked as a group to help the time pass more quickly.

As houses varied according to status and wealth, so did the daily diet of the ancient Egyptians. Archaeological, written and artistic evidence makes it possible to identify the food available. Food left in tombs for the deceased to enjoy was often in a raw, uncooked state, so we can only guess at how these ingredients were combined to make a meal. Moreover, food left in a funerary context was not the same quality or quantity consumed on a daily basis, which is evidenced by the absence of fish and pork in these contexts. It is well attested that both were eaten in the villages on a regular basis.

The staple food of the Egyptian diet was bread made from emmer wheat or barley, and there were over forty types of bread available.[55] The finer bread was made from wheat and is generally found in tombs. There were different-shaped loaves, indicating different ingredients. For example, sticky fruit bread in the Dokki Agricultural Museum, Cairo, was made with mashed dates between two layers of dough. Other loaves were rolled in cumin or sesame seeds, and could be coarse, fine, olive or fruit bread; often the dough was enriched with fat, milk, and eggs. Many loaves appear to have a hole in the centre, which could be to fill with jam or paste, or could simply be where the bread was pushed into the oven using a stick. Palm fruit or dates were made into a type of jam and used for flavouring or was spread on festival bread – a fine quality bread for special occasions.

Some bread was made in clay moulds which were put in the oven to cook. Often these broke when the loaf was removed, leaving only fragments in the archaeological record. Some complete moulds, however, were found in foundation deposits of temples, enabling the shape of the bread to be identified. The most common was a type of flatbread which is still made in Egypt today, and is made in the same way without the need for moulds.

Egyptian bread was very bad for the teeth, as the grain from which it was made was ground in sandstone querns and contained lots of stone grit and dust, which filled the air in Egypt at all times. This could enter the bread at any stage of production. All mummies have very worn teeth and this is often blamed on high grit levels in the bread (see chapter eight). In 1972, Leek carried out experiments on thirteen loaves of bread and discovered there were numerous inorganic particles embedded in the crumb. These were primarily desert quartzite sand, but also included other minerals, some several millimetres wide. It was suggested that as the bread that has survived in the archaeological record is from a funerary context, less care was taken in production as it was not intended for human consumption.[56] The general grain process included many levels of sieving, which eliminated any large inclusions, but this was clearly not carried out for the funerary bread. The sand present in the bread is likely to be wind-blown or from the querns when grinding flour,[57] and it has been demonstrated there was no need to add sand to the flour to aid grinding.

The other main staple was beer, made from the previous day's stale bread or partially cooked, fresh bread. The water in Egypt was unsafe to drink, so weak beer was drunk by everyone, including children. The beer was thicker and more nourishing than modern beer and needed to be strained through a sieve before consuming. It was often flavoured with fruit, primarily dates.

Wine was also popular in ancient Egypt. Egyptian wine was best drunk young, only a year or two after the grape harvest. A receipt from Deir el-Medina shows that the scribe Neferhotep paid twice the cost of barley beer for a jug of wine, showing it was an expensive commodity.[58] Studies carried out on six of the twenty-six wine jars from Tutankhamun's tomb by a Spanish team in 2006 showed all of them contained tartaric acid, a chemical produced by grapes. Five jars, however, did not contain syringic acid, which develops in aged red wine, suggesting they were white wine. This was unusual as white wine is not recorded in Egypt until the third century CE, indicating these were very special jars.

There were different quality wines, such as wine for offerings, wine for taxes, wine for merrymaking and a very popular heated wine called *shedeh,* which is often said to have been made from pomegranates flavoured with spices. However, analysis on residues in amphorae labelled as *shedeh* show it was in fact red grape based, although classified as separate from wine.[59] What the difference was is not yet clear.

Some wine and beer was flavoured with dom palm fruit, which tastes of gingerbread. These fruits are hard and woody and need to be soaked in order to extract the flavour. A label on a jar from the Malkata vineyard claims the wine within was 'blended', indicating they were also combining different grapes to produce different-flavoured wines.

The Theban region in the New Kingdom was well known for wine production and many tombs from the Valley of the Nobles show the vineyards and wine production in action. The Delta region and the Fayuum were also famous for their vineyards.

With such alcohol consumption Egyptians were known to get drunk, and in year 40 of Ramses III the absentee record from Deir el-Medina shows a man called Pendua took a day off work because he was drinking with Khons. Iyerniutef simply said he was 'drinking' and could not attend work on the royal tomb that day.

One notorious Deir el-Medina inhabitant, Paneb, was accused of behaving badly when drunk. On one occasion, just after Sety II's mummy had been placed in the sarcophagus, Paneb, drunk, climbed atop the sarcophagus – a shocking action as the king was considered to be a god incarnate. He was also accused of falling into rages and was threatening to kill not only his adopted father, Neferhotep, but also the foreman, Hay.

Charge concerning his [Paneb] running after the Chief workman, Neferhotep, although it was him who reared him. And he [Neferhotep] closed his doors before him, and he [Paneb] took a stone and broke his doors. And they caused men to watch over Neferhotep because he [Paneb] said 'I will kill him in the night.'[60]

It took a number of guards to drag the enraged Paneb away from his adopted father's door, and they stood watch just in case he returned. Unfortunately what the argument was about will remain a mystery. He also made a similar death threat to another foreman, Hay, by saying, 'I will get you in the mountains and kill you.' However, yet again he does not appear to have carried out the threat and this may also have been the result of a drinking binge. A further accusation against him was actually of murder, although he was not charged with it: 'He is keeping well although he is like a madman. Yet it was he who killed those men that they might not bring a message to pharaoh. Lo, I have caused the vizier to know about his way of life.'[61] Unfortunately the papyrus cuts off at this point, so if any more information was available about this murder it is lost to us.

The 'Instruction of Ani' (twenty-first or twenty-second dynasty) warns against such behaviour. 'Don't indulge in drinking beer, lest you utter evil speech and don't know what you are saying.'[62] However, being drunk was considered a part of daily life for both men and women and the consumption of alcohol was regularly depicted in tomb scenes. In the tomb of Paheri at El Kab, a female cousin demands of the servant, 'Give me 18 cups of wine; I want to drink to drunkenness; my throat is dry as straw.'[63]

While bread and beer were staples, the majority of people had very little meat in their diet, surviving primarily on vegetables and fish. Those fortunate enough to eat fowl enjoyed wildfowl, duck, geese, pigeon, egret and squab, all of which were roasted. Sometimes the birds were captured alive and fattened up at home before being eaten, and scenes in the tomb of Mereruka (sixth dynasty) depict geese and cranes being force-fed on grain. It is unknown whether the Egyptians just liked fatty fowl or whether they had a taste for *pate de foie gras*.

Beef was rarely eaten by anyone other than the elite. However, when it was eaten every part of the animal was used; the blood was made into a type of black pudding, the offal was dried and the bones were boiled up for stock and soups. Ox heads were often depicted on offering tables, indicating that this was the best cut of meat; a suitable meal for a god, in fact. Other meats included pork, goat and desert game,[64] although these were also expensive and reserved for special occasions.

Evidence from mummies, including those of Ramses II and his son Merenptah, demonstrates that the wealthy ate too much meat and animal fat, with them showing signs of arteriosclerosis – or hardening of the arteries – common with high cholesterol. Other causes have been suggested for this ailment, such as poor ventilation in the homes and temples where fires were lit and incense was burnt. Many people suffered from parasitic worms and other infections (see chapter eight); constant smoke inhalation from hearths and incense, causing similar damage to that of smoking in the modern world, could all have exacerbated arteriosclerosis.

Archaeological evidence shows the ancient Egyptians had spoons and knives but nothing that could be used as a fork, indicating they ate with their hands. Moreover, royal banquet scenes from the Amarna Period show Akhenaten chewing on a rib which he holds in his hand, and one of the princesses is biting down on an entire roast duck which she holds in her hands. As these are royal scenes it indicates that this was indeed the etiquette for the upper classes, and therefore no doubt for the lower classes too.

A great deal of meat, fowl and fish was dried using salt or by simply hanging it in the sun. In the eighteenth dynasty tomb of Nakht (TT52) ducks are shown being packed into jars which were filled with salt or pickling brine, for consumption in later months.

Fish were never offered to the gods and they are never depicted in offering scenes to the gods or the deceased. This is because the method of drying was too close to mummification to be considered sacred. Some fish were pickled in oil and there is a market stall image in the tomb of Ipuy (TT217) where a woman appears to be selling fishcakes, indicating fish was eaten.

A text from El-Lahun lists the numbers of fish gutted and prepared in the town, and although the name of the fish is missing the quantities are present and include more than 1000 gutted *rat*-fish and 400 *adj*-fish,[65] showing that for a population of about 3000 the fish intake was quite substantial. However, although it has been assumed that fish formed a staple for many people, recent studies have indicated that this may not in fact be the case. In 2014, results of a study carried out by a French team on forty-five mummies in the museum in Lyons were published.[66] They studied the carbon isotopes in the mummies and compared them to pigs that were given controlled diets, in order to ascertain what the Egyptians ate. The most surprising result was that there was in fact very little fish in the diets, with the main food group being of a cereal nature, which supports the general idea that most Egyptians consumed a mostly vegetarian diet. It would be interesting to know whether any of these mummies were priests who were unable to consume fish, at least while they were working, which would obviously skew the results.

For those who did eat meat, on the whole it was cooked in its own juices, although more than thirty different oils were used for cooking (including sesame, olive, almond, linseed and radish oil) and numerous spices were used for flavour, such as cumin, coriander seeds, cloves, dill, lettuce seeds, cinnamon, mustard, mint, fenugreek, rosemary and wild marjoram, all of which have been found in tombs.

In addition to fat, other by-products from animals were commonly used. Evidence shows they kept goats, cows and sheep for their milk. It is unknown whether they drank the milk on its own, but it was used in recipes and for making cheese, which was exchanged in the marketplace. There were two cheese types that are still served today: gebna and labna. Labna is made by straining salty yoghurt into a creamy consistency, and gebna is made from harder salted curds and kept for two to three days to firm. The tomb of Hor-Aha from the first dynasty yielded remains of a substance which could be identified with this cheese.

For the majority of people vegetables and pulses formed the basis of their diet, including lettuce, lentils and chickpeas (called hawk-face due to their shape), hummus and ful nabed (broad beans), ful madames and tirmis. Onions, which were smaller and sweeter than today, were eaten like apples, and there is an image from the non-royal tomb of Horemheb at Saqqara which shows a soldier eating an onion in this way. Food was garnished with garlic, radishes, leeks, cabbages, cucumbers and celery. An image from Tell el-Amarna shows a man eating his packed lunch, which comprised bread, cucumber and an onion, all washed down with beer. Evidence from El-Lahun indicates that many of the houses had a small garden to grow beans, peas and cucumbers. At Tell el-Amarna they were also trying to grow olive trees. Traditionally these had been imported and the people of Amarna clearly developed a taste for them.

The Egyptians also ate a great deal of fruit, which was used as a sweetener in food, wine and beer, as well as being used to make cakes and sweet desserts. The variety of fruit included watermelons, pomegranates, raisins, figs and dates. Although mandrake fruits are toxic it is thought they were used as narcotics at parties and are often shown being held to the nose of revellers. Most desserts were fruit-based, in particular dates. The equivalent of pastry chefs were known as 'workers in dates', and they produced such snacks as flapjacks or oatcakes made with crushed grain and oil or fat, sweetened with honey.

The fig, in ancient Egypt, had a religious as well as a practical association. The Lady of the Sycamore, a form of Hathor, provided figs and water to the deceased in order to ensure they lived for eternity. The sycamore fig, or wild fig, was small and yellow and had a more astringent taste than ordinary figs. Tomb images show traditional fig trees being cultivated in the gardens of the wealthy and wild trees by their tombs, indicating the fruit from both were savoured.

Excavations at El-Lahun and Deir el-Medina show the Egyptians also had carob from the powdered pods of St John's Locust, often used as a chocolate substitute. Carob had been grown in Egypt from the earliest times and could also have been used as a sweetener.[67]

The Egyptian love of food and flavour was rather similar to that of modern societies, and they were very good at producing banquets from minimal ingredients, using all parts of the animal or plant. They were a very practical people, in food production as well as in home improvements and improving their income through cottage industries. The Egyptians worked hard, but as we shall see in the next chapter, they also liked to relax and enjoy themselves.

2.

PASSING THE TIME

'I want to drink to drunkenness; my throat is dry as straw.' [1]

The Egyptian love of food and over indulging show it was more than a simple necessity for life and survival, and was in fact a favoured pastime in the form of elaborate banquets. Banquets were held for any number of reasons, including funerals, religious ceremonies or general celebrations. They are regularly portrayed in non-royal tombs showing numerous guests, often segregated by sex, seated on elaborate chairs or kneeling on the floor. Married couples, however, generally sat side by side, although as they were often related to the tomb owner and held some significance in the tomb scenes their preferential treatment is not surprising. Due to the peculiarities of Egyptian art it is unknown whether the segregated revellers were literally in separate rooms, sitting opposite each other or if this was simply an artistic characteristic bearing no resemblance to the reality of an Egyptian banquet.

One of the main problems with banquets as they are depicted in the tombs is the number of guests in relation to the house sizes discussed in chapter one. The rooms were all too small to accommodate many people, so it is suggested that large banquets were held outside in the town squares or in temporary structures[2] in the courtyard of palatial homes, perhaps around the central pool. However, if the banquets were held within the homes, this goes some way to explaining the segregation in the tomb images, with men and women in different rooms, rather than all the guests in one place. Such segregation could therefore have been a natural separation of people as they mingled throughout the house for a party, as often happens in modern day situations.

Regardless of the seating plan, servants made sure wine and beer flowed freely and tables were piled high with food. Many people overindulged, and in one eighteenth-dynasty tomb the servant encourages a guest, 'Drink this, my lady, and get drunk,' to which the lady replies, 'I shall love to be drunk!'[3] Not surprisingly some scenes show both men and women vomiting into vessels held by servants. While it seemed acceptable to overindulge on wine at these banquets, the Middle Kingdom 'Teaching of Khety' (otherwise known as the 'Satire of the Trades') insists this is not suitable behaviour: 'If you have eaten three loaves, drunk two jugs of beer and the belly is not yet sated, restrain it!'[4]

Musicians, both male and female, entertained the guests. There was often a lutist, a flute player, a harpist and a couple of girls keeping time with drums or by clapping. They were often led by a chironomist, who was a singer who made gestures at the musicians, rather like a musical director,[5] keeping them in time with each other. Sometimes he is depicted holding his hand to his ear, indicating he was singing. The music and singing was followed by dancers and acrobats, who were primarily women, wearing little more than a belt made of shells and a large weighted wig, which swung as they moved.

Singing was an essential means of entertainment, not only at banquets but also at religious ceremonies or daily activities, and agricultural workers even had songs to mark the passing of their daily chores. An Old Kingdom farming song, for example, which was possibly sung by two groups, follows thus:

Q – O West! Where is the Shepherd? The shepherd of the West?
A – The shepherd is in the water with the fish. He speaks with the *phagos*-fish and converses with the *oxyrhynchus* fish.[6]

This was possibly sung in a round between different groups. Another song for the harvest had a flautist in the field to accompany the singing;

Q – Where is the one skilled at his job?
A – It is I.
Q – Where is the hard-working man? Come to me.
A – It is I! I am dancing.[7]

There was even a song sung by Old Kingdom servants about carrying their master in his sedan chair: 'Happy are they that bear the chair! Better it is for us when full than when it is empty.'[8]

Ancient Egyptian people liked the outdoor life, and perhaps carrying a sedan chair outside was better in their mind than being inside a hot, stuffy building all day. Therefore, many recreational pastimes were conducted outside. In particular, hunting, fishing and fowling were common sports for the elite. The Fayoum was a popular place to catch birds using throw-sticks or to fish in the lake with spears. In fishing and fowling scenes in tombs from the Old Kingdom, the tomb owner is seen standing in a small papyrus skiff with his wife and children seated or standing at his feet. Their role was a subordinate one and often they are shown handing things to the tomb owner, such as spears or throw-sticks.

The throw-sticks were thrown at birds as they broke cover and it was necessary to disturb the birds in order to make them fly.

Either a cat was sent into the marshes, a servant shook the papyrus stems to disturb the birds or the tomb owner held a decoy bird – a tamed bird whose call attracted others to the area.⁹ Marsh-hunting was considered a demonstration of the virility of the hunter, and was such an important aspect of elite daily life that such scenes soon became essential for entering the afterlife. Spell sixty-two of the Coffin Texts states, 'Water birds by the thousands will come to you, which lie on your way. You hurl your throwing stick at them, and they are thousands that drop with the sound of its path through the air, namely *sa*-geese, green-breast birds, *trp*-geese and male *st*-geese.'¹⁰

The fowling scenes are always accompanied by a corresponding fishing scene, where the tomb owner, in the same vessel, thrusts a long spear into the water, catching the fish swimming past the boat. The papyrus skiff was a rather unstable vessel in which to stand upright while thrusting a spear into the water, and there is a certain amount of artistic license employed in these scenes. In order to spear the fish it would be necessary to bend at the waist and thrust from a crouched position, although this would not look as elegant in the images. The tomb owners are always shown standing tall. There were two prongs on the end of the spear and in some images there is a fish on each prong, presumably caught with a single thrust. This method of catching fish was particularly difficult and required a great deal of skill, further emphasising that fishing with spears and hunting fowl with throw-sticks were sports rather than a means of catching necessary food.

Those who craved more excitement hunted in the desert for lion, gazelle, wild ox, wild sheep, jackal, wolf, hare, fox, hyena and ostrich. In the New Kingdom desert hunting was carried out on a chariot, which was the easiest way to catch fast animals like gazelles and hares.

Imenemheb in his eighteenth-dynasty tomb (TT85) is depicted as a hippopotamus hunter, something that was previously only the prerogative of the king, showing that big-game hunting became the pastime of the rich as well. The king, however, was still the only hunter depicted killing wild bull from the papyrus thickets.[11] Generally, anything caught during the hunt was eaten and the skin, fur or feathers used.

For a riverine society one would expect swimming to be a popular pastime, or at least a common life skill, although it is not often depicted. In the 'Biography of Harkhuf' (sixth dynasty) he recalls when he brought a pygmy on his ship to entertain the king. The king is concerned about the pygmy's safety and tells Harkhuf that he is responsible for ensuring 'he doesn't fall into the water'. This indicates that should this have happened the pygmy may have drownd as he could not swim. In the Kadesh battle scenes of Ramses II, the Hittite king falls into the water and needs to be rescued, suggesting to the Egyptian propaganda machine that 'others' – or foreigners – were unable to swim, as a direct contrast to the Egyptians, who could.

Moreover, there are a number of cosmetic spoons depicting young girls stretched out with the bowl of the spoon in their hands. These bowls are often decorated with images of birds, indicating that they likely depict the girls swimming rather than simply lying down. These spoons are clearly erotic images but their realism suggests that some young women were able to swim. Clearer depictions of girls swimming can be seen on a twenty-second-dynasty silver bowl[12] from Tanis which depicts a number of girls swimming among fish, birds and flowers, and an ostracon, now in Turin, also shows a girl swimming. All of these girls are shown naked except for a large wig, and it has been suggested that as it would be impossible to swim in such a wig there was erotic symbolism to its depiction in these scenes.[13]

The Middle Kingdom nomarch Kheti boasts that he had swimming lessons with the king's children,[14] something he was clearly proud of, which tells us the royal children and therefore the king were also able to swim. However, generally people were only depicted swimming if it was necessary as part of their job. In the tomb of Djar at Deir el Bahri a fisherman is depicted underwater untangling a fishing net and adjusting the weights.[15] Swimming in the Nile was a dangerous activity as the crocodiles and hippopotami which lived within posed a great threat, perhaps limiting the appeal of swimming as a regular pastime.

Many people worked on the river and this obviously affected their free time and means of entertainment. While there are no records of boat races, there is no reason why they would not have happened. There is, however, evidence that boatmen enjoyed boat jousting, a rather boisterous, impromptu competition. Such scenes are depicted in New Kingdom tombs, and provide a snapshot of riverine entertainment. The boats were generally light papyrus skiffs, of the type used in marsh hunting, and the competition took place between two, three or four boats, depending on how many happened to pass by at the same time. The fishermen used the long rowing poles to push the men from the other boats into the water. Once they got close enough the men abandoned the poles and used their arms to achieve the same ends. Once someone fell into the water the competition was over. They then helped them back onto the boats. In one scene, an unfortunate man who has fallen into the water has been seized by a crocodile, emphasising the danger of such boisterous games on the Nile. Sometimes the participants took it too far and used their poles to beat their competitors, shouting things like 'break his skull open!',[16] indicating that perhaps some people were too competitive for such violent sport.

When the Egyptians were not feasting or hunting they were big fans of board games and, perhaps by association, gambling. There are at least three popular board games from the archaeological record: senet, mekhen and hounds and jackals (the shield game). Everyone could play these games, either with a purpose-made board or by scratching a makeshift board into the sand and using pebbles as pieces. On the roof of the temple of Khonsu at Karnak there are make shift senet boards scratched into the floor blocks in the shade of the pylon, upon which the priests played while they were on watch on the temple roof.[17] Unfortunately there are no surviving rules for any of these games.

The Egyptians did not have dice and used throw-sticks or knuckle bones instead. Throw-sticks had one dark and one light side, and knuckle bones, often from sheep, had four distinct faces (flat, concave, convex and twisted). The combination of each side thrown determined how many spaces could be moved. The pieces to be moved across the board varied with each game and were referred to as 'dancers'.

Mekhen, or the coiled snake game, is the oldest and was popular in the Pre-Dynastic Period and Old Kingdom. The board was constructed of concentric circles representing the coils of a snake, and the Pyramid Texts describe how the dancers should travel around the board from the tail to the head. There are slots along the body of the snake where the gaming pieces were placed. In the tomb of Hesy from the third dynasty, these pieces are depicted in the form of six small lions and six balls. It is thought the lions were used as pieces on the board and the balls were held in the hand and were used to determine the number of spaces moved, rather like dice, although how exactly this worked is not certain.[18] There was no standardised direction for the game to be played, as the snakes coil both clockwise and anti-clockwise.

In the First Intermediate Period the game of choice was hounds and jackals, or the shield game. The shield-shaped board consisted of a box or block of wood with sixty small holes drilled into it: twenty-nine for each player and a large central hole which both players shared. Into these the pieces were placed. Some of the holes had inscriptions next to them which identified positive or negative places to land. For example, the word *nfr* (good) is inscribed next to holes fifteen, twenty-six and twenty-seven.[19] Howard Carter believed the dancers or gaming pieces for this game were in fact hairpins due to their shape, which was long and stick-like with a decorative top. There were ten pieces in total, half with dog heads and half with jackal heads, making five pieces each.

The most popular game in ancient Egypt, however, was senet, a game played on thirty squares and thought to be similar to backgammon. The game was known before the first dynasty (2686–2613 BCE) and continued in popularity throughout the dynastic period; more than 120 gaming boards have been found throughout the ancient Near East and Egypt.[20]

It was known as Thirty Field Game or the Game of Thirty, in reference to the number of squares on the board. It was a game of strategy played by two players, with seven or five dancers. There were two different styles (cones or reels) in two colours, usually white and black, making it easy to identify each player's pieces. The objective of the game was to move all the dancers through the thirty squares to the end. Some of the squares were marked with a hieroglyph indicating whether it was considered a lucky or unlucky square, and there was likely some penalty or reward for landing on them. On some of the boards all thirty squares were inscribed, but on others only square fifteen, the House of Rebirth; square twenty-six, the Beautiful House; and square twenty-seven, the Field of Water, which was a negative square to land on, were inscribed.[21]

By the time of the New Kingdom the game had also taken on spiritual meaning and is represented in tombs, with the deceased playing an unseen opponent. If they won, the deceased continued into the afterlife, and presumably if they lost – although no one did – they were cast into oblivion and denied rebirth. This scene is used to represent chapter seventeen of the Book of the Dead and a senet board was an essential part of the funerary assemblage.

The Egyptians were not really very different to modern people, passing the time by playing games, drinking and chatting with their friends, and images of senet playing in tombs as a pastime rather than a representation of the Book of the Dead is accompanied by the inscription, 'You sit in the hall; you play the senet board game; you have wine, you have beer.'[22] It seems like a very civilised way to spend an evening.

Members of Egyptian society who were talented (or sometimes not-so-talented) artists sketched on ostraca and papyri, sometimes simply for the sake of drawing. Such sketches have revealed the Egyptian sense of humour and, to a certain extent, their cruelty. Many of the drawings involve poking fun at people – individuals and royalty – and religious practices. Like many people in ancient Egypt, these artists are anonymous and we can only imagine what they were thinking as they sketched these things. However, sometimes we are given little glimpses of individual moments in these anonymous artists' lives. One such moment was discovered in 1991–92 at Dra Abu el Naga. In the New Kingdom an artist decided to pack away his paints for a few moments, perhaps to take a break, have lunch or a nap. He dug a small hole in the ground and stacked his bowls of paint one on top of the other, with a little paintbrush laid gently in each pot. Three large pots were turned upside down to cover the stack, perhaps to prevent the paint from drying out or to prevent flies and dust getting into the paint. It seems he was only planning to be gone a short time, but he never returned.[23] What had he been painting? A tomb scene, a portable object, or a small sketch on an ostracon to entertain his friends and family? And what is more intriguing, why did he never return?

Most of the surviving drawings are not captioned, so what exactly is being presented it not always clear. However, one caricature is labelled as belonging to Pay and his wife Mereseger. Pay is shown drinking beer through a straw and wearing a knee-length kilt. He is depicted as tall and thin, whereas in contrast his wife is plump, depicted naked and without a wig, showing a short, stubbly hair style.[24] It is a less than flattering depiction of Pay's wife and could indicate she was not popular among his friends and colleagues.

Another stylised image of a woman with a wig, lotus flower and perfume cone on her head was amended by another artist, who added a small monkey pulling on her nose. Who the woman is – if she was in fact a known individual rather than a generic study of a woman – we will never know.

Even the king is sometimes shown in unflattering ways, with stubble or even shedding tears. Perhaps these were means of making the king seem less majestic than the divine being he was thought to be, or they may have been images of the king in mourning. The Queen of Punt was an interesting subject for one Deir el-Medina workman, who had seen the image in the temple of Hatshepsut and copied it onto an ostracon,[25] perhaps to show his friends and colleagues. By the time this sketch was drawn the original on the temple wall was more than two centuries old. It is intriguing to think of this artist showing his friends the sketch in the same manner as a modern person showing their holiday photographs.

Even religion was not off-limits to these satirical artists; they were not only drawn on ostraca but actually on the walls of the temple at Nag el Medamud, just north of Luxor. A banquet is depicted being held in the papyrus marshes and the noblewoman on her throne is actually a mouse holding a flower, attended by a cat servant. A figure stands before her which some believe to be a monkey and could even represent the king. The noblewoman is entertained by a crocodile playing a lute, with a naked woman on his back playing a harp. Why such an unusual scene is depicted in a temple is a mystery. The imagery of animals playing instruments, however, was not a new theme when this temple was decorated in the twenty-fifth dynasty. The much earlier Two Dog Palette from the Naqada III period shows a jackal playing a flute. This indicates that perhaps this imagery had a deeper significance than a 'reverse world'.

The subversion of the natural world was, however, a particularly popular theme and there are numerous images showing animals carrying out human activities. Popular animal pairs include lions and gazelles, cats and mice, and crows and hippos. The two former pairings are clear to understand due to the nature of these animals and their natural conflict. The Satirical Papyrus in the British Museum shows, for example, a lion playing senet with an antelope, a rather more mundane version of their normal predator–prey relationship. The lion looks particularly jovial and is probably winning the game. Another scene on the papyrus shows a lion having sexual intercourse with an animal which could be a donkey or an antelope, and it has been suggested that the scene depicts the same animals later in the day.[26]

A scene repeated in numerous places is that of a mouse judge who oversees the trial of some criminals and administers their punishments. One fragment shows a young boy being beaten by a cat, whereas there is another where the role is reversed and the boy is beating the cat. Another ostracon shows a fight between crows and monkeys over some dom nuts, perhaps a representation of a possible conflict that arose in the villages. The pairing of crows and hippos, however, is not so easy to explain. A rather peculiar ostracon shows a crow climbing a ladder to reach the branches of a sycamore fig tree. The branches of the tree are already occupied by a hippopotamus.

While the meaning of these images on the ostraca – if indeed there was one – is unknown, it has been suggested that they represented scenes from popular folk stories which were part of an oral tradition. Evidence suggests the Egyptians liked to tell stories and there are some elaborate Middle Kingdom tales which were popular. The most popular story seems to be the Shipwrecked Sailor, in which a sailor tells a rather farfetched tale of being shipwrecked on an island inhabited by a giant divine snake that disappeared, along with the island, once he left, meaning no one could return.

A. Cartoon on the satirical/erotic papyrus, Turin, showing a crow and a hippopotamus in a sycamore fig tree. (Drawing after Houlihan, 2001, fig. 68).

Another popular tale can be found on Papyrus Westcar, also known as Three Tales of Wonder, in which King Khufu is in need of entertainment and his sons all try to appease him. In one story he decides to go on a river trip. The boats are rowed by young, scantily clad girls, until one of them drops her fish pendant into the water. She refuses to continue rowing until it has been retrieved and so Khufu has to call upon his magician to help, who divides the water to retrieve the pendant. In the second story the king is entertained by a magician who can decapitate a goose and an ox and reattach the heads. The third story tells of the fantastic birth of the next dynasty of kings, aided by a group of deities. Although the final story may have been one of propaganda to legitimise the divinity of the kings of the fifth dynasty, these stories may have already been familiar to the Egyptian population in some form.

It is easy to imagine the ancient Egyptian workmen seated around a fire in the evening telling such stories, or mothers entertaining their children at bedtime with fanciful tales of magic and monsters in exactly the same way people do in the modern world.

Whatever the Egyptians were doing, if the tomb scenes are to be believed, they looked remarkably well turned out while they were doing it. Such tomb and even temple images provide clues to the fashions of the time, although it must be considered that these images were stylised and only represented the dress of the upper classes. Even if the scenes are of the middle classes from Deir el-Medina, they could represent clothes they wanted to own rather than those they actually had.[27] Therefore it can be difficult to ascertain from the tomb scenes alone what the ordinary Egyptian wore on a daily basis. Luckily, clothes have been discovered in tombs, which indicate that most people dressed simply in a short kilt or loincloth[28] or long linen tunics.

Even with the limited resources available it is possible to identify changing fashions in the elite society. In the Old Kingdom it was fashionable to wear tight sheath dresses with two shoulder straps. They would have proven difficult to move in and some take this as evidence that elite women were expected to be ornamental rather than useful. Although this dress style remained in fashion until the New Kingdom, as time progressed the dresses became more transparent and fuller, with large volumes of fabric. A very fine, transparent dress with dozens of folds and pleats was an indication of great wealth, although the artistic images bear no resemblance to the clothes discovered in elite tombs. These include the royal tombs of Tutankhamun, Thutmosis IV and Ramses II and the Deir el-Medina tomb of Kha, in addition to texts from Deir el-Medina describing the average wardrobe via messages to the dressmakers and laundry lists detailing garments and their quantities.[29]

The majority of ancient Egyptian clothes were made of linen, and for the most part were left undyed as it was expensive and difficult to make the dye colourfast. Linen came in various shades, from white to golden brown, depending on the maturity of the flax.

Tutankhamun, as king, had a number of coloured garments heavy with embellishment, including woven decoration, beads, discs and needlework. One shawl was striped with bands of red and blue and a row of ankhs along the edge in brocade.[30] Royalty also had tapestry decoration and a tunic from the tomb of Thutmosis IV shows elaborate tapestry images of open and closed lotus flowers, birds and purple mandrakes.[31]

Tunics were the most commonly worn garment in ancient Egypt and were similar to the modern gallabeya worn by Egyptians today. They are mentioned most frequently in the laundry lists, and they also appear in lists of market values. They were relatively cheap, at 5 deben each (1 deben is 91 grams of copper). In New Kingdom love songs women are described as wearing tunics[32] and children also wore them from the Middle Kingdom onwards. They were made of a single piece of rectangular linen folded in half and sewn up the side, leaving a gap for the arms. They came in two lengths, either reaching to the floor or waist length to be worn with a short kilt. There were different ways of wearing the tunic, which included tucking the bottom hem into a girdle underneath creating a puff-ball effect.[33]

Tunics formed part of a set with a triangular loincloth that was worn beneath as underwear. However, in the tomb of Tutankhamun over 145 loincloths were found and only 10 tunics, indicating either the ancient robbers stole a number of the linen tunics[34] or a tunic was worn for many days. In the Deir el-Medina tomb of Kha, he had what was considered a large number of garments for an ordinary citizen and this wardrobe included fifty triangular loincloths.

Tying a loincloth was simple; the two corners at the base of the triangle tied around the waist and the third point was pulled between the legs and tucked into the waist band, with the end hanging down the front as a flap. These loincloths were worn by men, women and children. Tutankhamun's examples were made of two triangular pieces of linen sewn together in the centre and were shaped at the waist to ensure a snug fit, whereas other examples were made of one piece of linen with a straight waistband.

Manual workers such as laundry men, fishermen, brick makers and wine pressers, as well as the more elegant dancing girls,[35] simply wore the loincloth on its own, as this prevented them from getting too hot and produced minimal amounts of washing. People performing such low-grade jobs may also have been unable to afford many other pieces of clothing.

Kilts were another staple to any wardrobe, and were worn as underwear beneath a tunic or over the loincloth as an overskirt. These were rectangular pieces of linen which wrapped around the waist. Over time the fashionable kilt length changed from covering the chest to the ankles to just the waist to the knees. Kilts were worn throughout the pharaonic period by rich and poor alike. They were wrapped around the waist and bunched and tucked up at the front making the front of the kilt shorter than the back. In images of men wearing kilts there are lines incised that denote pleats or folds. The kilt was held in place by a metal belt or a sash.[36] The more pleats there were on a kilt the greater the wealth of the individual, as this showed the kilt was made with a larger piece of fabric and was therefore more expensive.

In general the Egyptians loved the layered look, as the more layers of linen worn the wealthier you appeared. This led to the popularity of shawls, which were rectangular strips of linen approximately two metres long and one metre wide. These were tied over the torso, wrapped from left to right and tied under the breast. These were often worn over tunics and went some way to producing wide, draping sleeves.

All of these layers were tied in place using a sash and most people would have owned at least one. They varied in length to accommodate different waist sizes and were often sold in the market together with loincloths and kilts, as without one the kilt was at risk of falling down. Sashes were on the whole plain pieces of linen, sometimes with a fringe on the short end, although the wealthy may have possessed tapestry sashes decorated with geometric patterns. In the Amarna Period the sashes were wider at the back than the front and were tied under the stomach, giving the distinctive Amarna profile.

Even the poorer members of society dressed in a similar fashion. Labourers wore plain, knee-length kilts, no doubt made of a relatively short piece of low-quality material, a sash over their chest to catch sweat and a kerchief over their heads.[37] These headdresses were particularly important in order to protect their heads from the sun. It is likely that most Egyptians wore headdresses for this very reason, the most common of which was the kerchief. Even Tutankhamun was buried wearing a linen kerchief decorated with an appliquéd vulture on the crown, showing that this item of clothing was for all classes.[38]

Kerchiefs were made of linen which varied in length. In the marketplace the price varied between 7 and 25 deben,[39] demonstrating a variance in linen quality. Another common headdress was the *khat*-headdress and twenty-four examples were found in the tomb of Tutankhamun. A *khat* was a semi-circular piece of material with the curved end left hanging over the neck and held in place with a headband. The *khat*-headdress is also depicted in non-royal tombs, such as the fishing scene in the tomb of Ipuy (TT217), indicating it was another item of clothing worn by all levels of society.

No outfit was complete without a pair of shoes, and the shoes of choice in Egypt were sandals very close in design to the modern flip-flop. In the ancient Egyptian marketplace male sandals were twice the price of female sandals, presumably due to the size difference. There were varying qualities of sandals, with leather or papyrus shoes being stronger than the reed or grass sandals that most people wore. Examples of leather and papyrus sandals found at Qasr Ibrim show they were made up of layers of material to give them extra strength. Shoes were a valuable commodity, and should they break they were repaired rather than disposed of. At the market, buying the sandal thongs to repair them cost half of the price of a new pair. Making shoes was a relatively straightforward activity in the pharaonic period and did not require a specialist shoemaker;[40] some families produced them in the home to sell in the marketplace in order to boost their household income.

The people in ancient Egypt had the same attitude to clothes as we do today, even though they did not have clothes in anything like the quantities of a modern wardrobe. A letter, on an ostracon from Deir el-Medina, was written by a lady called Ese to her dressmaker, Nubemnu, regarding a shawl she had commissioned for the next procession of the deified Amenhotep I through the village. She pleads, 'Please weave for me that shawl, very very quickly, before the god Amenhotep comes, for I am completely naked. Make one for my backside because I am naked.'[41] Most western women today have uttered the same plea: 'I have nothing to wear!'

The festival of Amenhotep I was an important one in the village, when the statue of the deified king was taken from his shrine and carried around the village in a sedan chair, and even on occasion taken to the Valley of the Kings. This festival took place six times a year and was one of drinking and merriment: 'The gang rejoiced before him for four solid days of drinking together with their children and wives.'[42] Normally in processions of divine statues they were hidden from view, but Amenhotep I was visible to all. Many of the villagers approached the statue as an oracle and the god was able to answer directly.[43] It is clear Ese wanted the god to see her at her best.

The ancient Egyptians were conscious of their appearance and had very clear ideas of beauty and how to obtain it. The New Kingdom love poetry described the ideal body shape:

> Upright neck, shining neck,
> Hair true lapis lazuli;
> Arms suppressing gold,
> Fingers like lotus buds.
> Heavy thighs, narrow waist.[44]

This description resembles the figures portrayed by so-called concubine or fertility figures, which all have curvy hips, small waists and large buttocks. This was considered a healthy shape for childbearing and therefore the ideal shape of a potential partner.[45] This ideal body shape and idealised beauty all centre on the lower parts of the anatomy, bypassing the breasts, which are a modern focus of sexual attraction. Breasts were considered an important aspect of motherhood and milk provision, and were therefore not considered erotic. Instead hands, eyes, hair,[46] legs and a narrow waist were the focal points of erotic thought. The Egyptian idea of sexuality was more about tantalising glimpses of the body through fine, see-through linen, rather than full nudity.[47]

Diets were unheard of in ancient Egypt, no doubt because famine was a very real threat. There are some rather realistic images of famine depicted on the Old Kingdom causeway of Unas at Saqqara. The people are emaciated and some of the children have distended stomachs, which are common with malnutrition. It is generally believed the image itself does not represent Egyptians but instead shows how Unas helped another country in distress. However, the image demonstrates that the Egyptians had certainly witnessed, if not experienced famine. Furthermore it is recorded that they were also aware of the effect diet had on overall health, and believed many illnesses were due to indigestion and excess in eating.[48] Herodotus describes how 'every month for three successive days they [the Egyptians] purge themselves for their health's sake, with emetics and clysters, in belief that all diseases come from the food a man eats'.[49] This appears to be describing a detoxifying period where certain food was avoided for three days a month.

Although diets were unheard of, most people are shown as slim, the women with curving hips and large breasts. The exceptions are men of official status who are shown with stylised rolls of fat, as are blind harpists; in the New Kingdom tomb of Tjanuny, five Nubian mercenaries in the Egyptian army have podgy stomachs,[50] which are representative of a settled and rich life. Furthermore, mummies have provided evidence that obesity was not unheard of. One mummy, that of Horemkenisi – a scribe and chief workman at Deir el-Medina, and part-time wab priest at the temple of Ramses III at Medinet Habu during the reign of Pinedjem I (1070–1032 BCE) – had numerous folds of skin, which could be indicative of obesity. As discussed in chapter eight, it was unusual for Egyptians to have tooth decay due to a lack of sugar in their diets other than honey, but Horemkenisi had two caries which, coupled with his obesity, could indicate over indulgence in honey cakes.

Horemkenisi was not the only one; another mummy, Masaharta, also from the Third Intermediate Period, was so fat when he was embalmed that his hands could not be crossed over his pelvis, as was traditional, as they did not meet.[51]

Greek travellers to Egypt commented that Egyptians were very clean and bathed every morning after rising and often also after meals,[52] which, as discussed in chapter one, was necessary considering the lack of cutlery. They were also well known for using purgatives and enemas.

In Graeco-Roman Egypt a common sign of mourning was to deny oneself the luxury of bathing and adornment. In a letter of this period to a woman called Isidora from her husband, Serenus, whom she has abandoned, he writes, 'I have not bathed or anointed myself for a whole month.'[53] In the earlier periods of Egyptian history professional mourners threw dirt over their faces and pulled at their hair and clothes, showing themselves as dishevelled and dirty.

Herodotus records, 'Egyptians who shave at all other times, mark a death by letting the hair grow both on the head and on the chin.'[54] Just as washing and cleanliness were important, so was the removal of body hair for both men and women, and to abandon this practice was a sign of neglect and a suitable demonstration of grief. In the Middle Kingdom story of Sinuhe, when he was reinstated in the Egyptian court he claims, 'I was shaved and my hair was combed. In this may my squalor be returned to the foreign land, my dress to the Sandfarers. I was dressed in the finest linen. I was anointed with perfumed oil and I slept on a real bed.'[55] Sinuhe had been living in Syria as a tribal leader, and therefore the message he is giving here is that being clean, shaved and anointed was a luxury of the Egyptians. It was generally believed that the long beards and hair common to Asiatics was a sign of barbarianism and uncleanness.

On a daily basis the removal of body hair was important, both for hygiene and for ritualistic purposes. Tombs of both men and women have included knives accompanied by miniature whetstones, razors and tweezers. The razors were generally made of flint or metal, were kept in a sheath of bone or wood or a leather pouch and were stored with other cosmetic items.[56] As in the modern world, shaving was not for everyone and there are recipes for hair removal creams made from the boiled and crushed bones of birds, fly dung, oil, sycamore juice, gum and cucumber. It was heated up and applied, then ripped off when it had cooled.[57] The Egyptian priesthood, as part of their elaborate cleanliness rituals, shaved off all body hair, including their eyebrows, every three days, which ensured they were free from lice when entering the temple and the domain of the gods.

Keeping clean was important to people of all classes and some houses at El-Lahun and Amarna have separate bathrooms. Poorer people did not have such luxury and washed in a basin or in the Nile. Most people had washbowls in the house with matching jugs made of bronze, alabaster or pottery, depending on wealth.[58]

Soap was made from natron, soda and ashes, or niter (a type of potassium). Oil and lime were added to the water, which had the effect of soap but no doubt irritated and dried the skin. There were more than thirty types of oil designed to anoint the skin which may have soothed it, made by mixing vegetable oil with milk, honey salts, fragrant resins and aromatic flowers.[59]

Perfumed oils were considered such a necessity that they were included in the rations of the Deir el-Medina workmen.[60] The production of perfume oil is depicted in numerous tombs, including the fifth dynasty tomb of Iymery at Giza, and shows plant parts being crushed in a bowl before being placed in a cloth with two loops at each end. A rod was put into these loops and the cloth was twisted until all of the liquid had been squeezed out of the plant pulp.[61] This method only uses part of the plant and the perfumes, especially those with lily extract, had a shelf life of as much as twenty years. Myrrh-based scents lasted ten years and cinnamon and cassia lasted a little less.[62]

Like any modern individual, the Egyptians were concerned with growing old and oils were prescribed in the Ebers Medical Papyrus (1500BCE) as a cure for wrinkles: 'To remove facial wrinkles: frankincense, gum, wax, fresh balanites oil and rush-nut should be finely ground and applied to the face every day. Make it and it will happen!'[63] In order to improve the appearance further, cosmetics were a regular part of the daily routine for rich and poor alike, from as early as the Badarian Period (4000 BCE). In the temple cults where the statues were ritually washed and dressed, eye make-up was regularly used to give them a lifelike appearance.[64]

A New Kingdom love song demonstrates the extent make-up played in everyday life, as it is listed among the daily rituals of getting dressed and perfumed:

When I think of my love of you, it makes me act not sensibly,
It leaps from its place, it lets me not to put on a dress,
Nor wrap my scarf around me:
I put no paint upon my eyes,
I'm not even anointed.[65]

Eye make-up also had a medical function, as it repelled flies (which carried diseases), prevented the delicate skin from around the eyes from drying out and also reflected the glare of the hot desert sun. On some New Kingdom kohl pots, which were used for storing eye make-up, there were inscriptions like 'good for the sight', 'to staunch bleeding', 'to cause tears' or 'for cleaning the eyes',[66] identifying their medical properties.

From the Pre-Dynastic Period to at least the nineteenth dynasty, green malachite was popular, and then dark-grey galena, a lead-based mineral, was used for eyeshadow. Both minerals were imported from the Sinai, and malachite was also mined in the eastern desert. In later periods kohl was used, which was made from sunflower soot, charred almond shells and frankincense, and is still used in some areas of the Middle East today. The powdered minerals were mixed with water and resin and stored initially in shells and then later in elaborate kohl pots until it was needed. To apply it the kohl was dropped into the eye and the tear spread it to the underside of the lashes.[67]

In the New Kingdom the eyes were sometimes shaded with two colours, green applied to the brows and the corner of the eyes and grey to the rims and lashes. A dark line was drawn from the corner of the eye to the hairline and the eyebrow was extended to parallel this line.[68] New Kingdom tomb paintings also tell us that black galena was used on the lids and upper eye and green malachite was used on the lower eye as a defining line, as portrayed on the Old Kingdom statues of Nesa in the Louvre Museum, Paris.

In addition to eye make-up, the Egyptians also wore rouge and lipstick. The Turin Erotic Papyrus shows one girl applying lipstick with a lip brush while looking into a hand mirror, and the painted bust of Nefertiti shows her lips as distinctly darker than her face, which some have identified as the use of lipstick.

Rouge was made of hematite and red ochre mixed with vegetable oil or animal fat, and examples have been found in a number of tombs. The Ebers Medical Papyrus suggests a similar recipe to disguise the appearance of facial burns, indicating it was a cosmetic for the face. The tomb of Nefertari is the only tomb that clearly shows cheeks as a darker, circular patch indicative of rouge, although a relief from the Middle Kingdom which is now in the British Museum (1658) shows a woman wiping her face with a small pad, which could be the application of foundation or rouge.

A cleanser was discovered in the eighteenth-dynasty tomb of three princesses, comprising sediments of fat mixed with lime or chalk, and likely used to clean these cosmetics from the face. This cleanser probably caused as much damage to the skin as the cosmetics. In order to counter dry skin the Ebers Papyrus recommends 'gall bladder of a cow, oil, rubber and flour of the ostrich plume. Thin with plant oil and wash the face with it daily'.[69]

In order to complete a well-planned, fashionable ensemble the Egyptians dressed their hair. Hair was particularly important and had aesthetic, social and ritualistic importance. The ritual started in childhood, as heads were shaved except for a lock of hair on the right hand side as a sign of their infant status. All children, regardless of sex or class, wore the side-lock. The daughters of Akhenaten are all shown with side-locks, with the oldest having the longest and thickest one.

The king is often depicted as a child being suckled by Isis while wearing the lock of youth, showing that he is the divine son of the goddess, and in the Valley of the Kings the mummies of two princes were discovered with the side-lock still in place. One was the son of Amenhotep II, aged about eleven years old, and the other was a son of Ramses III, aged about five years old. When the child reached adolescence the side-lock was shaved off, perhaps in a coming of age ceremony (see chapter five). Sometimes this side-lock of hair was kept and in the British Museum (EA 62500) there is a plaited side-lock which was discovered in the sixth dynasty grave of a child.[70]

In adulthood many people shaved their heads to prevent lice, as well as to keep cool in the desert climate. During the day they wore simple linen headdresses (as discussed above) to protect their shaved heads from the sun. However, for banquets and memorable occasions elaborate wigs were worn. They were made of human hair, horse hair, sheep wool or plant fibres, depending on budget. The best quality wigs consisted of up to 120,000 human hairs woven into a mesh and glued into place with bees wax and resin, whereas wigs of poorer quality were made of red palm fibre.[71]

Artistic representations often show the wearer's natural hair line, which tells us that wigs could be worn over natural hair, should they have their own hair, or over a shaved head. The style of wigs changed over the millennia from the short-cropped, curly wigs of the Old Kingdom, which were constructed of small overlapping curls in horizontal rows over the forehead,[72] to the long, full wigs of the New Kingdom, which consisted of the hair separated into three sections, with one over each shoulder and a long, thick section down the back. In the eighteenth dynasty it was fashionable for royal women to wear Hathor wigs, which saw the hair divided into two even sections, which were brought to the front and bound with ribbon wrapping them around two flat discs. New Kingdom wigs were generally varied and complicated, with designs of curls and plaits.

While the majority of wigs were black, some were dyed a vibrant blue, green,[73] or red and yellow as depicted in the Old Kingdom tomb of Merysankh III on the queen's short wig.[74] Henna was a common means of dying the hair, hands and nails, and can be seen on mummified remains.

While greying hair is a simple fact of life, in ancient Egyptian art it is rarely depicted. In the tomb of Pashedu (TT3) at Deir el-Medina and the tomb of Ipuy (TT217) there are some unusual images of the tomb owner and family members with white hair, grey hair and salt-and-peppered hair. Although the hair is grey and denotes age and wisdom, the faces and the bodies are youthful. The Hearst Medical Papyrus includes a remedy to prevent hair from turning grey, which suggests cooking a mouse in oil and applying it to the greying hair,[75] whereas the Ebers papyrus recommends the placenta of the cat for the treatment of the same issue.[76]

Some people were also unlucky enough to lose their hair, and while it was fashionable to shave the head and wear a wig there were also remedies to prevent hair loss, which included one of a mixture of the fat of a lion, hippopotamus, crocodile, cat, snake and ibex: 'Mix as one thing, smear the head of the bald person with it.'[77]

In the New Kingdom, while wigs were popular, some people maintained their own hair and added hairpieces to thicken it, to both appear fashionable and to enhance thinning hair. A number of hairpieces have been found in funerary contexts. Wigs and hairpieces were a major part of everyday life for most Egyptians and archaeologists discovered a wig workshop in a room near the temple of Deir el Bahri. This has provided information regarding the care and manufacture of wigs, as many were in various stages of completion. Remnants of a waxy soap was discovered, which was probably used for washing the wigs and hair. It was made of natron and soda, and was very good for removing fatty substances like the perfumed cones. A dark brown substance of bicarbonate of manganese and quartz grains gave the hair body and shine, and if mixed with a waxy substance could have been used as a dye.[78]

Elite and royal women had servants to dress their hair, and there are images in tombs of wigs being rearranged by female servants.

For example, in the Cairo Museum there is a sarcophagus belonging to Kawait, priestess of the goddess Hathor; on it she is depicted sipping from a cup and holding a mirror in her hand while a servant curls her hair. Hair curlers were included in numerous tombs, as were hairpins and wooden or ivory combs.[79] In the eighteenth-dynasty tomb of Userhat (TT56) there is an image of a number of young men waiting to have their hair cut outdoors, indicating barbers worked in the open and travelled around different villages. However, being a barber was not considered a very good job, as the Middle Kingdom 'Satire of the Trades' describes.

> The barber barbers until nightfall.
> He betakes himself to town, he sets himself up in his corner,
> He moves from street to street looking for someone to barber.
> He strains his arms to fill his belly,
> Like the bee that eats as it works.[80]

Hair was seen as more than just a means of enhancing beauty; it was considered erotic, and was often used in literature and love poetry to symbolise sexuality. In the 'Tale of the Two Brothers' the younger brother interrupts his sister-in-law as she is braiding her hair, which at the time was as erotic as being caught in a state of undress. She propositions him but he refuses as he is loyal to his brother. However, she lies to her husband, claiming his brother had propositioned her and said, 'Come, let us spend an hour lying together: loosen your braids.'[81] This final line has also been interpreted as 'don your wig'[82], but both connect hair and sex. The act of braiding one's hair is also mentioned in a New Kingdom love poem.

> My heart thought of my love for you, when half of my hair was
>   braided;
> I came at a run to find you, and neglected my hairdo.
> Now if you let me braid my hair, I shall be ready in a moment.[83]

Hair was also used as a sexual tool by erotic dancers and acrobats. They wore long wigs that were weighted at the bottom, enabling them to swing their hair in an arc while dancing,[84] which focused the attention of the men watching. In one Middle Kingdom story that describes an encounter between a herdsman and a goddess, the herdsman describes his awe:

> See, all of you, I went down to a pool which is close [to] this lowland, I saw a woman there, whose physique is not that of [ordinary] humans; my hair went on end as I stared at her locks (?), for the smoothness of her skin I would never do what she had said (otherwise but) awe of her pervaded my body.[85]

The mere sight of the heavenly woman with her flowing hair rendered him immobile. Although this describes a goddess the description is one of eroticism, and conveys the ancient Egyptian idea of beauty to us.

In such a hot climate, especially after spending so much time and attention on their appearance, the Egyptians were rather conscious of their body odour, and there were numerous ways, in addition to applying scented oil, of combating this. Numerous tomb paintings show revellers at banquets with a small cone of fat on their heads. There are varying thoughts about this cone, one being they were made of animal fat and saturated with perfume, and as they slowly melted they gave off a subtle fragrance. Such cones may have been made by the cold-steeping technique, which comprised placing a number of flower petals (rose or jasmine are best suited), over a layer of animal fat placed between two boards. When the fat had absorbed the fragrance the petals were replaced with fresh petals. This process was repeated for a number of weeks until the fat layer was saturated with scent. Then it was moulded into cones.[86]

Some scholars believe, however, that these cones were not worn as a physical item but were purely an artistic representation to show the application of perfume. [87] This is supported by the overall eroticism of the banquet scenes, in which the revellers are anointed with oil, imbibing alcohol and watching dancers.[88] The shape of the cone has also led some scholars to believe there is in fact a spiritual element to them, the thought being that they were associated with the ba, an element of the spirit. The shape of the cone varies, developing from a standard loaf of bread shape, to a pile of corn, and back to a long loaf of bread of the type offered to the gods and essential for the survival of the ba in the afterlife.[89]

Egyptians were also regular users of breath freshener in the form of balls of cinnamon, myrrh, frankincense and rush nut, which one would chew on. Dental hygiene was minimal and teeth were cleaned by chewing on a twig or stiff reed.[90] Underarm deodorant was approached in a similar manner; small balls of incense and porridge were placed in elbows and armpits [91] and as they heated up they omitted a pleasant smell.

It is possible to see that the ancient Egyptians were not so different to modern societies in the way they passed their free time – drinking, going to parties, playing board games and listening to music – and the care they took in their appearance is something familiar to all societies, ancient and modern. Some aspects of the ancient Egyptian lifestyle are not, however, comparable to the modern world; this is most obviously their religious beliefs and household religious practices, which will be discussed in the next chapter.

3.

HOUSEHOLD RELIGION

'When I did a deed of transgression against the Peak, she punished me.'[1]

For the ancient Egyptians religion was more than simply a belief system; it was fundamental to their entire culture and comprised hundreds of deities who dealt with all aspects of daily life. These gods came in many forms, including animal and human, each with a specific role, their own imagery, mythology and cult practices. Contrary to popular belief, the Egyptians did not worship animals, but rather the anthropomorphic gods were believed to possess the characteristics associated with the animal represented; for example, Hathor, a cow-headed deity, was a mother goddess, as the cow was associated with life-giving milk and sustenance.

The pantheon was separated into state and personal deities. State religion was that of the king and is presented in temples throughout Egypt. These gods were concerned with the complexities of environmental cycles (solar and inundation), kingship succession, battles and cosmic equilibrium (Maat). Such concerns were too complex for ordinary people to comprehend, as their worries included primarily illness, fertility and childbirth. Therefore different deities that helped with such concerns were worshipped in the home. There were, of course, some deities who appealed to both king and commoner; Isis, for example, the mother of Horus and general mother goddess, or Ptah, a creator god worshipped primarily at Deir el-Medina as the god of craftsmen. Consequently there were deities who were members of both the state and household pantheon of gods.

Religious mythology was used in Egypt to explain environmental cycles and world formation, in the form of creation myths. Although the deities concerned were state gods, the whole population was familiar with the stories. There were, however, variants on the creation story, with different supreme deities dependending on the period and the city.

The primary myth concerns the Ennead of Heliopolis: the nine most important deities of the pantheon. According to this myth, creation took place in Heliopolis, just outside modern Cairo. In the time before creation the world was empty, except for darkness and the primordial waters known as Nu or Nun. Although there is a sacred lake in every temple in Egypt reminiscent of this primordial water, there are no temples or shrines dedicated to Nun in his own right.

A small mound of earth arose from the primordial water, upon which a lotus flower emerged. From this flower the solar deity Atum came into existence. Such a mound was familiar to the ancient Egyptians as these were the first visible land masses after the annual inundation started to abate. Every year, from July until October, much of Egypt was under water. This was essential for the fertility of the farmland, as the inundation brought with it rich silt which was deposited over the fields. As the water abated and the first mounds appeared, due to their freshly silted fertility, small shoots of plant life were visible on the top. Therefore, in the minds of the Egyptians, this was associated with the first mound of creation from which all life began.

Upon the first mound Atum, as a solar god, instigated the birth of the sun and the first dawn. Although male, Atum was able to self-reproduce through spilling bodily fluids. The next generation of gods, Shu and Tefnut, were created from spit and semen. Utterance 527 of the Pyramid Texts states, 'Atum is he who came into being, who masturbated in Heliopolis. He took his phallus in his grasp that he might create orgasm by means of it, and were born the twins Shu and Tefnut.'[2] This makes it clear that Atum masturbated to create the next generation of gods. However, Utterance 600 claims they were born from his mouth: 'You spat out Shu, you expectorated Tefnut, and you set your arms around them'.[3]

Shu was the god of air, whose name means void or empty. He is depicted as a man with arms raised to support the sky, filling the space between the sky (Nut) and the earth (Geb). Pyramid Text Utterance 222 states the bones of Shu were the clouds used by the king to descend to heaven. 'Go up, open your way by means of the bones of Shu, the embrace of your mother Nut will enfold you.'[4]

Tefnut, Shu's sister, whose name means 'to spit', was the goddess of moisture and was believed to be visible in the morning dew which purified the land. Shu and Tefnut then produced the next generation of gods, Geb and Nut. They formed the boundaries of the sphere which constituted the world, with Shu and Tefnut within and Nun the primeval water surrounding the exterior. The sun was unable to exist in the area outside this sphere. In the tomb of Ramses VI (1141–1133 BCE) the sun god is depicted travelling along Nut's body, to be swallowed at dusk in order to continue the journey inside her body until rebirth in the morning.

Nut and Geb's children were the most important gods in the pantheon: Osiris, Isis, Seth and Nephthys. The first five deities of the Ennead (Atum, Shu, Tefnut, Geb and Nut) explained the environment in a simplistic way, whereas the mythology of the final four deities explained the laws of kingship and succession.

The Turin King List (dated to Ramses II 1279–1212 BCE) records the time when Egypt was ruled by the gods; Ptah, followed by Ra (one of the many sun-gods), then Shu, Geb and Osiris. As king, Osiris taught the people how to farm, make wine, obey laws and believe in the gods.

> This he did by showing them the fruits of cultivation, by giving them laws, and by teaching them to honour the gods. Later he travelled over the whole earth civilizing it without the slightest need of arms, but most of the peoples he won over to his way by the charm of his persuasive discourse combined with song and all manner of music (Plutarch 13).[5]

Osiris's wife Isis taught wives how to make bread and beer. His brother Seth was envious of Osiris's popularity and plotted against him in order to take the throne for himself. The most detailed version of this story comes from Plutarch's *Isis and Osiris* (120 CE), although there are fragments in the Old Kingdom Pyramid Texts. Seth collected the bodily measurements of Osiris and built a box of priceless wood which fit them exactly. Seth then held a banquet and invited Osiris and a number of fellow conspirators to dine. In the middle of the banquet Seth presented the box to the revellers.

> The company was much pleased at the sight of it and admired it greatly, whereupon Typhon [Seth] jestingly promised to present it to the man who should find the chest to be exactly his length when he lay down in it. They all tried it in turn, but no one fitted it; then Osiris got into it and lay down, and those who were in the plot ran to it and slammed down the lid, which they fastened by nails from the outside and also by using molten lead (Plutarch 13).

Seth then cast the chest into the Nile and it floated away, drowning Osiris. When Isis heard about this she immediately began searching for the chest. She learnt that a casket had been found in Byblos and travelled there to retrieve it. After some time she located the chest, but discovered that the spirit of Osiris had entered a tamarisk tree which the king of Byblos had used for a pillar in his palace. Isis appealed to the queen of Byblos and eventually returned with the body and the casket to Abydos. After unloading the chest she fell into a deep sleep, only to be discovered by Seth, who was hunting crocodiles in the area.

> [She] bestowed the chest in a place well out of the way; but Typhon [Seth], who was hunting by night in the light of the moon, happened upon it. Recognizing the body he divided it into fourteen parts and scattered them, each in a different place. Isis learned of this and sought for them again, sailing through the swamps in a boat of papyrus (Plutarch 18).

The tears of Isis, instigated by the loss of her husband, were believed by some to be the cause of the first inundation. Greek records, however, state her tears were those of joy, at the discovery of her pregnancy with Horus.[6]

Isis and her sister Nephthys started to search for Osiris's body parts. They eventually found thirteen of the fourteen pieces.

> Of the parts of Osiris's body the only one which Isis did not find was the male member, for the reason that this had been at once tossed into the river, and the lepidotus, the sea-bream, and the pike had fed upon it; and it is from these very fishes the Egyptians are most scrupulous in abstaining (Plutarch 18).

Wherever they discovered a body part they built a tomb, the most important of which was Abydos, where the murder took place.

After discovering all the pieces of the body Isis resurrected Osiris and turned herself into a kite, using her wings to breathe life back into him. She modelled a penis from clay and became impregnated with her son Horus. After that final act Osiris was banished to the realm of the dead, where he remained as the god of the underworld. Seth then took over the throne of Egypt.

In the later periods of dynastic history the murder was ritually re-enacted annually to ensure that the cycle of life continued. In the Ptolemaic Period, this ritual re-enactment of the Sacred Mysteries was common and was dominated by priestesses rather than priests. Two priestesses were recruited in particular to play the roles of Isis and Nephthys. They had all their bodily hair removed in order to maintain their purity and wore wigs and headdresses to identify them with the goddesses. The names Isis and Nephthys were written upon each goddess's arm, to make it clear which role they were playing, and they chanted from sacred texts while shaking their sistra, which were bronze rattles sacred to the goddess cults. Performing a re-enactment at the burial place of Osiris was very powerful and ensured the cycle of birth and death was maintained.

In a similar Ptolemaic re-enactment at the Serapeum at Saqqara, the burial place of the Apis bulls, orphaned twin girls were known to have played the roles of Isis and Nephthys in the ceremonies surrounding the burial of this sacred Bull. The Apis Bull was thought to accommodate the ba of the creator god Ptah during its lifetime, and was treated as a god for all of its natural life. Even the mother of the Apis Bull was revered and kept in luxury. Both the bull and his mother were mummified and buried in stone sarcophagi with traditional canopic jars (see chapter nine) and offering stelae.

The twins, Taous and Tawe, had requested asylum at the Serapeum, where a friend of their father worked. Their mother had left their father and moved in with another man, who attempted to murder their father. He managed to escape, but died of grief after being separated from his daughters. His body was returned to their mother, 'but to this day Nephoris [their mother] has not troubled to bury him'.[7] Nephoris then sold his possessions even though the twins should have inherited them, and threw them out onto the street. They approached the Serapeum in the hope of refuge. 'At that moment the mourning for the Apis was declared, and they hired us to make the lamentations for the god.'[8] They performed tasks around the temple to pay for their upkeep, the most important and symbolic being the divine mourners at the Apis Bull funeral.

As the burial place of Osiris, Abydos was considered an important place of pilgrimage for many Egyptians. The journey to Abydos was depicted on the walls of numerous New Kingdom tombs, or model boats were placed in the tomb to enable the deceased's spirit to make the pilgrimage. However, despite the apparent importance on the walls of the tombs, it seems that not many Egyptians physically went on pilgrimage to Abydos in life. The images in the tomb acted as a substitute for a physical pilgrimage and ensured the deceased (the new Osiris) connected with the divine Osiris on a spiritual level.[9]

Horus was raised secretly by his mother Isis in the marshes until he was old enough to take his rightful place, as the son of Osiris, on the throne. However, Seth still wanted to rule and called for a tribunal held by the Ennead, which lasted for eighty years. 'The Contendings of Horus and Seth' describes this tribunal and is recorded on the Chester Beatty I Papyrus (twentieth dynasty).

Ra-Horakhti (another sun-god) presided over the tribunal and supported Seth, whereas the other deities believed, as the son of Osiris, the throne rightfully belonged to Horus. There were various judgments, each declaring Horus to be the rightful king, but Seth refused to accept the decision. He boasted that the throne was his by right on the basis of his personal strength, before challenging Horus to a battle, demanding they both turn into hippopotamuses and submerge themselves in the water for three months. The one to re-emerge should be given the crown.

After they submerged Isis was distressed, and made a fishing line with a copper barb and cast it into the water, where it pierced first Horus and then Seth. Both appealed to her for mercy, the former as her only son, the latter as her brother. Isis felt compassion for both of them and released them, incurring the wrath of Horus. He was furious that she had shown mercy to Seth and cut off her head in a fit of rage. Ra-Horakhti ordered that Horus should be punished. Seth found him asleep under a tree, attacked him, plucked out his eyes and threw him down the mountain. Hathor discovered Horus weeping in the desert and healed him by milking a gazelle into his eyes. She reported his injuries to Ra-Horakhti and the Ennead, who demanded Horus and Seth stop their arguing. Seth agreed and asked Horus to dine at his house that evening.

After the meal when Horus was sleeping, Seth inserted his erect phallus between Horus's thighs. Horus caught the semen in his hand and showed the revived Isis what Seth had done. Becoming angry, Isis cut off Horus's hands and threw them into the river, making new ones from clay. She then took Horus's semen and poured it over Seth's lettuce garden. When Seth ate a lettuce the next day he became pregnant. Lettuces were considered an aphrodisiac due to the white, semen-like liquid that poured from the stem when cut, and were the sacred vegetable of the fertility god Amun-Min. Seth reported the incident to the Ennead.

Horus decided to settle the argument with a race in stone ships. It was Horus's turn to cheat and he constructed his boat of pine and covered it with gypsum to resemble stone. Seth sliced off the top of a mountain and fashioned a boat from it. They started their race in the presence of the Ennead. Seth's boat sank and he transformed himself into a hippopotamus and attacked Horus's ship. Horus aimed a copper harpoon at him but the Ennead stopped him. Horus later complained that he had been in the tribunal for eighty years and was constantly winning against Seth but still was not king. After some deliberation and intervention by Osiris in the underworld, the Ennead arrived at the conclusion that the throne of Egypt should belong to Horus. As a consolation Seth was to accompany the sun-god on his solar barque to fight the enemy of the sun-god, the snake Apophis.

This myth introduces a number of deities and confirms the act of succession as well as the balance of order (Horus) over chaos (Seth), all of which were relevant, not only to the king, but also to the wider populace, as such concepts were important in daily life. There were numerous other myths which the Egyptians may have been familiar with, although they may not have had such an impact of their day-to-day lives.

However, during the reign of Akhenaten the religion of the king was to have a great, if not necessarily positive impact on the very foundations of society. Akhenaten decided to eliminate the rich pantheon of gods and replace them all with the Aten. The Aten was portrayed as a sun-disc with a uraeus on the lower arc and was androgynous in nature. Hands on the end of the sun-rays emanating from the disc often held the symbol of life (the ankh), which was offered to the mouth and nose of Akhenaten, his queen, Nefertiti, and their daughters. This was never offered to the ordinary citizens of Tell el-Amarna as only Akhenaten and the royal family were allowed to worship the Aten; everyone else worshipped the royal family.

The Aten does not appear in any myths and is androgynous, being neither male nor female. It is constantly present above the heads of the people and worship was carried out in the open air, with temples having rows and rows of open-air offering tables. One of the Amarna Letters (EA16) to Akhenaten from the Assyrian king complains about the treatment of the messengers at Tell el-Amarna: 'Why should messengers be made to stay constantly in the sun and to die in the sun?'[10] Clearly not everyone was happy with standing in the sun for hours on end. After Akhenaten's death the Aten returned to the role of a minor deity, leaving the pantheon open again for traditional deities.

Although the city of Tell el-Amarna was founded in order to worship the Aten and no other deity, there is little evidence this worship was carried out within the houses of many of the citizens, as statues and stelae dedicated to the traditional gods have been discovered, indicating many people were simply paying lip service to Akhenaten's new god. In one house in the workman village at Tell el-Amarna there was an image of four dancing Bes figures, all with different arm and head positions,[11] moving towards a figure of Taweret. In a house in the main city at Tell el-Amarna a cupboard underneath an altar also produced a stela of a woman and child worshipping a figure of Taweret,[12] and in another house there was a large wall mural showing four figures of Bes dancing, although whether they were dancing in front of another figure is not clear.[13] Bes and Taweret were still clearly worshipped in the homes at Tell el-Amarna despite Akhenaten's ban on any gods but himself and the Aten.

It is difficult for people today to understand how much of an upheaval this religious revolution would have been for the ordinary people of Egypt. The population of Egypt were essentially told that everything they had believed since childhood was wrong and they were to stop believing in the gods and only worship the royal family, whom most of the population never saw. It was doomed to failure from the outset. People continued to worship the gods they had always worshipped, which comprised a rich pantheon of household gods that they appealed to in times of trouble and who were a major part of their daily lives.

As the main temples throughout Egypt were not open for worship to the public, only being accessible to the king, priests and invited officials, everybody worshipped their gods within their own homes. However, should they know someone with access to the temple they appealed to that person to approach the god on their behalf.

When I was looking for you (the god) to tell you some affairs of mine, you happened to be concealed in your holy of holies and there was nobody having access to it to send it to you. Now as I was waiting to encounter Hori ... and he said to me 'I have access' so I am sending him to you. See you must discard seclusion today and come out in procession in order that you may decide upon the issue involving seven kilts belonging to the temple of Horemheb and also those two kilts belonging to the necropolis scribe ... now as for one who is the same position as you, being in the place of seclusion and concealed, he sends forth pronouncements, but you haven't communicated anything to me at all.[14]

It seems that this man's reason for wanting access to the god was to approach him as an oracle in order to settle a dispute about some stolen kilts.

Another person was unable to visit the temple due to illness even though he had been invited, so therefore appealed to someone else to go on his behalf:

Please call upon Amun to bring me back, for I have been ill since I arrived north and am not in my normal state. Don't set your minds to anything else. As soon as my letter reaches you, you shall go to the forecourt of Amun of the Thrones of the Two Lands, taking all the little children with you and coax him and tell him to keep me safe.[15]

While state temples were generally off limits to the majority of people, the community at Deir el-Medina solved the problem by building small shrines dedicated to state gods in the village. For example, in the eighteenth dynasty to the north of the village a small temple was built to the god Amun; while maintained and built by the villagers themselves, during the reign of Ramses II the king actually made improvements to it. There were smaller shrines dedicated to the gods Ptah, Hathor, Thoth, Khnum, Seshat, Taweret and Meretseger, some in the northern part of the village and others on the path over the cliffs leading to the Valley of the Kings. Also within the village was a terraced temple dedicated to the deified founder of the village Amenhotep I and his wife Ahmose-Nefertari. This temple housed the oracle of Amenhotep I and the villagers approached this in order to settle disputes, solve problems and ask for the god's help.

While those on the east bank could appeal to the main temples (should they have access) to settle disputes and to cure illnesses, and those in Deir el-Medina constructed their own temples that were open only to them, generally state gods were not approached for the trials and tribulations of everyday life. Household gods reflected personal concerns, and many were associated with fertility, pregnancy and childbirth, or with a particular locale, whether it be a nome (region) or a city. Like state gods, household gods often had their own associated myths, regalia, practices and taboos.

Household religion catered directly for the concerns of the householder, and one of the most common concerns was childbirth. Childbirth was one of the most dangerous times in a woman's life; approximately 1.5 per cent of mothers died[16] and infant mortality was as high as 50 per cent, so divine intervention at this time was essential. One of the most common childbirth gods was Bes. From the eighteenth dynasty he was shown as an achondroplastic dwarf with a lion's head and tail and was depicted facing forward with bowed legs, feet turned outwards, arms bent at the elbows and his hands placed on his hips. His lion face is sometimes thought to be a mask; a cartonnage mask was discovered at El-Lahun together with items used in childbirth, and a similar mask of moulded clay was also discovered at Deir el-Medina. They are thought to have belonged to a midwife, doctor or dancer.

Bes's lion's tail is sometimes replaced with a cape of lion skin and after the New Kingdom he often wore a panther skin, with the head and claws across the breast, instead of the traditional lion skin. In the eighteenth dynasty he was often shown with wings, especially on the apotropaic or protective wands (see chapter four) used in childbirth rituals in order to prevent evil spirits from harming the mother and newborn child. On these wands he is often shown holding a knife in order to represent his aggressive nature when scaring off demons. He is sometimes shown carrying the *sa* symbol of protection, a knife, or two snakes and a gazelle, indicating he defeated evil.[17]

Bes had many roles; he was the god of love, marriage, jollification, the guardian of Horus-the-child and consequently the protector of all children, and was therefore evoked during childbirth. '[The spell was] to be said four times over a dwarf of clay [a Bes amulet], [and] placed on the crown of the head of a woman who is giving birth under suffering.'[18] Through the process of singing, dancing and music he chased away snakes, scorpions and all forces of evil or malevolent spirits. His role as a musician and dancer connects him to Hathor, as the dance was sacred to her. In the Middle Kingdom he was given the title The Fighting Deity and was shown holding a knife, which focused on his violent nature. This was later reinforced in the Roman Period, when he was represented in Roman military costume as a war god.[19]

Throughout the pharaonic period there were no temples dedicated to Bes, but in the Ptolemaic Period at Saqqara there was a small Bes shrine. This comprised a few rooms next to a large enclosure wall surrounding another temple (which is now destroyed). The walls were a combination of mud-brick and limestone fragments and large-scale figures of Bes (1-1.5 metres) had been modelled from clay and painted. Next to these figures were others of smaller, nude ladies. There were also large platforms which could have been used for sleeping, indicating that dream therapy was practiced here.[20] This was when the devotees slept at the temple and the god sent them dreams which, once interpreted, helped with their problems. Excavations uncovered numerous limestone votive statues of Bes, some with a large penis indicating fertility was a major focus of this cult. The cult developed further in the Roman Period; the Roman historian Ammianus Marcellinus records an oracle of Bes was situated in Upper Egypt.

Although Bes has this deep-rooted connection with childbirth and fertility he is rarely shown with a wife or consort, as most other deities are; however, in later periods a female counterpart, Beset, was introduced. She is shown as full-size with a lion's head and is often holding a snake to show her protective nature. She was an Asiatic deity who had been adopted into the Egyptian pantheon.

Bes was closely associated with the goddess Taweret and they were often represented on the same objects, which included furniture, headrests, pottery vessels, kohl tubes, cosmetic spoons and mirrors. Taweret was a pregnant hippopotamus, normally shown standing on her hind legs with pendulous breasts and a protruding stomach. Her breasts emphasised her role of a nursing mother, and were in no way considered erotic. She bore the head of a hippopotamus, the four limbs and paws of a lion and a mane in the form of a crocodile's tail. She was also evoked during childbirth to scare away harmful demons and spirits.

As a fertility goddess, Taweret was associated with female sexuality and pregnancy and was affiliated with the goddess Hathor. Hence, she is sometimes shown wearing the cow-horn and sun-disc headdress common to Hathor. She was given the title 'She Who Removes the Birth Waters',[21] making her connection with childbirth clear. Like Bes, Taweret also carried the *sa* sign of protection, an ankh, a knife or a torch, the flame of which repelled evil spirits. In the funerary cult, Taweret was the 'Lady of Magical Protection', who guided the dead into the afterlife.

Childbirth deities were often associated with death and rebirth as the process was believed to be the same; one is the birth into life and the other is the rebirth into the afterlife. Hathor, for example, protected the western mountains leading to the necropolis, consequently protecting the deceased at the start of their journey. Therefore any female deities equated with her often held a similar role.

Amulets and their moulds of both Bes and Taweret have been discovered at numerous sites, including Naukratis and even Tell el-Amarna. Larger amulets were worn singly, whereas smaller ones were incorporated into necklaces or bracelets. They were worn during pregnancy and labour, and may have been hung around the necks of newly born infants as well as older children.[22] Amulets of Bes and Taweret were sometimes given as votive offerings to Hathor at her shrines.

At Deir el-Medina a particularly important god for the workmen was Ptah, the patron of artists, stonemasons and craftsmen. As a state god Ptah's role was that of Divine Creator, creating the world as a craftsman works. He is often depicted in a divine triad with Sekhmet and their child Nefertum. As a personal god he protected the creative industries, but he was also thought to cause blindness to those who did not uphold the laws of Maat. This was an ailment that frequently affected the workmen in the Valley of the Kings, as they worked in dark, dusty and confined spaces. Therefore there are numerous appeals to Ptah to remove the affliction of blindness which they believed was caused by offending him in some way, either through impiety or blasphemy.[23] The stela of the workman Neferabut from Deir el-Medina was dedicated to Ptah and describes such a curse: 'I am a man who swore falsely by Ptah, Lord of Maat; he made me see darkness by day ... He caused me to be like the dogs of the street, I being in his hand. He made men and gods observe me, I being as a man who has sinned against his lord.'[24]

Many people dedicated 'ear stelae' to Ptah, so called because these stelae were inscribed with between 1 and 376 images of ears. A god was thought to have multiple ears and eyes and the stelae appealed to all of them. Some examples have an inscription dedicated to 'He Who Hears Prayers' and the idea was that these stelae were a conduit for voicing prayers directly into the ear of the god. The god is emphasised as the focus, as the deity is named far more often than the donor: 'I am calling you, Mut, Lady of Heaven, that you may hear my petitions.'[25] As with many personal religious items they varied in material and craftsmanship, and there are wooden or stone examples. Although primarily dedicated to Ptah, some are also inscribed with images or inscriptions to Hathor, Amun, Mut, Thoth or Sekhmet and have been found at Deir el-Medina, Thebes, Giza and Memphis.

These stelae were erected at a Chapel of the Hearing Ear, which was situated outside the temple proper as ordinary people were unable to enter the temple. At Karnak temple – on the eastern side there were several of these chapels – the remains of one still standing is dominated by a large calcite statue of Thutmosis III and Amun.[26] It is referred to in a building inscription of Thutmosis III as a 'proper place of hearing for Amun-Ra' and there were wab priests and doorkeepers associated with this structure.[27] The concept of ear stelae and hearing chapels was popular from the Middle Kingdom to the Roman Period.[28] Inscriptions describing Ptah of the Hearing Ear have been discovered in Deir el-Medina, Thebes and Memphis. One devotee, the sculptor Ptahmose, asked that after his death he would be allowed to dwell in the temple of Ptah, indicating prayers were not always in anticipation of something in this life.

Another deity worshipped primarily at Deir el-Medina was Meretseger, a cobra goddess. The Valley of the Kings lies in the shadow of a natural, pyramid-shaped hill known as the 'Lady of the Peak' who was personified in the form of the snake goddess Meretseger. She was known as 'She who Loves Silence' and was worshipped over the whole of the Theban necropolis, although primarily at Deir el-Medina.[29] The workmen at Deir el-Medina set three-dimensional images of cobras at their doorways, and in the lower- or middle-class houses at Memphis they fashioned cobras from clay with offering bowls. In this manner the goddess protected the house.[30] She caused those who incurred her wrath to be bitten by a snake or afflicted with blindness and there are numerous inscriptions to her from the workmen in relation to this. One workman, Neferabut, laments,

> [I am] an ignorant and witless man ... I knew not good or evil ...
> when I did a deed of transgression against the Peak, she punished
> me, and I was in her hand by night as well as day ... I called out
> to the wind, but it did not come to me ... but when I called to my
> mistress, I found her coming to me with sweet breezes. She showed
> mercy unto me, after she had let me see her hand. She turned about
> to me in mercy.[31]

It was believed the truly repentant would be cured of their snake bite and would regain their sight. Neferabut clearly was uncertain as to which deity he had wronged, hence the stela was dedicated to both Ptah and Meretseger.

Another state deity worshipped as a household goddess was Hathor. In the home she was a goddess of sexuality and motherhood and protector during childbirth. In chapter 148 of the Book of the Dead she took the form of the Seven Hathors who pronounced the fate of the newborn baby.[32] The incantation addresses the cow-goddess directly: 'May you grant bread and beer, offerings and provisions which are beneficial to my spirit, may you grant me life, prosperity, health, joy and long duration on earth.'[33]

Hathor's connection with childbirth is reflected in her title Lady of the Vulva and her shrines were often approached by childless couples desperate to conceive, who left votive offerings of clay or wooden penises, necklaces, beads or three-dimensional female figurines. Hathor was connected with all aspects of female lives, but personified male as well as female sexuality. At Deir el-Medina domestic items, shrines, votive stelae, tomb paintings and amulets[34] were dedicated to Hathor by both men and women, although most of the votive cloths from Deir el Bahri name women and depict family scenes, indicating they were dedicated by women. The men making offerings were probably appealing for help and protection during the fertile aspects of their lives, as well as a cure for male sexual problems, including impotence or infertility. Ramose, a scribe at Deir el-Medina born in approximately 1413 BCE (see chapter one), sought a cure for such a problem.[35] He and his wife, Mutemwia, were childless and had petitioned various deities for children but to no avail. He dedicated stelae and statues to different gods, including Qudshu, the Asiatic goddess of love; Reshef, the Asiatic thunder-god; Taweret, the hippopotamus goddess of childbirth; Min, the fertility god; and Shed, the saviour and helper of mankind. He also dedicated numerous statues and a stone phallus to Hathor, the latter bearing an inscription that reads, 'O Hathor, remember the man at his burial. Grant a duration in your house as a rewarded one to the scribe Ramose. O Golden One, who loves when you desired the praised one, you desired one, cause me to receive a compensation of your house as a rewarded one.'[36] This was a plea by Ramose for fertility, and was perhaps a final act of a desperate couple. However, the couple still did not conceive and they were forced to adopt, as was traditional (see chapter four).

In the villages Hathor was worshipped as the 'Lady of Drunkenness', as it was believed that through drinking alcohol it was possible to experience the goddess and converse with her. Conversing with the goddess was made easier at the Temple of Mut at Karnak, which in the New Kingdom had a Porch of Drunkenness associated with Hatshepsut. Worshippers got drunk, slept here and were woken by drummers in order to commune with the goddess Mut.[37]

The Festival of Drunkenness enabled the villagers of Deir el-Medina to get drunk in the hope of communicating directly with the goddess Hathor. This festival was dedicated to Hathor in her form of Sekhmet, as a means of ensuring her return. On the Ptolemaic gateway to the Temple of Mut at Karnak, it is described that the beer drunk at this festival was red in order to look like blood, and makes reference to the myth of the 'Destruction of Mankind', where Sekhmet gorged on the blood of mankind.[38] All festivals dedicated to Hathor involved playing instruments, especially the sistra, singing and dancing. Moreover, most festivals at Deir el-Medina dedicated to the goddess also involved alcohol and drunkenness, which no doubt also led to singing and dancing. Some festivals also had a sexual nature; one included the transportation in procession of a large phallus, and another was called the Festival of Opening of the Bosoms of the Women, which may very well have ended in an orgy.[39]

Hathor was also worshiped in a funerary function in her form as Lady of the West or Goddess of the Western Mountain. In these roles she protected the necropolis and all those in it. She is often depicted in this form as a cow emerging from the cliffs or overshadowing the tomb. As the Lady of the Sycamore, Hathor provided nourishment for the deceased in the form of a sycamore fig tree. She is depicted in this form in both royal and non-royal tombs, sometimes emerging from the tree as a woman bearing a tray of food or pouring water into the tomb owner's hands, demonstrating her role in the continuance of the afterlife. Sometimes, as in the tomb of Thutmosis III, Hathor is shown as a tree with a breast nursing the king, showing her status as mother goddess and nurturer of the king.

Although all families worshipped all or some of the deities discussed, primarily they worshipped their own ancestors, who upon death and rebirth into the afterlife became Excellent Spirits of Re (*akh ikr en Re*). These spirits were thought to be able to affect the life of the living as well as influence the gods of the afterlife.[40] The ancestors worshipped were within two or three generations: parent, spouse, child or sibling,[41] presumably those within living memory. However, in the tomb of Paheri at El Kab there are, rather unusually, five generations depicted, including the tomb owner and his wife, their children and grandchildren, as well as the parents and grandparents of the tomb owner and his wife, and their aunts, uncles and cousins.[42] It is quite likely that if the women of the family had their children at a young age all five generations were in fact known to each other, which renders this scene well in keeping with the traditional number of generations.

Normally the ancestors worshipped were depicted on a small stela (approximately 25 centimetres in height), holding a lotus flower and standing before a deity, or seated and being worshipped by their living relatives. These stelae were often dedicated to men, and may have been placed in the second room of the house – the masculine room[43] (see chapter two). In some cases the ancestor is depicted on more than one stela and worshipped in multiple homes within the community,[44] either representing extended family worship or a wider reverence for a particular individual.

These stelae were often accompanied by ancestor busts consisting of small (less than 30 centimetres) human heads on a base made of stone, clay, wood or faience. Some figures were bald and others had natural hair or large tri-partite wigs. The only other adornment was a collar with lotus blossoms and buds hanging from it. Over 150 ancestor busts are known, mostly from Deir el-Medina, but only five have hieroglyphic inscriptions, two with the title Lady of the House and a name and another with the name and titles of Hathor, suggesting the goddess was portrayed in this particular case[45] rather than a family member. A number of them have red-brown skin indicative of male figures, although these busts represented both men and women.

Such ancestral busts were designed to be placed in temples and shrines and were the focus for religious offerings. Food and liquid libations were brought and placed in front of the statue in order to appease the ancestors and encourage them to help the family in daily life. When in the homes they were used as protection against evil forces as well as for the family to appeal to them for favours.[46] A number of them were found north of the Hathor temple at Deir el-Medina, indicating they may have been part of a procession to the chapels and shrines in and around the village.[47]

It is thought the villagers took part in the Beautiful Festival of the Valley, when the statue of Amun was taken from Karnak in procession to the necropolis on the west bank and joined the procession carrying the ancestor busts where they were worshipped alongside the gods at the tombs.[48] The Beautiful Festival of the Valley was a festival of the dead between the harvest and the inundation. One element of this festival was that the ithyphallic form of Amun-Re visited the temple of Deir el Bahri and 'spent the night' with Hathor. Couples may have used this time to invoke blessings on their sexual relationship and associate themselves with the divine couple. Couples may have slept at the Hathor shrine on this night in the hope of receiving a dream of the goddess[49] or even to conceive. They possibly thought that having intercourse at this time would result in conception. It is quite likely that Ramose and his wife also attempted to conceive at this time, but were not fortunate enough to be blessed by the goddess.

The existence of a large number of the stelae and busts in the home suggest that the ancestors were considered to be a part of the world of the living and it was believed that the Excellent Spirits of Re could intercede on behalf of the living in matters of daily life and also in concerns of the afterlife. Often the families appealed to the deceased in the form of letters to the dead, in which they asked for help in various matters. These letters were often left at the tomb following feast days and celebrations, in the form of clay bowls filled with offerings. The idea being that once the spirit of the ancestor had gained nourishment from the food they would then see the letter and feel obliged to grant the requests. Some letters are written on linen or papyrus, although the majority are on such bowls.

One letter on a pottery bowl was from a man called Shepsi to his dead parents, asking for them to intervene over a property dispute.[50] On the inside of the bowl the inscription reads,

Shepsi speaks to his father Iinekhenmut. This is a reminder of your journey to the dungeon [?], to the place where Sen's son Hetepu was, when you brought the foreleg of an ox, and when this your son came with Newaef, and when you said, 'Welcome, both of you. Sit and eat meat!' Am I to be injured in your presence, without this your son having done or said anything, by my brother? [And yet] I was the one who buried him, I brought him from the dungeon [?], I placed him among his desert tomb-dwellers, even though thirty measures of refined barley were due from him by a loan, and one bundle of garments, six measures of fine barley, one ball [?] of flax, and a cup- even though I did for him what did not [need] to be done. He has done this against this your son evilly, evilly. but you had said to this your son, 'All my property is vested in my son Shepsi along with my fields'. Now Sher's son Henu has been taken. See, he is with you in the same city. You have to go to judgement with him now, since your scribes are with [you] in the same city. Can a man be joyful, when his spears are used [against his own son (?)].

Here he is clearly unhappy that he did everything he should have done for his brother in regard to funerary rites, even though there was an outstanding debt. As this brother is in the realm of the dead, Shepsi wants his father to intervene in order to solve the problem. On the outside of the bowl he writes to his mother about the same complaint.

> Shepsi speaks to his mother Iy. This is a reminder of the time that you said to this your son 'Bring me quails for me to eat', and when this your son brought to you seven quails for you to eat. Am I to be injured in your presence, so that the children are badly discontent with this your son? Who then will pour out water for you? If only you would judge between me and Sobekhotep! I brought him from another town, and placed him in his town among his male and female dead, and gave him burial cloth. Why then is he acting against this your son, when I have said and done nothing, evilly, evilly? Evil-doing is painful for the gods![51]

It seems he had to bring the body of Sobekhotep from another town to be buried in the appropriate cemetery, and yet he feels he is being victimised by him and clearly wants his parents to intervene.

There are only about fifteen of these letters in existence and all are written to recently deceased relatives. They date from the Old Kingdom to the New Kingdom and perhaps reflect a much wider practice than the small survival numbers suggest. These letters are often written under stress, which is reflected in the handwriting and the unplanned nature of the requests. They are thought to derive from the oral tradition of going to the tomb to ask the spirits for help, and perhaps indicate an increasingly literate population. They are not 'chatty' letters, written solely to communicate with the dead, but rather raise more urgent matters, such as problems encountered in this world or anticipated in the next.

Unfortunately, not all Egyptian religion was of a positive nature; curse figures have been discovered, which were made of wax or clay and were inscribed with a single name or group of names. Often these figures were broken, which was believed to cause harm to the named individual. During the Harem Conspiracy against Ramses III the conspirators made wax figures of the palace guards in order to overpower them.

> And he began the ritual of consulting the divine oracle so to delude people. But he reached the side of the harem of that other great, expansive place, and he began to use the waxen figures in order that they be taken inside by the inspector Adi-ram for staving off one gang of men and spellbinding the others so that a few messages could be taken in and others brought out.[52]

In the British Museum there is a wax figure with a thread running through it which may have been used to curse someone. Although this is thought to be dated to the Roman Period,[53] the method described in the Harem Conspiracy Papyrus appears to be the same. While the physical evidence of wax curse figures is lacking, the idea was one familiar to the Egyptians; in Papyrus Westcar a man accused of adultery was thrown into the Nile with a wax figurine of a crocodile, which turned into a real crocodile and devoured him as soon as it hit the water. While this is a fantasy tale, aspects of reality are often used to make stories believable.

Perhaps the limited evidence for curse figurines reflects a less hateful nature than the political propaganda texts concerning foreign enemies suggest. The worship of ancestors perhaps made it more natural for the Egyptians to turn to their deceased family to help them fight an enemy, rather than the use of such dark magic. On the other hand, as the figures were constructed with wax perhaps they simply did not survive the passing of the millennia in a desert climate.

As the ancestors worshipped slipped out of living memory and were replaced, so to were the wider pantheon of gods. New gods were created as community needs changed and old gods fell out of fashion. Deity worship and the associated rituals varied from town to town, and each town had its own religious cult and specific rituals. Egyptian religion was flexible, meeting the changing needs of the worshippers. Should there be a gap in the pantheon a new god would be created or an ancestor invoked who could address this need. Egyptian religion was therefore totally inclusive for all Egyptians. They could choose who they worshipped and how, and everyone from the poorest farmer to the king had their favourite deity whom they worshipped above all others.

They could purchase beautifully crafted statues or stelae or they could fashion them themselves out of clay, and they worshipped wherever they wanted to with no need for elaborate temples or shrines if they were unavailable. The result was that the pantheon of gods was was an evolving entity, accessible to everyone, which was always able to address their particular problems or requirements.

4.

LOVE, SEX AND MARRIAGE

'Man is more anxious to copulate than a donkey.
What restrains him is his purse.'[1]

Sex in ancient Egypt was an integral part of life and was not considered shameful or taboo. The Egyptian language had at least a dozen words for intercourse,[2] with numerous hieroglyphic signs for male genitalia, although there were none for female genitalia.[3] Not only was the penis used as a determinative hieroglyph for numerous words, but it was also used in votive offerings and religious art to represent fertility and rebirth.

Sex also features prominently in the New Kingdom dream interpretation texts. The Egyptians believed that while asleep they were open to messages from the gods, which were transferred in the form of dreams. However, these messages were complex and a dream about sex could be a positive or a negative omen.

> If a man sees himself in a dream his phallus becoming large: good.
> It means that his possessions will multiply.

> Having intercourse with his mother: good: His companions will
> stick to him.
> Having intercourse with his sister: good. It means that he will
> inherit something.
> Having intercourse with a woman: bad. It means mourning.
> Seeing his phallus erect: bad. It means that he will be robbed.
> Having sex with his wife in the sun: Bad. The god will see his
> miseries.[4]

Sex was considered important for women too and in the medical texts the recognised cure for most female gynaecological problems was penetrative sex; it was thought that if a woman was not sexually active she would be open to all kinds of maladies.[5] This does not, however, indicate that extramarital sex was encouraged. Rather, it was expected that all women were married and had intercourse regularly, but only with their husbands. Furthermore, while it was expected that women would dream about sex, the interpretations were always negative.

> If a woman dreams she is married to her husband, she will be
> destroyed. If she embraces him she will experience grief.
> If a horse has intercourse with her, she will use force against her
> husband.
> If a donkey has intercourse with her, she will be punished for a
> great sin.
> If a he-goat has intercourse with her she will die soon.
> If a Syrian has intercourse with her, she will weep for she will let
> her slaves have intercourse with her.[6]

While dreaming about sex may have been enough for some members of the community, others pursued physical contact, and sex manuals have been discovered at Oxyrhynchus from the Graeco-Roman Period that aided men in this quest. None of the ideas are new. One clearly follows the premise of 'treat them mean, keep them keen': *'Concerning Seductions.* Accordingly the seducer should be unadorned and uncombed, so that he does not seem to the woman to be too concerned about the matter in hand.'[7] Another section encourages the use of flattery, 'saying that the plain woman is the equal of a goddess, the ugly woman is charming, the elderly one is like a young girl'.[8]

Should such blatant attempts at flattery and seduction be unsuccessful, the medical papyri offered medicinal means of snaring the woman of your dreams. One such remedy said to make a woman love her husband was to 'grind acacia seeds with honey. Rub your phallus with it and sleep with the woman'.[9] Another spell was to enable a woman to enjoy intercourse. The man was advised to 'rub [his] phallus with the foam of the mouth of a stallion and sleep with the woman'.[10] Presumably the virility of the stallion was thought to be transferred to the man, who would then prove to be irresistible to all.

Marriages often took place between young girls and older men, meaning it was likely that girls were expected to be virgins to ensure there was no doubt regarding paternity of the first child, but the same was not expected from men.[11] Men were expected to copulate from a young age, and Ankhsheshonq claims that 'man is more anxious to copulate than a donkey. What restrains him is his purse.'[12] Whether he is speaking metaphorically or literally about paying for sex is not entirely clear, but it is likely that men in ancient Egypt visited prostitutes. Most of the evidence for brothels comes from Graeco-Roman Egypt, as prostitution was taxed, meaning a central register probably existed. It is likely, however, that the profession was much older.[13] Visiting prostitutes was a common enough pastime to be considered in the Teaching Texts, as one scribe comments to a student, 'Here you are spending all your time in the company of prostitutes, lolling about ... Here you are next to a pretty girl bathed in perfume, a garland of flowers around her neck, drumming on your belly, unsteady, toppling over onto the ground, and all covered in filth.'[14]

Herodotus records that King Cheops, the builder of the Great Pyramid, actually forced his daughter to take payment for sex in order to build her own funerary monument. This pyramid is said to be the one in the middle of the three smaller pyramids near the Great Pyramid at Giza, and was probably owned by Queen Meritetes. However, Herodotus was writing some two thousand years after the pyramids were built and the story may have been propaganda, or even at this point legend, surrounding an unpopular king.

A section of the cemetery at Deir el-Medina that housed the burials of unattached women and their children has caused some debate. Manniche states there are documents from Deir el-Medina hinting at the existence of prostitutes, naming women who were not wives or mothers but belonged to the 'others'.[15] However, she does not elaborate on what these documents are and they are not identifiable among the available texts from Deir el-Medina.[16] The population of the village comprised men with a function in the building of the tombs and their families, so unattached women were conspicuous unless they provided a service. Graves-Brown has suggested these women were unmarried or divorced.[17] In general women were buried with their husbands, and this section in the poorer part of the necropolis reserved solely for these unattached women and their offspring separates them from the rest of the community. This could possibly suggest a prostitute class, as Manniche believes,[18] or as Bruyère initially thought, it could indicate the separate burials of dancers and female musicians.[19]

The Turin Erotic Papyrus, produced in Thebes in 1150 BCE, is the most compelling evidence of New Kingdom prostitutes. It was initially thought the papyrus recorded the adventures of a Theban priest of Amun and a prostitute, although it is likely to be a number of men as each is depicted differently. They are all elderly, with varying stages of baldness and different facial hair. They are wearing simple, undecorated kilts, are common- to lower-class men – servants, field labourers and workmen – and all have 'a huge phallus which swings pendulously between the couple'.[20] The women are all wearing different wigs, hip belts, jewellery and make-up and occasionally a lotus flower in their hair. Their lower regions are emphasised with narrow waists and large hips, but their breasts are small. The images do not tell a continuous story but rather are a collection of scenes, which indicate what went on in a Theban brothel, punctuated by short inscriptions such as, 'Oh, sun, you have found out my heart, it is agreeable work,' or 'Come behind me with your love.'[21]

Although sex was an important element in the life of ancient Egyptian men (and also, to some extent, women) it was considered more important to get married and start a family. As soon as a child was considered an adult they were eligible for marriage. For a girl this was at the onset of menarche, which some estimate was approximately fourteen years old as the age of menarche has decreased over the centuries and was much later in the ancient past.[22]

According to the 'Instruction of Ani' and the 'Instruction of Ankhsheshonq' it was best to get married while still a young man, although there was no mention of the most appropriate age for girls to marry.[23] However, the phrase 'to make her a wife and teach her to be human' does indicate a young girl, as the latter part of the phrase is often related to raising children. Boys became adults at approximately twelve years old, but often married after they started their careers and accumulated enough wealth to maintain a family. This idea was emphasised in the Middle Kingdom 'Teachings of Ptahhotep', who claimed, 'Love your wife with proper ardour ... Fill her belly and clothe her back!'[24]

Although a boy officially became a man when he was circumcised, socially they were considered adults once they obtained their first paid position, whether as a scribe, a soldier or working independently of their father. Therefore this age varied from boy to boy and from profession to profession. A boy inheriting a position may be older than a soldier starting in the army and training at a young age. Once they had settled into their new role they could consider marrying and starting a family.

There is a common misconception that in ancient Egypt sibling marriages were the norm. In actual fact this was only practiced by gods and royalty. Royal marriages included brother–sister, father–daughter or even grandfather–granddaughter alliances. However, these marriages were often political and meant to reinforce the royal line, and it is unknown if they were all consummated. For ordinary Egyptians, such close-kin marriages were unacceptable. That is not to say relatives did not marry. Jaroslav Černy studied 490 marriages from the First Intermediate Period to the eighteenth dynasty and was able to identify two which appeared to be sibling marriages. On the contrary, half-brothers and sisters or cousins[25] could marry, primarily to ensure family possessions remained within the family, and this was not uncommon. At Deir el-Medina there were three cousin marriages in the family of Sennedjem, and five other cousin marriages in the Ramesside Period.[26] Additionally there are two possible cases of uncle–niece and one of aunt–nephew marriage. Unfortunately this does not provide enough information to ascertain how widespread this practice was. Some of the identifications may also be tenuous as such research is based solely on names, which can be problematic.

Marrying within the same class and financial background did not seem to be a requirement and there are numerous examples of people from different social backgrounds getting married. For example, Amenhotep III famously married Tiye, a girl from a non-royal family. A less lofty example is that of the sculptor Neferenpet from Deir el-Medina, who got a household slave pregnant. It is unclear if he married her but he certainly encouraged his family to take care of her.[27]

Hardjedef offers some advice on the sort of woman who makes a good wife: a hearty woman, one who is joyful and who is known in her town.[28] Once he is married, according to Ptahhotep, a man should love her, feed her, clothe her and keep her happy.[29] Ani suggests the best way to keep her happy was to appreciate her skills. 'Do not control your wife in her house when you know she is efficient. Don't say to her "Where it is? Get it!" when she has put it in the right place. Let your eye observe in silence, then you recognise her skill.'[30]

It is believed that for the elite, marriages may have been arranged by the families, and dowries were paid in these situations. If this was the case a marriage contract was often drawn up. However, it has been suggested that the sheer number of divorces, separations and remarriages at Deir el-Medina indicates arranged marriages were not that common, as family-arranged marriages were more difficult to dissolve than love marriages.[31]

The personal records from Egypt give us lots of little snippets of information about individuals and their marital status, enabling us to form a clearer picture of married life in ancient Egypt. A Ptolemaic stela in the British Museum belonging to a woman called Taimhotep explains how she married Psherenptah, a man more than thirty years her senior. He was the High Priest of Ptah at Memphis and in marrying him she 'obeyed her father', who was also a High Priest of Ptah at the same temple. It appears that this marriage was arranged by her family to maintain the family's position in society by ensuring she married someone of equal status to her father; it may also have been partly political, in the sense that she married her father's colleague.

Such an age difference as that between Taimhotep and Psherenptah may not have been unusual in ancient Egypt, as men often postponed getting married until they were settled into a career.

Many people, whose status in society was not as consequential as it may have been for Taimhotep's family, married for love. However, there were traditions to be upheld even for love matches. The New Kingdom love poetry, although probably written by professional scribes, describes desire and longing for a potential husband or wife. The following comes from the songs entitled 'the beginning of the songs of pleasant entertainment for your beloved the chosen of your heart when she comes from the field', and eloquently describes love and desire.

> O beauteous youth, may my desire be fulfilled
> To become the mistress of your house.
> With your hands resting upon my breasts,
> You have spread your love over me
> I speak to my innermost heart.
> With the prayer that my lord may be with me this night.
> I am like one who is in her tomb
> For you are not alone my health and life.
> Your touch brings the joy of my well-being,
> The joy of my heart seeking after you.[32]

Conversely, the second stanza of Papyrus Chester Beatty I, another poem, laments what appears to be unrequited affection: 'He knows not my wish to embrace him, or he would write to my mother.'[33] The sixth stanza of the Papyrus Chester Beatty I records something similar: 'If only my mother had known my heart, she would have gone in.'[34] These are rather interesting as they indicate that should a man wish to marry a young woman he was expected to get permission from her mother, rather than her father as is traditional in the western world. However, other texts indicate that the potential groom first spoke to the girl's father. It could be the case that the suitor could in fact speak to either the mother or father, as bridal negotiations may have been carried out with the bride's family as a unit.[35]

Generally, happy relationships do not tend to end up in the archaeological record, but glimpses of loving relationships have been found. A number of canopic jars bought by George Legrain in 1904 display the nicknames of the female owners, which include 'The much sought after one', 'The cat-like one' and 'She [who is] hot-tempered like a leopard'.[36] Someone other than the women gave them these nicknames and they show dimensions of these ancient relationships and characteristics which are often lost to us today. Other terms of endearment have been discovered from Old Kingdom tomb chapels; one husband praises his wife, 'She did not utter statement that repelled my heart, she did not transgress whilst she was young in life,' and another wife is complimented as being 'one who speaks pleasantly and sweetens love in the presence of her husband'.[37]

Sadly, not all love matches were successful, and the 'Wisdom Text of Ankhsheshonq' warns against the duplicitous nature of women. He was a priest who wrote the text while in prison for conspiring against the king. The bitterness towards women indicates he may have been betrayed by a woman, perhaps resulting in his imprisoned state.

Do not open your heart to your wife. What you have said ends up in the street.

Do not open your heart to your wife or your servant. Open it to your mother. She is a woman to be trusted.

Teaching a woman is like having a sack of sand with the side split open.

What a wife does with her husband today she does with another man tomorrow.[38]

The contrast here between the wife and mother was particularly important to the Egyptians, as they were a rather pragmatic people and believed you could only be certain of who your mother was, not your father. Ani tells us to 'double the food your mother gave to you. Support her as she supported you. She had a heavy load in you but she did not abandon you. When you were born at the end of your months, she was yet yoked to you.'[39]

There seemed little problem with illegitimacy in ancient Egypt, as while it was important to have a son to take over the role of the father and care for the parents in old age it was not necessary for this person to be a blood relation. It was totally acceptable to adopt a son to take this role. However, illegitimacy was not a desirable state and in the tale of Truth and Falsehood an illegitimate boy is mocked for this status.[40]

While marriage was very important and something that people aspired to, there was no formal wedding ceremony, either religious or legal. In fact, there was no word in the Egyptian language for 'wedding', and phrases like 'sitting together', 'to be together with', to eat with', 'entering a house' or 'bringing the bundle' could mean to move into the marital home or the transference of a dowry,[41] or the phrase 'to make as a wife' could mean the male role in forming a wedding alliance.[42] There is very little reference to marriage itself in the texts, although a love poem, Papyrus Harris 500, states, 'My heart [desires] your property as the mistress of your house, while your arm rests on my arm, for my love surrounds you.'[43] This could be a reference to the desire to be married to a man and become his support as she manages his home.

The texts are also silent on wedding celebrations until the Ptolemaic Story of Setne Khamwas (I), which tells of Ahwere and her brother Naneferkaptah, the children of the pharaoh Merenebptah. They loved each other and wished to marry. Initially their father forbade it, as he wanted to expand the family by marrying them to other people. Once he relented, the celebration of the wedding is described thus:

'Steward, let Ahwere be taken to the house of Naneferkaptah tonight and let all sorts of beautiful things be taken with her.'

I was taken as a wife to the house of Naneferkaptah [that night and Pharaoh] sent me a present of silver and gold, and all Pharaoh's household sent me presents. Naneferkaptah made holiday with me and he entertained all Pharaoh's household. He slept with me that night and found me [pleasing. He slept with] me again and again, and we loved each other.[44]

Although no ceremonial aspects are discussed, this text indicates a party marked the occasion, as well as extravagant gift giving. With no legal or religious arrangements this emphasises weddings were purely social events.

As was the case with Ahwere and Naneferkaptah, for a couple to get married the woman simply left her parents' home and moved in with her new husband. This could be the home of her husband's family or the home of her husband himself. Whether this was marked by a procession through the streets is not recorded, although it would be unusual for such an event not to be celebrated in some way. However, an Ostracon (Nash 6) from Deir el-Medina provides evidence of a man trying, unsuccessfully, to move into a woman's home, proving sometimes marriage was not so straightforward. Twice he took a number of goods, including food, furniture, clothing and jewellery, and twice he was unsuccessful. He complains that she would not even 'provide clothing for his backside'.[45] Unfortunately, no further information is available about this encounter, although he was obviously persistent: 'I went again with all my property in order to live with them. Look she acted exactly the same way again.'[46] As the family are described as throwing him out it is possible he had successfully married the daughter and was divorced, twice over.

As a new bride moving into her husband's home with his parents and siblings it is not surprising that marital strife could follow. A letter from Takhentyshepse to her sister Iye is a wonderful example of the stresses of having to deal with extended families.

> I shall send you barley, and you shall have it ground for me and add emmer to it. And you shall make bread with it, for I have been quarrelling with Merymaat (my husband) 'I will divorce you', he keeps saying when he quarrels with me on account of my mother questioning the amount of barley required for bread. 'Now your mother does nothing for you' he keeps telling me and says, 'although you have brothers and sisters, they don't take care of you' he keeps telling me in arguing with me daily.[47]

As marriage was easy, with no legal documentation, divorce was just as straightforward. To divorce, either party declared, 'I divorce you,' the man declared, 'I repudiate you,' or the woman stated, 'I will go,' before she left her husband's house to either return to her family's home or set up on her own. Some parents helped their children to set up a home with their new spouses and the 'Autobiography of Wedjahorresne' states, 'I fed all their children and I established all their homes.'[48] Then there was a public oath in a local court,[49] which cleared the couple of the marriage in the eyes of the people. Finally, the property was divided, with the woman receiving a third of the property accumulated throughout the marriage as well as the possessions she arrived with at the start of the marriage.

Families were not obliged to accept the daughter back into their home, or in the case of the small homes in Deir el-Medina they may not have the room to accommodate her. One workman, Horemwia, promised his daughter Tanetdjesere that should she be thrown out of her marital house he would let her have a room in his storehouse. It appears that the state owned the house, whereas Horemwia built and owned the storehouse, meaning there were no restrictions on how it was used,[50] 'and no one in the land will throw you out'.[51] Although it is unlikely that the state monitored house occupancy there was clearly some restriction, either socially or legally, as to why Horemwia's daughter could not move into his house should she be divorced.

Although women could divorce men, evidence from Deir el-Medina suggests men were more likely to divorce than women with a ratio of 12:3.[52] Due to the ease with which divorce could be administered some people were concerned enough to introduce an early form of pre-nuptial agreement:

> Make Nakhtemut take an oath of the lord, life, prosperity, and health that he swore 'As Amen endures, as the ruler endures, if I go back on my word and abandon the daughter of Tenermonthu in the future, I will receive one hundred blows and be deprived of all the property that I will acquire with her'.[53]

Documents were generally only produced for wealthy families where a dowry had been paid upon the marraige. Such documents discussed returning the dowry during a divorce.[54] A dowry comprised gifts given to the bride upon her marriage and therefore legally belonged to her. Families perhaps believed they held more influence in the marriage through this provision of gifts to the bride. In comparision, a bride price comprised gifts or services provided to the bride's family in lieu of the wedding.[55] How such services or gifts were agreed on, or the period of time within which they should be carried out, is not mentioned in the texts.

One such wedding contract on Papyrus Louvre E7846 (546 BCE) has the lady Tsendjehuty outlining appropriate property reimbursement should she get divorced from her husband, Iturekh son of Petiese. Should he divorce her for another woman he promised to give her maintenance:

> If I repudiate Tsendjehuty ... and if I am the cause for this harsh fate that will beset her, because I wish to repudiate her or because I

prefer other women above her – except in the case the large crime that is (usually) found in a woman – I will give her two deben of silver and fifty sacks of grain.[56]

Divorce had no stigma attached to it and a divorced man or woman could remarry, although evidence indicates that women who divorced after the age of 30–35 tended to remain single. Perhaps they were financially self-sufficient and did not need to marry, could no longer have children or had children already and were therefore not considered good marriage material.[57]

In the case of couples with children divorcing it is unknown who gained custody. However, the workman Userhet from Deir el-Medina swore an oath[58] that upon the divorce from his wife Menat-Nakhti his three children should not be taken from him. He paid for a wet nurse and a doctor in order to care for them, which indicates that upon their divorce he gained custody of the children.[59] Another record, the Stato Civile, shows children are sometimes identified as having the same father but different mothers, and this could indicate that after the mother left the house following a divorce the children stayed with their father and were raised by his next wife. An alternative interpretation could be that following the death of the first wife the children remained with the father, who later remarried.[60]

Although it does not appear to be the norm, there is evidence of alimony being paid to an ex-wife. Details from Deir el-Medina inform us that the workman Hesysunebef divorced his wife Hunro following her affair with Paneb. He gave her a small grain ration every month for three years, which was not enough to make her self-sufficient but no doubt helped. When they divorced he tried to sell a scarf she had woven at the east bank market for her, but no one wanted to buy it. He was told it was low quality. He therefore gave her six times the value for it out of his own income. The information we have about Hunro indicates the divorce was her fault as it is recorded that before she married Hesysunebef she was married to Pendua. Their divorce was the result of an earlier affair with Paneb, the same man named in Hesysunebef's divorce documents.[61] Perhaps if Paneb had met Hunro before he married his wife Wa'bet the situation could have been very different. However, interestingly enough, Hesysenebef was Paneb's adopted brother, both of them having Neferhotep as an adopted father. Was this act of adultery with his sister-in-law all part of an on-going feud between Paneb and Neferhotep's family? Wa'bet could have chosen to divorce Paneb over his adultery but records show they were married a long time and had more than ten children.

In these records Hunro was divorced for her adultery, but the penalty could have been far more severe. A woman could be disowned or even lose her life for committing adultery.[62] This depended on the wishes of the wronged husband as adultery with a married woman was seen as an affront to the husband. However, a married man and a single woman having an affair hardly raised an eyebrow.

The foreman Paneb was accused of three counts of adultery, two of these accusations with Hunro, his sister-in-law, although no punishment is recorded for him. One of the accusations came from his son Aaphate, who ran away from Paneb's house and went to the doorkeeper, saying, 'I cannot bear with him; my father made love to the Lady Tuy when she was the workman Kenna's wife, he made love to the lady Hunro, when she was with Pendua and when she was with Hesysenebef. And after that he debauched her daughter too.'[63] This accusation is recorded among others against Paneb on Papyrus Salt, which was written by Amennakhte, the brother of Paneb's adopted father. He was angered that his brother Neferhotep's role should be passed on to Paneb when he felt it should be his as a blood relative. This led him to list a number of accusations against Paneb which were collated in this papyrus. The validity and accuracy of some of the accusations can be questioned and this accusation in particular is rather suspicious as the daughter mentioned was approximately three years old at the time.

There is no doubt that adultery was considered unacceptable in society and was even included in chapter 125 of the Book of the Dead, the so-called negative confession, as it was obviously something they did not want to be accused of in the afterlife in case it affected their rebirth.

In literary texts adultery is a popular theme. In the New Kingdom 'Tale of the Two Brothers', the wife of Anubis, the older brother, tries the seduce the younger brother, Bata, when he enters the house during the day to get seed for sowing the fields. She was impressed by the number of seed sacks he was able to carry and

> She said 'There is great strength in you. I see your vigour daily' and she desired to know him as a man. She got up, took hold of him, and said to him, 'Come let us spend an hour lying together. It will be good for you and I will make fine clothes for you.'
>
> Then the youth became like a leopard in anger over the wicked speech she had made to him; and she became very frightened. He rebuked her saying, 'Look, you are like a mother to me; and your husband is like a father to me. He who is older than I has raised me. What is this great wrong you said to me? Do not say it to me again! But I will not tell it to anyone. I will not let it come from my mouth to any man'.

The wife was worried he would tell her husband so she ruffled her clothing and put dirt on her face to give the appearance of being attacked, which is how her husband found her. She told him that his younger brother had propositioned her and when she refused saying, 'Am I not your mother? Is your elder brother not like a father to you?' Bata became angry and beat her. She then stated, 'Now if you let him live, I shall die! Look when he returns, do not let him live. For I am ill from his evil design which he was about to carry out in the morning.'[64] Anubis waited for his younger brother in the stable with a spear, but luckily Bata was warned by his cows, who told him that Anubis was there. He fled and lived in exile from his brother. Eventually Anubis realised his wife was the one to blame, so he killed her and mourned the loss of his brother.

In all the literary tales concerning adultery the guilty party always ends up dead, to show that justice has been done. A papyrus in the British Museum (BM10416) records a real event where punishment was meted out to a woman who committed adultery in an eight-month affair with one of their relatives. The group of people claimed, 'We are going to beat her, together with her people.' The narrator of the text, possibly the woman's son, suggests the man go to court with his wife to sort out the matter instead of succumbing to violence.[65]

There was, however, no need for adultery in ancient Egypt as evidence indicates that polygamous marriages happened, although they were not the norm. In the ninth-dynasty tomb of Mery-aa from el-Hagarseh six wives are depicted, five who had given birth to his children. The sixth wife Isi, who did not have any children, was more prominently placed than the others in the tomb and it is suggested she was perhaps his first wife, who had remained childless. It is unlikely that these women were all ex-wives, as divorced wives were generally not depicted in tombs, and he would have been a particularly unlucky man to have lost five wives, indicating this is evidence of polygamy.

Another clear example of polygamy is in the Tomb Robbery Papyrus where there is a list of women involved in the robbery. One woman, Herer, is the wife of a guard of the King's Treasury. The next woman on the list is described as 'his other wife, which makes two'.[66] There is little ambiguity in this text, and it seems apparent that this guard had two wives living contemporaneously with each other.

It was very unusual for people not to get married, and a study of ninety-three New Kingdom funerary contexts show only three burials were of unmarried men. It was clearly considered the social norm to marry, and anything that deviated from this was seen as a deviation from Maat and could invoke a hostile response.[67]

Such social expectations must have been difficult should a person have been homosexual, and there is evidence of homosexuality in ancient Egypt among married and unmarried men. Homosexuals were known as *nkkw*, fucked man, or *Hmiw*, back-turners or cowards, which is related to the word *Hmt*, woman, indicating the passive element of homosexuality.[68] It is this passive role that was opposed rather than the attraction, and the complaints rarely concerned the instigator of homosexual sex, but rather focused on the recipient of it. It is this passivity which defined the person in a negative way, not their homosexuality.

In chapter 125 of the Book of the Dead it states, 'I have not done wrong sexually or committed homosexuality.'[69] This supports the idea that homosexuality was not approved of and therefore needed to be included in this negative confession. In this chapter of the Book of the Dead homosexuality is associated with adultery ('done wrong sexually') and therefore may have been viewed in the same way, as a deviation from Maat but not necessarily a crime.[70] It is also mentioned in literary texts, indicating it was an acknowledged fact of life. However, the modern concept of heterosexual and homosexual was not one the Egyptians were familiar with. As Parkinson eloquently describes it, 'Sexual preferences were acknowledged but only as one would recognise someone's taste in food.'[71] Homosexual desires were seen as a natural weakness of man and therefore something that should be overcome or ignored. 'Let him not spend the night doing what is opposed. He shall be cool after renouncing his desire.'[72] This section from the 'Instruction of the Vizier Ptahhotep' (32nd Maxim) actively encourages suppressing such desires as the only thing that will bring true peace of mind.

In the 'Contendings of Horus and Seth', the homosexual encounters between Horus and Seth are always instigated by Seth, the god of chaos.

Seth said to Horus, 'How beautiful are your buttocks, how vital! Stretch out your legs'. Horus said, 'Wait that I may tell it ...' Horus said to his mother Isis, 'Seth wants to know me.' She said to him, 'Take care. Do not go near him for that. Next time he mentions it to you, you shall say to him; "It is too difficult because of my build, as you are heavier than I am. My strength is not the same as yours."' She says, 'When he has aroused you, place your fingers between your buttocks ... the seed which has come forth from his penis without letting the sun see it'.[73]

Isis, rather than totally discouraging the action, tells Horus what to do once he has been aroused, indicating Seth is the problem, as he is instigating homosexual intercourse as a display of power which presents Horus as the weaker rival in the activity.[74]

A Middle Kingdom literary tale tells the story of Pepy II and General Sasanet and their homosexual relationship. The story tells of a man called Tjeti who was mocked when he tried to speak in the palace. In his anger he followed the king on his nightly journeys to try and gain valuable information about his activities.

Then he noticed the Person of the Dual King, Neferkara going out at night, all alone with nobody with him. Then he removed himself from him without letting him see. Hent's son Tjeti stood thinking; 'so this is it! What was said is true. He goes out at night.' Hent's son Tjeti went just behind this god – without letting his heart misgive him – to see all that he did. He [Neferkara] arrived at the house of the General Sasanet. Then he threw a brick and kicked the wall so that a ladder was let down for him. Then he ascended. Hent's son Tjeti waited until His Person returned. Now after His Person had done what he desired with him, he returned to his palace with Hent's son Tjeti behind him. When His Person returned to the palace, Tjeti went back to his house. Now His Person went to the house of General Sasanet when four hours had passed of the night [i.e. 10 p.m.], he had spent another four hours in the house of General Sasanet, and he entered the palace when there were four hours to dawn [i.e. 2 a.m.]. And Hent's son Tjeti went following him each night – without his heart misgiving him; and each time after His Person entered the palace Tjeti went back to his house ...[75]

The king is not criticised for having a relationship with a man, or even the low status of his lover, but rather the neglect of his duties while spending four hours every night in pursuit of carnal pleasures.[76] Homosexuality was perhaps viewed as decadent and in this case a dereliction of duty for a frivolous reason. As the king is keen to keep this relationship secret, in the sense that he was sneaking to the general's house and refused to allow the man to speak in the palace, this indicates it was something considered taboo.

Even in the 'Contendings of Horus and Seth', Horus threatens Seth with, 'Watch out; I shall tell this!' In the story of the General Sasanet it is assumed, as he was an unmarried man and of a low position, that he was the passive partner in the royal liaison, which was seen as the negative position. This could be why the king was not criticised for the act, but rather for the neglect of his duty.

Homosexual love also appears in the New Kingdom love poetry, where the narrator has fallen in love with a young charioteer.

> On the way I met Mehy on his chariot,
> With him were his young men.
> I knew not how to avoid him:
> Should I stride on to pass him?
> But the river was the road,
> I knew no place for my feet.
> My heart you are very foolish,
> Why accost Mehy?
> If I pass before him,

I tell him my movements.
Here I'm yours I say to him,
Then he will shout my name,
And assign me to the first ...
Among his followers.[77]

It is not clear why the narrator feels he cannot approach Mehy, perhaps because he is worried that he will not feel the same way.

Since the discovery in the 1960s of the fifth-dynasty mastaba tomb of Niankhkhnum and Khnumhotep, there has been extensive debate about the unusual depictions of the two tomb owners embracing. They both held the title Manicurist of the King and Inspector of Manicurists of the Palace during the reign of King Neuserre (2453–2422 BCE). Khnumhotep is depicted in feminine poses – smelling lotuses and standing on the left of Niankhkhnum, the traditional position of the wife – indicating there was a male–female duality to their representation.[78] In the tomb it is only Khnumhotep and the women who are shown smelling lotus flowers, and he is one of only three men in the fifth dynasty shown in this position. It is clear that stylistically he is holding the position of 'wife' in this tomb.[79] Their affection in the form of embracing and having their faces touching or holding hands is something normally only demonstrated by married couples.[80] Due to the nature of the images it has been suggested they had a homosexual relationship, although their wives and children are also represented in the tomb. However, in one banquet scene the wife of Niankhkhumn has been erased and Khnumnhotep's wife is completely omitted.

The most accepted theory is that they were twins[81] and therefore closer than average siblings, which is emphasised by their exaggerated displays of affection. Some even go so far as to suggest that they were conjoined twins. However, the dominance of Niankhkhnum in the tomb could be because it appears that Khnumhotep died first and therefore Niankhkhnum was responsible for the decoration of the tomb. The fact that Khnumhotep died first puts pay to the theory of conjoined twins, as it is highly unlikely that Niankhkhnum would have survived separation surgery at this time. It is only in their own tomb that they are depicted side by side, and in the tomb of the vizier Ptahshepses at Abusir the two men are shown in isolation of each other, indicating that they were not viewed as 'one person' and were able to function separately. This casts doubt on the theory that they were twins as surely this perception would have been shared by others in the community. Without the bodies of Niankhkhnum and Khnumhotep it is impossible to identify whether they were related or not, but the images in the tomb strongly support a deep same-sex affection unprecedented in any other Egyptian tomb. It may never be possible to categorise this relationship as just good friends, brothers or lovers.

While homosexuality between men was considered a natural, if not necessarily ideal part of life, homosexuality between women was considered to be a bad thing. While being extremely poorly documented, the dream interpretation book on Papyrus Carlsberg states that if a woman 'dreams that a woman has intercourse with her she will come to a bad end'.[82] Relationships were intended to be procreative, so any in which this was not possible was considered to be a waste and actively discouraged.[83] This expectation for relationships to be productive and result in the birth of children was a major concern of ancient Egyptian adults. A prayer inscribed on some scarabs expresses the hope that 'your name may last, children may be granted to you'.[84] Should a couple not be able to produce a child the husband could be ridiculed, as was the case of Nekhemmut, who received a letter from an angry colleague: 'You are not a man since you are unable to make your wife pregnant like your fellow men. A further matter; you abound in being exceedingly stingy. You give no one anything.'[85]

It was considered socially important to have as many children as possible in order to ensure that the parents were cared for in old age in the absence of any adequate state scheme to care for the elderly. However, where there were no children many couples adopted, as was mentioned in the letter to Nekhemmut: 'As for him who has no children, he adopts an orphan instead to bring him up. It is his responsibility to pour water onto your hands as one's eldest son.'[86] Adoption could be in the traditional sense, where an orphaned child was raised by their adoptive parents, or an adult could be adopted (even if his parents were still living) in order for the adoptive father to have a son to pass his role or business on to after his retirement.

Some men even adopted their wives, either to enable her to inherit all of his possessions rather than only the third legally required, or in order to care for a barren wife while obtaining a child through other means. The latter scenario is described in the Adoption Papyrus dated to the reign of Ramses XI (1098–1070 BCE). The man Nebnefer adopts his wife Naunefer before fathering three children with a household slave. Naunefer then adopts the three children as her own. Her brother marries the eldest of the three and Naunefer adopts him as well.[87] This would no doubt have been a difficult situation for Naunefer, but it technically made her life easier than if her husband had simply divorced her.

Married women spent most of their adult years pregnant or recovering from childbirth.[88] Although it was more desirable to have boys to take over the father's role and to bring a wife into the family, offering extra care for the elderly, girls were not exposed or abandoned as they were in other ancient cultures.

Infertility was such a concern for married couples that an entire fertility cult arose around the goddess Hathor, and there were numerous votive offerings made by both men and woman in the form of model breasts, vaginas, phalli and fertility figures.[89] She was approached to help in all sexual matters and graffiti left at the temple of Thutmosis III at Deir el Bahri by a Priest of Mut, Paybasa, asks Hathor, 'Give to him love in the sight of every man and every woman. Cause that his phallus be stronger than any woman ... Give to him a good wife who will be his companion.'[90] This priest obviously wanted his sexual performance to improve as he believed this would result in him finding a wife.

As discussed in chapter one, for many the houses were inadequately small, perhaps with three generations living in just four rooms, meaning it was difficult for newly married couples to be alone. No one had their own bedroom so at night other people were always present, potentially making intercourse a rather public affair.[91] Some depictions of sex on ostraca from Deir el-Medina often have other people in the vicinity, perhaps servants, indicating that even for the rich with large houses, sex was not a private act.[92] However, privacy may have been achieved through snatched moments alone, and perhaps by using the box-beds in the first room of the house. The woman were generally pregnant soon after marriage. If this did not happen there were tests to ascertain whether the woman was fertile, although there were none to check male fertility. In the Kahun Gynaecological Papyrus seven of the thirty-four cases were associated with determining the fertility of the woman.[93]

In order to conceive it was necessary to have open passages from the vagina to all body parts, and it was important to test for blockages. The Kahun Gynaecological Papyrus suggests the woman should sit over a concoction of beer and dates. If she vomited her tubes were open and she would conceive, and if she did not her tubes were blocked and she would not fall pregnant.[94] The number of times she vomited indicated how many children she would have. Another fertility test instructs the woman to insert an onion into her vagina. If the next day her breath smelt of onions she would conceive. The concept of easy passage from the vagina to the head was also apparent if a woman's neck was aching and she had sore eyes, as this was diagnosed as a 'discharge of the uterus in her eyes', which it was treated by fumigating her eyes with goose leg fat and her vagina with incense and fresh oil, as well as ensuring she consumed the fresh liver of a donkey.[95]

The Berlin and Carlsberg VIII Papyrus provided pregnancy tests which necessitated urinating over barley and emmer seeds. Should the barley sprout first the baby was a boy, if the emmer sprouted first then it was a girl, but if neither sprouted the woman was not pregnant.[96] It has been suggested that the only reason they chose barley to prove a boy and emmer a girl is because these words were masculine and feminine in ancient Egyptian.[97] The idea itself is one that is used in modern pregnancy tests, which look for indications of increased hormones associated with pregnancy. Experiments were conducted in 1968 where forty-eight urine samples were used: two from men, six from non-pregnant women and forty from pregnant women. These were poured over barley and emmer. Neither grew with male urine or that of non-pregnant women. However, in twenty-eight of the forty samples watered with the urine of pregnant women there was growth from one or both seeds; the sexing of the baby only proved correct in seven of the twenty-eight cases.[98] The conclusion was drawn that should either cereal grow then the woman was pregnant, but should neither grow this did not eliminate the possibility of pregnancy.

Once pregnancy was established, spells were recited over knotted fabric; this was placed inside the vagina as a tampon in order to prevent blood flow, which the Egyptians identified with the start of a miscarriage. The spell was thought to prevent any blood from soiling the fabric.[99]

There was a very high mortality rate among infants. It is estimated that 20 per cent of pregnancies failed, 20 per cent of newborns died in the first year and 30 per cent did not survive past five years old.[100] The highest death rate was in the first few days of life;[101] the threat slowly decreased in the first month and then again after the first year. A woman may have ten children with only half surviving into adulthood. The New Kingdom 'Instruction of Ani' warns, 'Do not say "I am too young to be taken," for you do not know your death. When death comes he steals the infant who is in his mother's arms, just like him who reached old age'.[102]

Childbirth itself was a very dangerous time in a woman's life and many women died during or shortly afterwards. At the base of the eastern necropolis at Deir el-Medina, at the lowest point of the hill, was a cemetery dedicated to very young children, including the burials of infants, neonates, foetuses, placentas, viscera and bloody cloths. In general, the higher up the cliff the burial was situated, the older the individual. Each of the child burials was in a small pit only 40–90 centimetres deep, and included simple grave goods such as beer, plates of food and ceramics for use in their afterlife. Very young children were buried in a variety of ways, including in amphora, baskets, boxes or coffins, and resembled, to a certain degree, a mini adult burial. As the New Kingdom progressed, children and adolescents were buried in the family tombs and benefited from the spells and images within.

A similar children's cemetery was discovered at Gurob, which Diana Craig Patch studied along with other cemeteries, showing that 50 per cent from Gurob, 48 per cent at Matmar and 42 per cent at Mostagedda were children's graves, demonstrating the high infant mortality rate.[103]

There were three categories of childbirth: *Htp*, satisfactory; *bnd*, difficult; and *wdf*, protracted.[104] The medical papyri offer numerous remedies to ensure a safe birth for both mother and child. The Kahun Gynaecological Papyrus had remedies for, among other things,

> Causing a woman's womb to go to its place.
> Recognising good milk.

> To loosen the child in the belly of a woman.
> To separate a child from the womb of its mother.

The birth could be speeded up by burning resin near the abdomen or massaging saffron powder steeped in beer to reduce the pain. The Ebers Papyrus also postulates that should a newborn's first cry be *ny* then he would live, but should it be *mb* then he would die.[105]

During birth the woman was aided by a midwife, and it is suggested it took place in a special room or an external bower. Images of such bowers have been discovered on ostraca decorated with a vine, which most identify as the convolvulus leaf, although Harer suggests it is the *aristolochia* which grows wild in Egypt and is often used for uterine contraction. To give birth the pregnant woman crouched with her feet, or perhaps, as Harer suggests, her buttocks,[106] resting on sacred birth-bricks; there is an image of this at the mammisi (birth house) at the temple of Hathor at Denderah.

An example of a birth-brick was discovered in Abydos near fragments of an apotropaic wand in the mayor's residential building.[107] The brick was discovered with a number of seals bearing the name of princess Reniseneb, and it is thought she lived here during the second half of the thirteenth dynasty and was married to the mayor.[108] It may have belonged to her or one of the other women in the household. The brick was 35 centimetres by 17 centimetres wide and was decorated with a woman holding a baby boy, flanked by Hathor standards. Protective deities, of the same type discovered on apotropaic wands, decorate the other sides of the brick, clearly showing the important protective nature of these items.[109] The top surface of the brick is extremely worn, which is to be expected as this was the place where the woman placed her feet during childbirth. The wear on the brick could indicate much use over multiple births.

B. Middle Kingdom birth-brick, Abydos. (Drawing after Szapakowska, 2008, fig. 2.1).

It is suggested the image of a woman giving birth balanced on the bricks resembles the hieroglyphic sign of the horizon, which is the sun rising between two mountains.[110] The baby's head represented the rising sun and therefore connected all babies with the sun-god. The few depictions and written descriptions of childbirth indicate someone stood behind the pregnant woman to support her and the midwife was in front encouraging the birth.

Ritual prayers and activities may have been carried out with a ceremonial ivory apotropaic wand engraved with images of Bes, Taweret and other protective deities. The names on the wands are normally of the mother and the child, normally a boy, and indicates that either the child was named during gestation or the wand was inscribed with the child's name after the event. Wileman suggests that the child was in fact named at birth and the mother was responsible for choosing the name.[111] However, many child burials do not include a name, simply calling the child 'The Osiris', indicating that perhaps names were given at a later date. This may have been dependent on the individual family. The spells inscribed on the wands were designed to protect the mother and child: 'Cut off the head of the enemy when he enters the chamber of the children whom the lady has borne.'[112]

Although it is unknown exactly what role it played, it is assumed the apotropaic wand needed to come into contact with the woman and to remain in the room with her and her baby after birth. A number of them have been found in tombs, ritually broken in two, presumably to prevent the harmful spirits from escaping. The edges of some wands are worn away and it is suggested they were used to draw a magic circle around the child. Some also have holes pierced into them with a cord threaded through, perhaps to carry them. On tomb walls wands are shown being carried by nurses, but their presence in a funerary context also indicates they were important for rebirth too.

Men were not present at the birth, although their help in the home may have been required afterwards and the absentee record of Deir el-Medina states, 'Second month of inundation, day 23. Kasa his wife being in childbirth and he had three days off.'[113] It is likely that Kasa's wife was having a difficult birth and therefore he needed to be with her in case she died.

Even if the mother did not die in childbirth, there was danger of infection. The medicinal means of soothing an injury to the perineum were recorded in the Kahun papyrus: 'Instructions for a lady suffering in her pubic region, her vagina and the region of her vagina which is between her buttocks. You shall say concerning it: very swollen due to giving birth. You should then prepare for her: new oil, 1 henu [450 ml] to be soaked into her vagina.'[114]

After birth, in an attempt to keep mother and baby safe, they were kept secluded in a room called a *hrryt* for two weeks. In a house at Tell el-Amarna in a small room under the stairs there were two female figurines, two model beds and a stela dedicated to Taweret, which led many to believe this was an example of a *hrryt*.[115] While there is little doubt of a confinement period, whether this is carried out in the seclusion of a small room is not clear. A letter from Deir el-Medina makes arrangements for a servant woman who has given birth to be provided with bread, meat and cakes, *sgnn*-oil, honey, wood and water,[116] indicating they were well fed and cared for during this period.

In wealthy families where the absence of the women was not so marked, woman also confined themselves in the *hrryt* during menstruation. It is interesting to note that some of the workmen at Deir el-Medina were absent from work because women in their household were menstruating, indicating they were needed at home during this confinement.

Upon leaving the confinement the new mother resumed her daily life. There is no doubt the birth of the child was celebrated, and there are records from Deir el-Medina describing how the birth of a child was celebrated in the Place of Hard Drinking. Both men and women took part in this celebration.[117] The new mother breastfed the child for up to three years as a means of ensuring healthy food for the baby. If a nursing child was ill the medicine was fed to the mother, as ancient Egyptians appreciated the connection between health and mother's milk.

If the family were wealthy, the mother had died in childbirth or was unable to produce milk, a wet nurse was hired. In the New Kingdom this was a sign of status[118] and some officials used the lofty title of Milk-Brother with the King to show a shared wet nurse. From the Middle Kingdom it was not unusual to name the nurse on a funerary stela alongside other family members, showing her revered status within the family. However, the contracts between a family and a wet nurse were rather strict. The child should be shown to the mother at regular intervals so she could monitor its health and progress. The wet nurse should not feed any other children, except for her own, and she should not fall pregnant or participate in sexual intercourse while feeding the child.[119]

There seems to have been little stigma surrounding breastfeeding your own child, and Papyrus Lansing (a schoolbook) praises the practice by comparing it to that of writing: 'more enjoyable than a mother's giving birth, when her heart knows no distaste. She is constant in nursing her son; her breast is in his mouth every day.'[120] However, elite women are never shown breastfeeding their children; only goddesses are ever shown in this state.[121]

Not all women wanted to get pregnant again straight after giving birth and prolonged breastfeeding was thought to prevent this from happening. However, other contraceptives were also available. These included such things as 'crocodile dung, chopped over *hesa* and *awyt* liquid'[122] as suggested in the Ramses IV Papyrus and the Kahun Papyrus. This was inserted into the vagina and the dung acted as an absorbent sponge,[123] and was probably expected to act as a deterrent for the man.[124] Honey was also used, which may have had some spermicidal characteristics; others included fermented vegetables, which produced lactic acid, a substance used in modern contraceptive jellies. An oral contraceptive used beer, celery and oil, which was heated and drunk for four days. According to scientific reports it is proven to have anti-fertility effects.[125]

Despite such methods women still became pregnant and gave birth to numerous children. Once the child was born it was the mother's responsibility to ensure they had a happy and healthy childhood.

5.

CHILDHOOD

'You smote my back and so your teaching
entered my ear.'[1]

Childhood in ancient Egypt was not much different to that of a modern child, albeit somewhat shorter, with adulthood starting in the early teens for both boys and girls. It would appear the main difference is that children in ancient Egypt had far more responsibility than those today, and could be found working in the family business, temples or construction sites from a very young age.

In tomb art children past the age of puberty are almost indistinguishable from adults, as they are depicted in exactly the same way, albeit sometimes on a smaller scale than their parents. Younger children, however, are clearly differentiated as they are not only presented on a much smaller scale, at times only reaching the knees of the adults, but they are also often depicted as being naked. Evidence shows that this was simply an artistic method meant to denote childhood, as a number of child-sized tunics have been discovered, demonstrating that children did wear clothes.

One of the main age markers was the side-lock of youth (discussed in chapter two), which was a curled or plaited lock of hair on the right-hand side of an otherwise shaved head.

With the men working in the tombs, temples or fields throughout the week, it was the women's responsibility to care for the children in the home. Raising a child was known as 'to make into a human',[2] presumably meaning through the teaching of the appropriate and right ways to act and behave. Tomb images show women carrying babies in slings across their backs, keeping the baby close to the body while still enabling them to do their chores. Mothers held a very special place in the heart of ancient Egyptians and the 'Instruction of Ani' emphasises this bond:

> Double the food your mother gave to you. Support her as she supported you. She had a heavy load in you but she did not abandon you. When you were born at the end of your months, she was yet yoked to you. Her breast in your mouth for three years. As you grew and your excrement disgusted, she was not disgusted, saying 'What shall I do?' When she sent you to school, and you were taught to write she kept watch over you daily with bread and beer in her house.[3]

From this it is clear that mothers were responsible for all aspects of raising children, from breastfeeding to organising education and protecting the children from harm. Although this text makes it clear that breastfeeding lasted for three years, evidence from the Upper Egyptian Palaeolithic site of Wadi Kubbaniya shows that by the time children were able to crawl they were weaned and were eating mashed vegetables.[4] However, from such an early site the practices cannot automatically be assumed to have still been valid in the pharaonic period. What are thought to be weaning cups were discovered by Petrie at El-Lahun and comprised a small, Nile-clay bowl with a pinched spout that made it easy to pour food into the mouths of young children or even the infirm.[5]

Children played an important role in the household and participated in many of the same activities as their parents, enabling them to learn their expected roles in life. A proverb states, 'You shall not spare your body when you are young: food comes about by the hands, provision by the feet,'[6] making it clear that the Egyptians had a very strict work ethic. Only very young infants would not have an active role to play, and girls helped their mother cook, clean and take care of the younger children. As some women worked at making linen, shoes or pottery, their daughters trained alongside them; perfect examples of children learning from their parents are among the mourners at funerals, when the women were accompanied by their daughters dressed as miniature adults.

Girls are often depicted in a family and household environment, serving drinks and helping with domestic chores, and therefore they were unlikely to have had an education. The boys, once old enough, helped their father with his work, so their activities varied depending on their father's occupation. One young boy, described in a New Kingdom schoolbook,[7] worked with a baker. His role was to prevent the baker from falling headfirst into the bread oven by holding his feet as he placed the bread on the fire: 'If ever he slips from his son's grasp he falls into the blazing fire.'[8] A Middle Kingdom tomb also shows an apprentice working in a bakery, whose role was less responsible than the boy in the above text; he was only charged with informing the customers their orders were ready.[9] Another young lad working in a meat kitchen is told, 'Get to work, that you may summon the lads to eat,' to which he eagerly answers, 'I'll do it.'[10] Another example of a young boy helping his father out was discovered at Abydos in the form of children's footprints in the mud plaster around the mortuary complex of Khasekhemwy, indicating that very young children were present,[11] possibly carrying water or tools for the workmen.

The temple singer, Tjatasetimu, from the Temple of Amun at Thebes during the twenty-second dynasty, was only seven years old when she died, but was buried as an adult in an adult-sized coffin. The adult depicted is slender and wearing a tight-fitting dress with one arm across her chest and the other down by her side. Her hairstyle reveals she no longer wore the side-lock of youth and had a hairstyle often associated with girls of marriageable age but who were not yet married. Her role was to sing in accompaniment to her own harp or lute playing for the cult of Amun.[12]

Despite having responsibilities at such a young age, children were still children, and an image from the tomb of Neferhotep (TT49) shows a nanny looking after a little boy and girl. She is taking at drink from a jar, oblivious to the doorkeeper waving a stick at the children as they passed. One wonders how the children had antagonised him.

Although literacy was low in ancient Egypt, estimated at less than 1 per cent, school was essential for certain careers and was seen as a rite of passage. Papyrus Sallier states, 'Man comes forth from his mother's womb and runs to his master.'[13] At towns like Deir el-Medina literacy was probably much higher, and McDowell has suggested that forty percent were educated and literate.[14] However, as Szpakowska points out, there is a scale of literacy, with some people able to read and write to the extent of producing documents, and others only able to write their own name so that they could sign and witness documents. All could be considered literate, but this obviously skews the literacy estimations.[15]

The earliest reference to a school or House of Instruction is from the Middle Kingdom and it is only from the New Kingdom that school texts and student writing tablets give an insight into how the system worked. For middle class and elite boys who were expected to enter into government administration or upper levels of priesthood, a school education was necessary. As women were unable to hold administrative positions, girls were not schooled in an official capacity. This is not to say that women were uneducated, and there is evidence that there was a female student at the school at Deir el-Medina. Another female student is mentioned in the Late Ramesside letters, the daughter of Khonsu-mes. She was encouraged to study hard and even to write a letter to the scribe Djehuty-mes.[16]

From Deir el-Medina there is evidence of literate women in the form of notes between villagers written by women. They are often regarding mundane items that would have been easier to communicate verbally rather than the expensive and time-consuming effort required to employ a scribe to write the note, and then another to read it. If we take the example of Ese (see chapter two) writing to her dressmaker to hurry along her order for a shawl, we can see the banality of some notes, which supports the idea of female literacy. Furthermore, in some New Kingdom tomb images scribal equipment is depicted under the chairs of the women rather than their husbands. These women were obviously educated at home by their parents rather than partaking in the same system offered to the boys.

There were a number of official scribal schools during the New Kingdom, situated at the Mut complex and the Amun temple at Karnak, the Ramesseum, Deir el-Medina (although only during the twentieth dynasty when the inhabitants were staying at Medinet Habu), Memphis and Sais. These official schools were primarily for the children of the upper elite, although the Middle Kingdom 'Instruction of Khety' for his son Pepi (also known as the 'Satire of the Trades') tells of their journey from Sile in the Delta to 'the school for scribes, among the children of the magistrates, with the elite of the Residence'.[17] This suggests children of non-elite families could be admitted to central schools. This particular Theban school appears to have been for those expecting a future career in central government, whereas other schools specialised in the priesthood, medical profession or the army. In the New Kingdom literary text 'The Story of Truth and Falsehood', a boy was 'sent to school and learnt to write well and practised the arts of war, surpassing his older companions who were at school with him'.[18]

Boys not fortunate enough to be admitted to one of these institutions were educated by their fathers, or were adopted by a local scribe in order to inherit the position after him. Although the young protégé was given the title 'son' or 'staff of old age', they were adopted as an apprentice rather than a biological son. It is thought that once adopted, even in this work relationship, the child may have resided at the house of their adopted father in order to fully absorb the career path they had chosen.

Most of the identified teachers from Deir el-Medina were draftsmen, scribes or chief workmen. They were more than likely the most educated in the village and were also able to employ assistants.[19] These assistants were probably also students of a high-ranking official.

Although it is not specified in any way how long the education system was, through a study of tomb biographies it is possible to put a suggested time frame in place. Boys started their education at five years old. They were beaten regularly, as it was believed 'a boy's ear is on his back; he hears when he is beaten'.[20] In the 'Miscellanies' (a collective book of teaching materials) a pupil praised his teacher for such methods: 'You smote my back and so your teaching entered my ear.'[21]

Children were taught reading, writing and arithmetic. The writing material used in school was limited, comprising ostraca (limestone or pottery sherds), a gesso-coated wooden or stone tablet, which could be wiped clean after use, and a reed pen. For arithmetic a wooden counting stick was discovered at El-Lahun, formed using a broken piece of furniture, and was used to teach children to count up to 100. While reading was an exercise to be spoken aloud, arithmetic was a silent subject, as the *Miscellanies* explains: 'On another happy occasion you grasp the meaning of a papyrus roll ... you begin to read a book, you quickly make calculations. Let no sound of your mouth be heard; write with your hand, read with your mouth. Ask from those who know more than you, and don't be weary.'[22]

Contrary to modern practice, ancient Egyptian pupils were taught hieratic (cursive writing) first and then, should they excel at this shorthand form of the language, they progressed to hieroglyphs. In the modern world we learn hieroglyphs first and then progress to hieratic. Initially they started on hieratic phrases before progressing onto famous Middle Kingdom texts. These were written in an archaic form of the language, almost indecipherable to New Kingdom children and perhaps equivalent to modern children reading Chaucer. These texts included model letters which helped to improve writing, spelling, ability and accuracy. They consisted of advice for moral behaviour and it was hoped the students would learn from them. Their studies therefore had an emphasis on honesty, humility, self-control, good manners and respect for parents. One such instruction, that of Ptahhotep, emphasised the importance of moderation in speech. 'Be prudent whenever you open your mouth. Your every utterance should be outstanding so that the mighty men who listen to you will say, "How beautiful are the words that fly from his lips."'[23] Such ideals were difficult to live up to but were instilled in children from a young age. Texts were chanted aloud and a 'Miscellanies' text indicates they were accompanied by instruments: 'You have been taught to sing to the reed pipe, to chant to the flute, to recite to the lyre.'[24]

Once they had learnt the texts they wrote them down on gesso-coated wooden or stone tablets. It is often possible to see the corrections to the composition in red ink, and despite the common misconception that they wrote from dictation the mistakes are rarely a result of mishearing. The corrections were often thought to be the work of the teacher but closer inspection has identified that the corrections are often in the same hand, indicating self-correction or the teacher discussing the text at the end of the exercise and the students checking their own work.

Other common aspects of the school literary curriculum was the production of lists, such as grammatical structures, royal names ordered in chronological sequence or, more arbitrarily, a list of names which held no relevance to people resident in the village at the time (the significance of this list will remain speculative). Such lists obviously held some significance to the students and perhaps aided them in spelling or recording techniques.

Students of a higher level were also given homework to do and a text from the scribe Piay to his student Amenmose states, 'A third chapter is ready for you,' to which Amenmose responds, 'I will do it! See I will do it!' Piay encourages him, 'Bring your chapter and come.'[25]

At approximately nine years old the child, if a talented scribe, considered pursuing a career in the temple, central government or military. They then entered an apprenticeship to train on the job in preparation for taking the role at the death or retirement of their father or mentor. This apprenticeship lasted for ten or twelve years, depending on the complexity of the role or the apprentice's personal ability.

At this important time of their life 'The Satire of the Trades' encouraged the child to choose the role of a scribe over all others: '... the greatest of all callings, there's none like it in the land. Barely grown, still a child, he is greeted, sent on errands, hardly returned he wears a gown. I never saw a sculptor as envoy, nor is the goldsmith ever sent.'[26] This description makes it clear that even a young scribal apprentice received wealth and respect and was sent on errands others were not to be trusted with. This idea of education bringing respect and wealth is emphasised in the 'Instruction of Hori' which states,

Set your heart to writing very, very greatly; it is an excellent office
  for the one who executes it.
Your father possesses the hieroglyphs, and he is shown respect in
  the street.
He does well possessing it, his years are plentiful like sand;
He is well-provided during his day on earth, until he reaches the
  Other side.
Be a scribe that you might become like him, so that the strength of
  your wealth may be plentiful for you.[27]

Papyrus Lansing appealed to the weaker, non-sporty boys who
were considering joining the army, encouraging them to enter the
less glamorous but stable scribal career:

Be a scribe! Your body will be sleek, your hand will be soft. You will
not flicker like a flame, like those whose body is feeble. For there is
no bone of a man in you. You are tall and thin. If you lifted a load
to carry it, you would stagger. Your feet would drag terribly, you are
lacking in strength. You are weak in all of your limbs, poor in body.
Set your sights on being a scribe, a fine profession that suits you.[28]

These documents appear to have been part of a wide-scale
recruitment campaign to boost the number of scribes, who were an
anonymous but essential element of the administration of the state.

Archaeologically, no school buildings have been identified from
the dynastic period, so it is unknown whether there was a
designated place for learning or if classes took place in private
homes or public areas. We also do not know how many students
were in a class at any one time, but from 'The Satire of the Trades'
we know school either had a break for lunch or finished at lunch
time, as the text warns the boys to use their afternoon wisely: 'If
you leave the school when midday is called and go roaming in the
streets ...'[29] Unfortunately the end of the sentence is missing so we

will never know what happened to young boys who wasted their afternoons. However, the lazy school boy was to live a life of hard work and manual labour:

Come, let me tell you the miserable occupations of the maladroit fool who does not listen to the instruction of his father to become an excellent scribe. He is in the boat and he is handed over to the cable on his head and to the water. He has become one with the crocodiles and the hippopotami. Every man is dragging for himself.[30]

As children were pushed to use their time wisely and were involved in working in the home or farm from a very early age there was limited time to enjoy games or play with toys, but that is not to say they did not indulge when they were able. El-Lahun has been a great source of children's toys, especially clay examples made by the children themselves. Examples of these clay models are hippopotami, pigs, a pack donkey complete with bags, crocodiles, an ape with beads inserted for eyes and a boat with two seats, one of which was pierced for a mast and has the remains of a rudder. The hippopotami toys were the most popular, although it is clear that some children were more talented with modelling clay than others. These toys were easy to make as they were modelled for the mud available from around the house, and once the toy was broken or no longer needed it could be remodelled by adding water.

More complex figures can be seen in the British Museum in the form of a wooden cat and a mouse with a moveable jaw, or in the Cairo Museum in the form of ivory dancing dwarfs. This particular toy was discovered in the tomb of a little girl call Hapy, from el-Lisht. The dwarfs were attached to a wooden block with lengths of cord, which when pulled made them dance; one puts his hands together as if clapping, the others have their arms out at shoulder level.[31] As this item is of such high quality it is possible it was not intended as a toy.

A number of jointed dolls were discovered in a house at El-Lahun, which Petrie named the 'doll factory', although some of them were decorated with small lines of tattoos indicating they were fertility figurines. This factory also included a number of wigs made with flax of about fifteen centimetres long, threaded with clay beads and inserted into holes in the dolls' heads. A doll found in the tomb of Sitrennut at Hawara was complete with both jointed limbs and a wig, similar to those found in the doll shop.[32] The Petrie Museum has two rag dolls from El-Lahun, both made from linen. Neither doll has removable clothing and the limited detailing indicates they were real toys rather than symbolic or ritual items.

Both sexes liked to play ball games and a number of wooden and leather balls have been found. Balls were made of as many as twelve leather strips sewn together and stuffed with straw, reeds, hair, yarn or chaff.[33] Some are so well played with they were repaired in the past. Normally ball games were played by girls and there are tomb scenes showing girls juggling with three balls, sometimes with crossed arms to demonstrate their skill. There is also a game of catch, depicted in the Beni Hasan tomb of Kheti, played while riding on the back of another child. It is possible that a dropped ball meant the riders became the carriers. Another scene shows two groups of three girls standing opposite each other. The girls in the centre throw the ball to each other, while their companions clap to keep rhythm.[34] The objective of the game is not clear. An Old Kingdom child at Naqada (Tomb 100) was buried with a skittle set comprising nine calcite and breccia skittles with four porphyry balls, a portable game that could be played inside or outside.

Children played a number of games outside, including what is believed to be a version of the British game 'piggy'; this involved wooden tip-cats of approximately 16 centimetres, which were thrown into the air. The child who hit the tip-cat the furthest using a stick before it hit the ground was the winner. Szpakowska makes an interesting point that had Petrie not been the archaeologist who discovered these toys at El-Lahun the games may have been interpreted differently.[35] As was common at the time, archaeological interpretations were made based on the archaeologist's culture, in this instance British, and the childhood games they were familiar with.

Other games did not require equipment and therefore could be played by all and could be considered a form of acrobatics. For example, in the tomb of Mereruka at Saqqara there is an image of a boy balancing on the shoulders of his friends. Another such game was the 'donkey game'. An Old Kingdom tomb scene shows an older boy on all fours carrying two younger children on each side like saddle bags. The young children had to hold onto each other to remain on board. Another fun outdoors game was 'erecting the wine arbour' in which two boys stood in the middle holding onto two or four other children (girls or boys). They spun them around as they leant back on their heels, inducing a feeling of dizziness that perhaps resembled the feeling of overindulging in the produce of the wine press. The text above the game states, 'Whirl, four times,' presumably after which they would wander around as if drunk. This is one of the few games that were played by both sexes together.

Another game played by the children of ancient Egypt (and children today) was 'the kid in the field', in which two children sat opposite each other with the soles of their feet touching. They lifted their arms up, creating a hurdle over which other children could jump. To make it more difficult the children creating the hurdle would raise their arms higher and spread their feet wider, creating a longer space over which the others were required to jump.[36] The boy waiting to jump would call, 'Hold tight, look, I'm coming comrade.'[37]

Another simple game was a type of 'blind man's bluff' in which one boy sitting in the middle of a group of other boys with his eyes closed guessed who had hit him. In the tomb of Baqt III the scene is accompanied by the words, 'Give one blow on the hand. Give one blow to the head.'[38]

A particularly interesting game, which some Egyptologists believe was also a rite of passage, is the 'hut game', in which four young boys stand inside a hut or arbour. Two stand with their right hand in the air and another pins the fourth boy to the floor. This boy reaches his hand out of the enclosure to a fifth boy, who is leaning down towards him. The caption above indicates he needs to escape by himself: 'Rescue you alone from it, my friend.'[39] This game is represented in a number of tombs and only ever involves boys. The second aspect of this game is what appears to be a ritual dance around a fertility figure, showing there were deeper levels to the game; what the significance is will remain a mystery.

Other games and ways of passing the time may have derived from the training young boys received in the military. On the tomb walls at Beni Hasan there are elaborate scenes of young men wrestling using a number of holds and positions. While this formed part of the military training it is likely the boys practised in the streets, or demonstrated their skills to their friends and family when they were not training.

Many children also had small pets, such as a monkey, a chick or a bird. The most common pet after the dog and the cat (see chapter one) was the monkey, and there were two popular types: the Green Monkey and the Hamadryas Baboon. They first appear prior to the first dynasty and remain prominent until the Roman Period. They were kept as pets due to their comical appeal, as they emulated human behaviour and were often depicted in odd stances. For example, in the tomb of Rekhmire (TT100) one is depicted riding on the neck of a giraffe, and another shows a monkey riding a dog like a horse, as well as others grasping the tails of birds or dressed in women's clothes.[40] They were also trained as performers and could dance and, some say, play musical instruments, although the latter is rather unlikely.[41] One baboon is shown carrying a stick as part of its dance routines and the caption states, 'The monkey carries the stick, though its mother did not carry it,' in reference to its ability to learn new tricks.[42] Children would have enjoyed hours of fun playing with these active and amusing pets.

However, monkeys could be aggressive and were therefore also used as guards; in one Old Kingdom marketplace scene from the mastaba of Tepermank (fifth dynasty) a baboon is shown clinging onto the leg of a thief who has attempted to steal some fruit from a basket. A similar scene is also depicted in the tomb of Khnumnakht and Niankhkhnum, although the baboon has actually sunk his teeth into the leg of the thief in this image. Other suggestions for a working role of baboons is that of fruit gatherers, based on the images of the baboons scaling tall trees to get the fruit at the top, although whether they are helping or hindering the fruit gatherers really is left up to interpretation.

However, the fact that they were beloved pets is demonstrated by the names that have survived which were given to these pet baboons: 'His Father Awaits Him', 'When the Foreign Land is Pacified, the Land is Happy'; powerful names for entertaining animals.[43]

Other, less boisterous pets included the dorcas gazelle. One was found in the Deir el Bahri royal cache (DB320) in a coffin shaped like its body, and another was found curled up at the feet of her mistress in her twenty-third-dynasty pit burial.

Other docile pets are birds and both boys and girls can be seen, particularly in fishing and fowling scenes, clutching a hoopoo, lapwing, turtle dove or duck by the wings, such as in an image in the fifth-dynasty tomb of Nefer and Kahay at Saqqara, which shows a little girl clutching a lapwing.[44] Young girls can often be seen holding a small chick in their hand, although some scholars believe these images are more about eroticism than pets. However, if anyone has seen a young girl confronted with a little, yellow Easter chick, there is little doubt that they were more than likely kept as pets by the young girls.

As children behaved like children, so teenagers behaved like teenagers, and in one New Kingdom text a teacher tries to encourage his students to be more restrained:

> When I was of your age, I spent my life in the stocks. It was they that tamed my limbs. They stayed with me three months, I was imprisoned in the temple, whilst my parents were in the fields, and my brothers and sisters as well.[45]

The stocks he refers to were wooden blocks placed around the ankles, generally used to hold criminals while they were in prison. They were thought to be an effective way of curbing unruly teenage behaviour. Such reckless behaviour was expected to stop once the boy became a 'man' with responsibilities.

A boy became a man in his early teens, and this transition appears to have been marked by a ritual circumcision. There are three images of a circumcision from ancient Egypt, although only one of them is thought to be of a real event. This appears in the sixth dynasty Saqqara tomb of Ankhmahor. The boy is held firmly from behind by a servant as a kneeling priest puts ointment on his penis to numb it, saying, 'Hold him firmly. Don't let him swoon.' There has been some debate as to why Ankhmahor depicted this scene in his tomb and Macy Roth has suggested an alternative interpretation of the scene. She interpreted the hieroglyphs in front of the kneeling man as meaning 'circumcising the ka priest' rather than the 'ka priest is circumcising', indicating this could be a ritual scene showing the initiation of the priest.

As a rule the priesthood all had to be circumcised as part of their cleansing rituals before performing their duties in the temple, and it was considered an honour to sponsor such an event. Such sponsorship could explain why this was included in Ankhmahor's tomb. A stela from Denderah, for example, states, 'I buried its old people, I circumcised its young people,'[46] indicating that this ceremony was considered an honour. The scene in Ankhmahor's tomb is depicted on a door thickness as you enter the chapel of the tomb, which is not a place where religiously significant scenes are normally depicted and could represent a personal, family event. The boys being circumcised may be Ankhmahor's two sons, as they were initiated into the priesthood and Ankhmahor was proud to have sponsored such an event.

The scene on the left could then be interpreted as the pubic hair being shaved as part of the purification ritual. Macy Roth suggests the use of a flint knife rather than a razor for this task was an indication of the ritual aspects of this ceremony. If this scene depicts shaving then the phrase above it that says, 'I will make it comfortable [well/pleasant/sweet],' makes more sense.[47] Circumcision may have been carried out in order to prevent a number of infectious diseases[48] rather than simply being a socio-religious endeavour.

The other two images are from divine-birth scenes in the temple of Mut at Karnak and that of Hatshepsut at Deir el Bahri. The king is shown being circumcised alongside his ka, which could show preparation for his coronation when he effectively becomes the high priest of all temples.

In order to further investigate the ritual behind circumcision we must turn to the texts. In a First Intermediate Period text a man from Naga ed-Dier says, 'When I was circumcised together with 120 men.' This suggests an entire age group was circumcised at the same time, clearly as a public ritual, which supports the theory that it was an initiation into the priesthood. Circumcision can be difficult to identify on mummies and therefore it is hard to ascertain how widespread the practice was. The evidence that has been collected from mummies suggests that circumcision was only ritual for people of status (for example, Amenhotep II, Thutmosis

IV, Ramses IV and V) and for certain ethnic or social groups.[49] Despite the lack of concrete proof, however, it is still widely believed most boys were circumcised in the pharaonic period, although it became less common as time went on.

There is no proof that female circumcision (clitoridectomy) was carried out in ancient Egypt, although one text on the twelfth dynasty sarcophagus of Sit-Hedj-Hotep, in the Cairo Museum, states, 'But if a man wants to live, he should recite it [the spell] every day after his flesh had been rubbed with the Balephd [unknown] of an uncircumcised girl and the flakes of skin of an uncircumcised bald man.'[50] There is some debate whether the word 'uncircumcised' is translated correctly, and could be translated as 'smear'. It is therefore assumed the general rite of passage of girls from childhood to adulthood was when they started their menstrual cycle, or their 'time of purification'. Obviously, this age varied from girl to girl, and whether this was publically acknowledged is unknown.

Once childhood was over for both boys and girls they stepped into adulthood and needed to take on the responsibilities that this life-stage brings, which included marriage and starting a family, as well as the more laborious task of finding work and earning a living.

1. The village of Deir el-Medina, looking towards the Ptolemaic temple. Photograph courtesy of BKB Photography.

2. The abandoned public well at Deir el-Medina.

3. View of Deir el-Medina, showing the cemetery in the background.

Above: 4. An Amarna house, Tell el-Amarna.

5. Shower stall
at the palace at
Medinet Habu.

6. Funerary banquet of Paheri, El Kab. Photograph courtesy of BKB Photography.

7. Boat Jousting, tomb of Iymery, Giza.

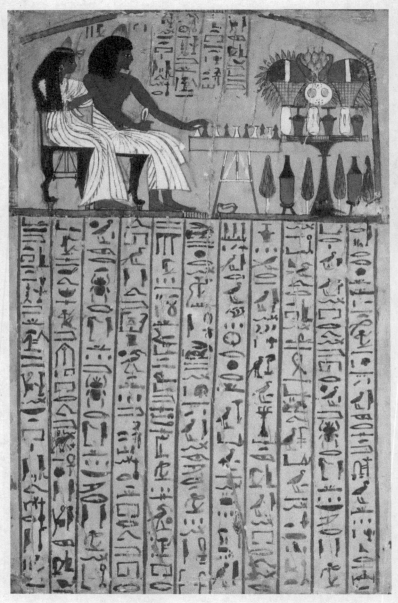

8. Sennedjem and his wife playing senet. Photograph courtesy of Mamienefer, Wikimedia Commons.

9. The Queen of Punt, Deir el-Bahri.

10. Depiction of famine sufferers from the Causeway of Unas, Saqqara.

11. Perfume Making, Tomb of Iymery, Giza.

12. Osiris as as king, showing the people how to farm, Medinet Habu.

13. Terraced temple of Amenhotep I, Deir el-Medina.

Above left: 14. Bes, the dwarf god, Denderah.

Above right: 15. Hathor columns, Kalabsha.

Below: 16. The mountain, Meretseger, seen from the Valley of the Kings.

Opposite: 17.
Min Festival,
Medinet Habu.
Photograph
courtesy of BKB
Photography.

Right: 18. The
Seven Hathors,
Medinet Habu.

Left: 19. Niankhkhnum and Khnumnakht embracing. Photograph
courtesy of the Egypt Archive and Jon Bodsworth.

Right: 20. Hatshepsut's mother when pregnant, Deir el-Medina.
Photograph courtesy of BKB Photography.

21. Hieroglyph showing childbirth, Edfu. Photograph courtesy of BKB Photography.

22. A family portrait showing a small naked child standing before his father, Giza.

23. Hathor
breastfeeding the
king, Edfu.

24. Ahmose's
wife's pet monkey,
tomb of Ahmose
son of Ebana, El
Kab.

25. Circumcision in the tomb of Ankhmahor. Photograph courtesy of Werner Forman Archive via Heritage Image Partnership Ltd.

26. Farmers gathering the harvest, tomb of Khaemhat (TT57). Photograph courtesy of BKB Photography.

27. Military training, Deir el Bahri. Photograph courtesy of BKB Photography.

28. Priests carrying the god in procession, Edfu. Photograph courtesy of BKB Photography.

29. Mourners with mourners in training, tomb of Khaemhat (TT57). Photograph courtesy of BKB Photography.

30. Ay's wife, Tiy, a royal wet nurse, Tell el Amarna.

31. A blind harpist from the tomb of Nakht. Photograph courtesy of the Yorck Project, Wikimedia Commons.

Below:
32. Funerary procession, tomb of Khaemhat (TT57). Photograph courtesy of BKB Photography.

33. Ramses II offering Maat to the god Amun, Karnak temple.

34. Relief showing surgical instruments, Kom Ombo.

35. Double false doors of Niankhkhnum and Khnumhotep.
Photograph courtesy of Horemweb, Wikimedia Commons.

36. Opening of the Mouth ceremony, tomb of Remini, El Kab.

6.

WORKING FOR A LIVING

'Man comes forth from his mother's womb and
runs to his master.'[1]

From a very young age, perhaps as young as nine years old, boys
had to make a decision about their future career. To a modern
western child this would be an impossible task, as there are so
many potential career paths open to them. However, in ancient
Egypt the options were somewhat limited. Generally a boy
followed in his father's footsteps, taking on his role upon death
or retirement. A lone text from Deir el-Medina, however, suggests
that some workmen left their jobs in order to enable their sons
to take over the role, with the understanding that the son would
contribute some of his rations to the upkeep of his father.[2]

Such hereditary roles included the priesthood, administration,
the military, farming and craftsmanship. Such crafts were varied
and included carpentry, stone masonry, bricklaying, basketry,
pottery, flint knapping, faience making and metalwork. All of
these industries could have been carried out in the home on a small
scale or in larger workshops if working for the state. One of the

more unusual workshops at El-Lahun was that of the doll maker, which was discovered with unfinished dolls and locks of hair that were still to be attached. The dolls themselves appear to have been a combination of fertility dolls, with their pubic areas highlighted, and jointed dolls, which may have been foreigners used in execration rituals, rather than dolls used as childhood playthings. However, regardless of their purpose this workman was an expert doll-maker, a role he probably hoped to pass on to his son.

Uneducated boys of the lower classes had even less choices than their middle-class counterparts and likely followed their fathers into farming or other unskilled manual labour. Their lives were hard and they relied heavily on the environment for a successful harvest year on year. Farmers were paid a percentage of the crop that was not required for taxes and land rent.

At the end of the sixth dynasty there was a change in status and farmers were exempt from some taxes, although they were still monitored carefully by state scribes. Farmers were able to sell and rent out their own land, but the owners were still ultimately responsible for the payment of taxes on the yield of the land. Farmers were reliant on a quick harvest and they often hired cattle from breeders to help with harvesting the crop, which they needed to pay for out of their income. 'You have satisfied my heart with the compensation for my red female ploughing ox, which is called by the name of Ta ... That I gave you to ploughing with from regnal year 14 to regnal year 15. My heart is satisfied with its compensation.'[3] To prevent any problems with the identification of the cows when it was time to return them, each cow was branded with an image unique to the cattle farmer. Many farmers, in addition to owning cattle who could pull the plough and speed up agricultural activities, owned a donkey, a classic beast of burden often depicted carrying an 'ass-load' upon his back. They were also loaned out to the peasants at harvest time to help with the back-breaking work. While some donkeys may have helped with pulling the plough across the fields, they were mostly used to carry the grain to the threshing floor and then participate in the threshing activity. Donkeys lived and worked for as long as forty years and were closely associated with hard work, as demonstrated by the proverb, 'When there is work to do, get the donkey, when there is fodder, get an ox.'[4]

A useful but probably not a very well-paid or desirable job was that of fisherman, who were responsible for catching, cleaning and preserving the fish. They were either independent fishermen, who fished as they needed for their families, or full-time fisherman, who caught more than they needed and were able to make a business out of it. Fishermen worked as a team and were paid a percentage of the catch, meaning it was difficult for an individual to climb the career ladder.[5] While fish were essential for the daily diet of the Egyptians there was no ritual element to the role of fisherman, as fish were never offered in temples. It was therefore almost impossible to hold a state position in this role.

Fishermen worked in close proximity to fowlers – groups of men who were responsible for catching ducks, geese and other small birds. Commercial fowlers used dragnets. They worked in a team with a lookout who signalled the time for the hunters to pull the net together, capturing the birds. However, the weight of the nets and the necessity for speed meant this was a difficult job and required stealth and excellent team work.[6] If the timing of the net-pullers and the communication with the lookout were not perfect, the birds were able to escape.

All jobs, even those of the fisherman and farmer, were liable for tax, which was paid in kind. Tax collectors were prone to violence and beating the payee was a recognised form of collection. They were armed with sticks and visited each farm, calculating, measuring and collecting the amount due. If someone failed to pay then 100 blows was administered with the stick. The first recorded tax-evader was Mery, from the eighteenth dynasty, who was given

100 blows for defaulting on his tax payment.[7] Anyone interfering with or hindering tax collection could be punished by having their nose or ears amputated.

Although collecting tax was a violent role there were controls in place in the New Kingdom to curb some of their enthusiasm. Furthermore, there are records of them using false measures, taking more than was required and keeping the excess for themselves, a crime the state tried to prevent.

The physicality of working outside in the hot Egyptian sun was wearying and both farmers and fishermen were plagued in their role by mosquitoes, which carried numerous diseases including malaria and even Elephantiasis.[8] The Ebers papyrus suggests, 'To prevent mosquitoes from biting; fresh moringa oil. Smear oneself with it."[9] How effective this would be is questionable.

In tomb scenes where glimpses of lower levels of society are depicted, such as farmers, fishermen and boatmen, we are offered a fascinating insight into this anonymous class. It is rare to know the names of these labourers and their depiction in non-royal tombs is in order to provide the tomb owner with food for eternity, rather than providing for his own mortuary cult. However, some of the captions above such images provide glimpses into lost moments. For example, in the fifth-dynasty tomb of Ti at Saqqara two boatmen are arguing and one yells at the other, 'Come on! You fornicator.' It seems this type of language was not considered inappropriate to be recorded in a tomb for eternity.[10]

Other unskilled but necessary work included that of laundrymen. Some household laundry was done by the women of the house but the professional launderers were always men,[11] who collected the clothes from the houses to wash down by the Nile. The clothes were rubbed vigorously against stones or trodden against the pebbles in the shallows. It is suggested the role was carried out by men because cloth when wet is heavy and therefore best suited to the strength of a man, although many female household tasks included such heavy lifting.[12] The laundrymen, who were more than likely illiterate, kept a record of the clothes they collected from each household on ostraca, marked with an image of the item (a tunic or loincloth, for example) with dots marking how many of each had been collected. It can be presumed that not everyone was able to afford to pay someone to wash their clothes for them, so this was a job carried out by the poor for the middle classes.

Although unskilled roles had little opportunity for advancement, the skilled roles were the opposite, with strict hierarchies encouraging new recruits to aspire for promotion. So, for example, if you worked as a scribe you aspired to hold a royal title such as seal bearer of the king, sole companion of the king or even vizier, the highest administrative post available. These roles, like most others, were passed on from father to son, but in the New Kingdom if someone caught the eye of the king they could bypass this hereditary system, as he would simply place them in the role he felt they were most suited for.

An excellent career, especially in the New Kingdom, was in the military, and it appealed to athletic boys as well as scribes looking for adventure. A military scribe followed the army into battle and recorded campaigns, manoeuvres, captives and booty. A military scribe never had to engage in combat, so therefore was not trained in military manoeuvres, but still found himself in a certain amount of danger.

Military training was rigorous and there were harsh penalties for poor effort. A new recruit was trained in chariotry and horsemanship, as well as handling weapons like spears and bows while travelling at speed. This required extensive target practice, such as shooting arrows or thrusting spears at a wooden or copper target while on the move. Stick fighting, target practice, sword fighting and wrestling prepared the recruit for hand-to-hand combat, providing a full range of skills for all military scenarios.

One of the earliest depictions of wrestling can be found on the pre-dynastic Cities Palette (3200–3000 BCE) although the majority of depictions can be found in the Middle Kingdom tombs at Beni Hasan. In the tomb of Baqt III (2134–1991 BCE) the figures are distinguished from each other by colour, with one light and one dark making it clearer to make out the different holds. The accompanying text in the nearby tomb of Khety includes phrases like, 'I grab you on the leg,' and 'I cause your heart to weep and to fill with fear.'[13] Although it was primarily for military training and hand-to-hand combat in a battle situation, it is likely that the soldiers also participated in wrestling competitions just for fun.

Stick fighting is often depicted in close proximity to wrestling, showing this was also included in military training. Stick fighting seems to be similar to fencing and the combatants wore wristguards and a leather band over the forehead and chin to protect themselves from being hurt. An image in the nineteenth-dynasty tomb of Khons (TT31) shows two stick fighters standing within a marked ring on a boat, hinting at some form of competition.[14] Whether there was some significance to the competition being carried out on a boat is unknown, although the unstable surface may have provided an extra element to their fight as they tried to maintain their balance.

Personal guards of the king and foot soldiers needed to be able to run for long distances, so stamina was also an element of military training. The Running Stela of Taharqa (690–664 BCE) tells of a race the king organised for the soldiers, enabling him to see who excelled at running. In order to motivate them, the king joined them in the race;

> The king himself was in his chariot to inspire the running of his army. He ran with them at the back of the desert of Memphis in the hour 'She has given satisfaction'. They reached the Fayum in the hour 'sunrise'. They returned to the palace in the hour 'She defends her master'. He distinguished the first among them to arrive and arranged for him to eat and drink with his bodyguard.[15]

The race was from the capital city of Memphis to the Fayum, via the desert route – a distance of approximately 50 kilometres in each direction – so the 100 kilometres was completed in approximately 9 hours.[16] The first half of the race was completed at night, and after a two hour break the runners started the return run to Memphis.

The measurement of time was not a simple procedure in ancient Egypt, and there were three available methods. To tell the time during the day, shadow clocks were used; although this did not consider that the earth spins faster in the winter it gave a rough means of measuring the twelve hours of the day. At night, star clocks were used, albeit generally in a religious context, where the rising in the east of eight particular stars enabled the viewer to identify the hour. For telling the time inside the house, when it was not possible to see the sun or the stars, water clocks were used. A large bowl with a scale measured the passing of time by the speed of the water flowing out through a hole in the side.[17] All of these methods were rough estimations and involved too many variants to be as accurate as timekeeping in the modern world. Moreover, hours were not the same length and varied from season to season.

The winner of this race was rewarded by King Taharqa. This race was not for public viewing and was solely for the king to gage the talent of his soldiers, as well as being an important element of their stamina training. Training was extremely difficult in the New Kingdom military and was not suited to all boys. Papyrus Anastasi III, copied from an earlier document during the reign of Sety II, describes the hardships of the army to a potential recruit, Inena;

> What is it that you say they relate, that the soldier's is more pleasant than the scribe's profession? Come let me tell you the condition of the soldier; that much exerted one. He is brought while a child to be confined in the camp. A searing beating is given to his body, a

wound inflicted on his eye and a splitting blow to his brow. He is laid down and beaten like papyrus. He is struck with torments.

Come, let me relate to you his journey to Khor [a general term for Palestine and Syria] and his marching upon the hills. His rations and water are upon his shoulder like the load of an ass. His neck has become calloused, like that of an ass. The vertebrae of his back are broken. He drinks foul water and halts to stand guard. When he reaches the enemy he is like a pinioned bird, with no strength in his limbs. If he succeeds in returning to Egypt, he is like a stick which the woodworm has devoured. He is sick, prostration overtakes him. He is brought back upon an ass, his clothes taken away by theft, his henchmen fled ... turn back from the saying that the soldier's is more pleasant than the scribe's profession.[18]

As one would expect, Inena decided not to enter the military and became a scribe instead.

Campaign life was difficult but the rewards of foreign travel may have been a deciding factor. To travel by river from Memphis to Thebes in daylight took between twelve and twenty days, and was a dangerous journey, with sandbanks, hippopotami and thieves along the way. The soldiers needed to carry all their food and equipment, including weapons, upon their backs, making the walking elements of the journeys even more arduous.

Life in the army was a combination of the excitement of being on campaign and the tedium of guarding desert trading posts. The latter lasted for twenty days at a time and soldiers marked the days until their shift was over on the rocks surrounding the guard posts. Other practical, domestic jobs carried out by the military included transportation of large stone blocks for construction work, as well as helping with the harvesting in times of need.

Soldiers were paid in food rations while on campaign, which provided the food they needed to survive, and when they returned to the barracks they received the excess. At the Middle Kingdom fortress of Uronaroti, in Nubia, wooden tokens have been discovered, which were exchanged for bread. The different-shaped tokens identified the number of loaves they could be exchanged for and was no doubt an easier way of providing the soldiers with their daily rations. They could exchange the tokens as and when they needed to.

On the battle field soldiers increased their wealth with plunder from conquered enemies, which included gold, cattle and even slaves. Soldiers who excelled in their role and caught the attention of the king were awarded golden flies (a sign of endurance and persistence) or gold collars of valour, known as *shebyu* collars, which were the equivalent of medals. Not only were the recipients made wealthy by these gifts, but they also gained recognition for their service. Such possibilities of wealth and fame no doubt persuaded a number of young boys to enter the army rather than another career.

While there is little doubt that the Egyptian army were well trained, many died on the battlefield. In 1923 a tomb was discovered at Deir el Bahri which contained the bodies of sixty soldiers who died in the Middle Kingdom civil wars. Only two of them were buried in coffins, and it is presumed these were the officers; the other soldiers were simply stacked on top of one other. All of the bodies had been wrapped in linen although none were mummified, and none were named. Tomb robbers had ransacked the tomb, separating the bones and making it impossible to reconstruct the full skeletons. The soldiers had all died in battle, either from arrow wounds or being struck on the head with stones. From the battle wounds it is possible to reconstruct their last moments. The soldiers were initially showered with arrows and one of these was embedded in the left eye socket of one of them. Those who survived this onslaught were able to scale the fortress walls on ladders or siege towers, only to have large rocks thrown on them from above. The enemy then caved in the face of any injured soldiers with a rock, and on many skeletons the left side of the face and head was destroyed. Before being collected, some of the bodies were left on the battlefield long enough for the carrion birds to start pecking at the flesh. When they were collected they were quickly rubbed down with sand and wrapped in linen. None of the soldiers were killed in hand-to-hand combat, indicating this was a siege using distance weapons.[19] Their burial in the valley of Deir el Bahri was a final sign of respect and honour for these soldiers, who were fighting for their pharaoh, Mentuhotep II, whose mortuary temple was in the same valley. However, this death and anonymous burial was almost certainly not what the young recruits were hoping for when they enrolled in the army.

Another sector which offered many opportunities for both educated and non-educated boys was the priesthood. The role of the priest was not a vocational calling and they were not expected to preach to or convert the uninitiated.[20] Egyptian priests were known as servants of the god, as their role was to provide for the god rather than to worship him or her. The titles were either passed down from generation to generation or the office was given as a gift by the king.[21] The family of the high priests of Ptah at Memphis, for example, the last of which died in 30 BCE, had held the same titles for 300 years, with the men as high priests and the women holding the title of songstresses of Ptah in the same region.

Prior to the New Kingdom the priesthood was organised on a part-time basis, with the temple staff working for one month in four on a rotational basis. For the remainder of the year they returned to their primary job. Even after the introduction in the New Kingdom of a permanent priesthood they were still operating on a part-time rota basis.[22] It was expected that their daily occupation dictated the priestly role issued. For example, doctors became priests of Sekhmet, the goddess of epidemics; lawyers would become priests of Maat, the goddess of truth; and scribes became priests of Thoth, the god of writing.[23]

It is only from the Late Period that we have any information regarding initiation rites into the priesthood. A Late Period papyrus states that new recruits had to pass an exam on religious topics before they were initiated into the role. Whether this was applicable to earlier periods is unrecorded.[24] The Ptolemaic Period records that for the initiation into the priesthood of Amun the new recruit should wash thoroughly before entering the temple and plunging into the sacred lake. They were then presented to the gods and initiated into the sacred texts and knowledge.[25] The Roman cult of Isis insisted new priests fasted for ten days and dressed in new linen before entering the holy sanctuary and learning the rites of the cult. These initiation rites were translated from older hieroglyphic texts and were therefore older traditions.

Through all periods the ritual of purification was the most important for the priest before entering the temple, and the most common, yet lowest, level of the priesthood were the wab priests, or 'the purified ones'. They were required to wash twice daily and twice nightly in the sacred lake of the temple and purify their mouths with natron diluted in water. Herodotus records that in addition to washing regularly priests also shaved all of their body hair every other day to prevent lice. Through these rituals the priests were daily cleansed and renewed.[26] The role of the wab priest included the carrying of the sacred barque, cleaning the temple and supervising painters and draftsmen. If they themselves were craftsmen they may have been given the task of making sandals for the deities. For a large temple like Karnak even the wab priests had a hierarchy, with the 'foremost of the pure ones' being in charge of the lower wab priests.

This strict hierarchy of all level of priests meant it was possible to progress through the ranks. The priesthood of Amun at Karnak was divided into five ranks, with the first prophet (high priest) being the highest and fifth prophet being the lowest. There was only one first prophet, but there were a number of people at one time holding the lower-ranking titles.[27] The first and second prophet titles were obtained through heredity, personal ambition or political and royal favour. Those who held the top positions in the priesthood of Amun were very wealthy; they owned a house and land and were held in high esteem.[28] The high priest was the most important in the temple and acted as a substitute for the king, performing the rituals on his behalf. According to tradition, the king, as the high priest of every cult, was personally responsible for carrying out all rituals in every temple in Egypt on a daily basis. Of course this was not physically possible and he hired high priests to act as stand-ins for him. It was therefore a greatly revered position.

Reaching this much coveted role of high priest or first prophet was beyond the reach of most priests, but there were plenty of other roles for them within the temple. Karnak temple at the end of the reign of Ramses III employed a total of 81, 322 personnel.[29] These ranged from priests concerned with the toilette and dressing of the divine statue, who were called stolist priests or priests of the loincloth, to priests of the House of Life, who were scribes and scholars working on the sacred texts.

The House of Life has often been referred to as a university or library, whereas it was actually more of an archive where religious and magical texts could be written, restored, archived and consulted. The House of Life discovered in Tell el-Amarna was near the archive for royal correspondence and seems to have acted as a library.[30] However, such institutions were not open to the public and were only consulted by specific priests, administrators or the king himself.

Numerous texts have been discovered that record the information stored in the House of Life, which included religious knowledge, temple plans for building and decorating and spiritual secrets. In the Famine Stela at Sehel (332–31 BCE), the king asks the lector priests where the dwelling of the god of the Nile inundation, Hapy, was and the priest says he will consult the books from the House of Life: 'I shall enter the House of Life, unroll the scrolls of Re, I shall be guided by them.'[31] These scrolls revealed all the knowledge required to stop the drought causing the famine.

Most large temples had a House of Life, including Memphis, Abydos, Tell el-Amarna, Akhmim, Koptos, Esna, Edfu and Karnak. There is at least one mention of a teacher of the House of Life and in the 'Story of Setne Khamwas (II)' a young boy is put in school,[32] indicating instruction may have been given there: 'He grew big and strong; he was put in school. [After a short time he surpassed] the scribe who had been given him for instruction.'[33]

Many of the priests at the House of Life were also lector priests, who may have been trained physicians and scholars. The lector priest carried the sacred book during rituals, recited the prayers and was present during the divine oracles. Furthermore, in society lector priests were regarded as magicians and were greatly revered, if not actively feared.

Sem or funerary priests were particularly sought after as they provided all the rites and rituals on the body before burial, as well as prayer recitations, water sprinkling, lighting of incense and the Opening of the Mouth ceremony.[34] After death ka priests were responsible for maintaining the cult of the ka of the deceased (see chapter nine).

A tantalising insight of how funerary priests made a living is provided by the archive of Djekhy. Djed-khonsu-iuf-ankh, known as Djekhy, and his son Iturech lived in the Theban area in approximately 590 BCE and were funerary priests (choachytes), responsible for carrying out rituals and making offerings to the dead on behalf of others. Their fee often took the form of land which was then rented out to others, meaning they earned a living from the rent. It is thought that in addition to working as funerary priests they also acted as trustees for important documents belonging to colleagues, as well as maintaining their own records. Their archive covered documents of land leasing, harvest tax receipts, private letters, a marriage contract, hostile takeover of a tomb, donation of land, business conflicts and the purchase of a son; on the whole these connected indirectly with their funerary priest business.

The funerary business was cut-throat in this politically and economically unstable time, and one document discusses a hostile tomb takeover. Another priest, Petosiris son of Iturech, and two other men were spreading the news that he had been commissioned to service a new tomb in the Theban Necropolis. However, this tomb 'belonged' to Djekhy and his colleagues. Djekhy clearly was not happy and raised this as a legal issue, after which Petosiris had to relinquish any claim on the tomb, passing it back to Djekhy and his colleagues. He had to file an oath before the god Khonsu-em-was-nefer-hotep to say he agreed to the terms:

> The place of the mountain [the tomb] of which I have said 'I have
> [...] received [...] Ankhhor son of Iturekh'- you are its choachytes,
> bonded with these Great Ones [the mummies in the tomb] ... I have
> no longer any authority over it from today onward. There is no one
> with us: brother, sister, master, mistress, or anyone else who will be
> able to approach you about this matter, unto eternity.[35]

Another document deals with Iturech's acquisition of two new mummies to perform funerary rites for, further increasing his income. Iturech and a partner, Khausenmut, signed a contract to split the role, completing half the practices and receiving half the payments each: 'Anything that will be given in their name, viz., bread, offerings, and all else that will be given in their name, half being yours and half being mine, and we will share their services between us, the two men, half being yours and half being mine, to complete the specification.'[36] These new mummies brought the recorded 'clients' of Iturech to four or five for whom he was expected to carry out the funerary rites, prayers and offerings on a daily basis. What is rather intriguing about the funerary cult is that it was possible for families to pay for someone else to do what was essentially family duty to their ancestors, and that the service was popular enough that people like Djekhy and Iturech were able to make a living from this.

Not all roles in the priesthood had such an impact on the community, but they were still considered as important to the maintenance of the cult. For example, during religious processions the god was transported in his sacred barque on procession and required as many as thirty bearers to carry it. Each held the title of bearer of the barque. Although a low-grade position it was one which enabled the priest to get close to the god, and one Ramesside priest declares, 'I carried Ptah at the length of my arms, may this god grant that I may be beatified with his fervour!'[37]

Each temple also had a number of auxiliary workers who were not priests, including caretakers, janitors, workmen, bakers, butchers and florists, all essential to the successful running of the temple. Of these auxiliary roles one of the most influential was the butcher, or 'one who slaughters animals and makes sacrifices', as he was responsible for the ritual killing of the food for the gods and the palace. Even butchers who were not employed by the palace had a high status and were often attached to large estates. There are jars which originally held meat labelled by the butcher and estate where he worked. It was a sign of immense importance to have their work labelled in such a manner. As with most positions in Egypt these were hereditary roles passed on from father to son. The ritual nature of the position is apparent as butchers held the title of veterinary priests and not only checked the health of the animals but also checked the entrails for messages from the gods.[38] At Tell el-Amarna one of the known butchers' yards was located in the temple of Aten, showing it was considered a ritualistic activity. In the house of Panehsy, the keeper of the cattle of Amun next to the temple of Aten, 43 kilograms of animal bone were recovered, primarily of cattle, with the most popular cut being the hind legs.[39] Through studying the butchery marks on the bones it was possible to identify that some of the animals were slaughtered by inexperienced butchers, perhaps trainees. It is thought that the cattle were killed in the sacred confines of the temple and then brought to the vicinity of Panehsy's house for dismemberment and preparation, indicating his was a practical rather than an administrative role. In a nearby house meat labels were discovered demonstrating the meat was not for immediate consumption but was to be potted and stored for a later date.

However, such a high status was only attached to butchers of cattle; poulterers were considered almost as unskilled labourers, because anyone was thought capable of killing a bird. Even Akhenaten is depicted wringing the necks of birds to offer to the Aten.

The priesthood also offered employment opportunities for women, both educated and uneducated. From the fourth dynasty women were priestesses mainly for the cults of Neith and Hathor, but could in fact work for the cult of any other god.[40] The first known priestess of Hathor was Neferhetpes, a daughter of King Radjedef in the fourth dynasty. In the Old Kingdom more than 400 women held this title. It appears that these women were members of the elite, as many owned their own tombs and it is unlikely their wealth was acquired carrying out the role of priestess.[41] There were tombs and chapels in the region of the temple of Nebhetepre Mentuhotep II for at least eight women, some of whom were priestesses of Hathor, indicating this king had a special relationship with them. There are even images of the king embracing two priestesses, Ashayt and Sadeh, which is unusual although not unique.[42]

Like the priesthood, the priestess positions were also hereditary and some were passed down for generations. Priestesses primarily acted as impersonators of goddesses or played instruments during temple rituals. Old Kingdom evidence shows that women could also act as funerary priestesses. The earliest reference of the role of choachyte carried out by women dates to the twenty-fifth dynasty.[43] An archive from the Persian Period (517 BCE) tells us of the career of Tsenhor, a female funerary priest, and a Ptolemaic Papyrus (P. Berlin 5507 and 3098) comments that Shakhepery, another female funerary priest, serviced thirty-six tombs; this included not only the tomb owner but also his family, which may have numbered 150 mummies. The job entailed praying for the deceased every ten days and making offerings to them of food and water. With so many tombs being the responsibility of one person there was likely a rota system for the funerary rituals. Sometimes choachytes shared a tomb and one person may only be responsible for quarter or half of a tomb, meaning they did not need to carry out the rituals as frequently. One stela (Cairo CG 22022) shows a choachyte on their daily rounds carrying a pole with a jug on each end over their shoulders. These jugs held everything needed for the libations and rituals.[44]

The most common temple roles for women were singers, dancers, chantresses or priestesses. The head of these groups taught novices the skills needed for the role.[45] The relative importance of these positions depended on the size of the temple, so a chantress of Amun at Karnak was more important than a chantress of a small shrine in middle Egypt. Singers and musicians were particularly important in all temples as all prayers were sung or chanted. By the New Kingdom so many women held the generic title of priestess it lessened the importance of the position at a time when the male priesthood was a profession held in great esteem. In the same way as male priests, priestesses worked one in four months on the same rotation system. Both male and female priests were paid the same for their services to the temple and were entitled to some of the food offered to the gods, which was divided among the priesthood once the god had taken spiritual nourishment from it.

Although female funerary priests had an important role in the funerary cult, the main role for women at a burial was that of professional mourner. They were hired for royal and noble funerals to throw dust over their heads, tear at their clothes, scratch their cheeks, wail and expose their breasts. It was considered unseemly for the women of the deceased's family to be shown in such grief, so they hired women for the occasion. These mourning rituals were ancient in origin and reflected the mourning of Nephthys and Isis for Osiris. Pyramid Text utterance 535 states, 'Nephthys has indeed seized the tip of (her) two breasts because of her brother ...'[46]

In the groups of professional mourners there are often images of young children, indicating girls who would inherit the role from their mother learnt on the job. On one stela from Deir el-Medina a mother and daughter refer to themselves as 'mourner' as a title, indicating it was an occupation[47] every bit as important as any other. Although the role of mourner was normally one carried out by women, in the tomb of Kenamun (TT162) there is a depiction of a male mourner.[48]

As mentioned in the previous chapter, girls were not generally educated and were unable to work in central administration, but, as we have seen, that is not to say that women did not work. There were other jobs open to them outside the temple enabling them to be self-sufficient or to contribute to the household economy. As most women spent the majority of their time in the home, many of their jobs were centred around household industries. Tomb images show that winnowing was generally carried out by women, and they were also responsible for grinding the grain and making it into bread and beer. Women could also help out in the fields during the harvest, and girls were frequently sent to the fields to glean.

Although women could not hold bureaucratic positions in the central government, in the Middle Kingdom they often held titles such as treasurer, major doma and superintendent of the dining room in private homes. In the central bureaucracy women held positions of authority in departments dominated by women, such as overseer of singers, overseer of amusements, mistress of the royal harem, overseer of the house of weavers or overseer of the wig shop. [49] Earlier in the Old Kingdom women held administrative titles like steward of storehouses, food supplies and cloth or the bearer of the seal, who held the authorised seal of the house [50] and was therefore in a position of great responsibility and trust. There is only one example of a woman holding the title of vizier from the sixth dynasty, although it is suggested that the title was probably honorary. These positions of authority were generally in the service of other women, as women were not allowed to oversee the work of men. [51]

Some industries were dominated by women, such as the linen trade, where both workers and supervisors were often female. Nephthys was the goddess of weaving and coupled with her funerary associations gave mummy bandages the name 'Tresses of Nephthys'. [52] The New Kingdom royal harem at Gurob was responsible for the production of a large amount of linen and the royal women trained and supervised the textile workers, [53] who were mostly foreign women sent to Egypt to marry the king as part of the diplomatic parties. The chief of weavers at the site was a woman called Tiy. [54]

A papyrus from El-Lahun suggests that several servant women were employed together in the same house as weavers, and another document records that twenty or twenty-nine servants in one household were also employed in weaving. [55] In the 'Tale of the Two Brothers', Bata's wife offers to make clothes for Anubis if he sleeps with her, indicating it was normal for women to produce cloth in their own home throughout the New Kingdom and beyond. Furthermore, such linens produced by women could be used as currency at this time. [56]

From the Old Kingdom women were visible in all aspects of the linen trade, including harvesting flax and spinning it into linen. Spinning was also carried out by children, as it did not require the same skill levels as weaving. It took three spinners to provide enough thread to be worked by two loom weavers and was an activity that required very little space, meaning it could be carried out anywhere inside or outside the home.[57]

Spinning and weaving were depicted in four Middle Kingdom tombs at Beni Hasan in addition to models demonstrating spinning. As home production of linen was an important part of ancient Egyptian life it was therefore a requirement in the afterlife.

Spinning is attested by numerous spindles, made of wood, stone or pottery, dated from the Middle Kingdom onwards, and spindle whorls have been discovered in El-Lahun, Deir el-Medina and Tell el-Amarna, showing it was a widespread household activity.[58] They used drop spindles with the whorl at the top. There were three methods of spinning using such drop spindles, all shown in the twelfth-dynasty tomb of Khety at Beni Hasan. These methods were used for spinning yarn from flax or sheep's wool.

Often the use of wool is dismissed in ancient Egypt due to Herodotus stating, '[It was] contrary to religious usage to be buried in a woollen garment, or to wear wool in a temple.'[59] Archaeological evidence, however, belies this, indicating wool was definitely used in Egypt for clothes and Diodorus Siculus (1st century BCE) records that Egyptian sheep yielded 'wool for clothing and ornament'.[60] Even Herodotus mentions wearing Egyptian woollen mantles over his tunic, indicating his earlier reference was purely in relation to the priesthood. Wool has been discovered in both domestic and funerary contexts from as early as 2000 BCE. Evidence from El-Lahun and the workmen's village of Tell el-Amarna show sheep's wool was dyed and spun on site.

The supported spindle technique of spinning necessitates rolling the spindle down the thigh to start it spinning in mid-air as the rove[61] was drawn through the left hand. A model from the tomb of Meketre at Deir el Bahri depicts numerous women standing on one leg holding their spindles, perhaps for balance. The grasped spindle technique shows the rove pulled from a basket through a ring or a forked stick and spun onto the spindle, which is rolled between the hands. This method is depicted in the eighteenth-dynasty Theban townhouse of Djehutynefer.

Everyone seemed to be involved in the production of linen, with women, men and children weaving and spinning. Men were generally responsible for beating flax stems and sometimes for twining the spun thread into two or three ply yarn, although in the tomb of Khnumhotep III (twelfth dynasty) a young girl is shown performing this task. The entire family could become involved with the industry of spinning yarn, both in the home or in professional workshops. However, the 'Satire of the Trades' describes the role in less than glowing terms: 'The mat-weaver in the workshop, he is worse off than a woman [in childbirth] with knees against his belly he cannot breathe out. If he skips a day of weaving he is beaten with 50 strokes; he gives food to the doorkeeper, to let him see daylight'.[62]

Different types of spun yarn were discovered at El-Lahun, from course wool to fine thread, and these were considered valuable enough to be used as bribes. In the nineteenth dynasty, during the reign of Merenptah, 'the workman Rahotep [who] shaved the hair of the scribe Kenherkhopshef [...] he gave a loincloth of 15 cubits and he gave him 9 balls of yarn after his [Kenherkhopshef] concealment of his [Rahotep's] misdeeds'.[63] Although we do not know what these misdeeds were it is clear that yarn had a market value high enough to constitute a bribe. Despite the value of the yarn the majority of woollen items date to the Late Period, although a woollen blanket was discovered at the workman village of Tell el-Amarna dated to the New Kingdom. This blanket comprised two-tone wool and another in the village had strings attached to the corners.[64] It is possible these were horse blankets rather than covers for the home, although it is also quite possible that wealthy Egyptians wore woollen cloaks in the winter.[65]

There are numerous socks from the Coptic Period (fourth century CE) in, among others, the Royal Ontario Museum, Toronto; the

Louvre, Paris; the Victoria & Albert Museum, London; and the Petrie Museum, London. All of the socks are of the same design, with two separate toes – one for the big toe and one for the other toes – so they can be worn with sandals. In 2009/10 I led an experimental archaeological project called 'Sock It!' at the Petrie Museum of Egyptian Archaeology, along with Dr Debbie Challis, with the aim of reproducing the socks from the Petrie Collection (UC16766) (*c.* 400–500 CE) using ancient techniques.[66] Studying all of the socks indicated they were made using a method with a similar result to two-needle knitting, but each stitch had a twist. No artefacts have been found suitable to be used as knitting needles, although there are many copper, bronze and bone needles with a large eye at one end, dating from the Pre-Dynastic Period through to the Graeco-Roman period. With such large-eyed needles and a length of yarn it is possible to create these socks using an extension of basic basketry or netting technique, known by various terms including looped-needle knitting, knotless netting, needle coiling, cross-knit looping, naalebinding or single needle knitting. Using this method produced a hard-wearing material which was easier to mend than two-needle knitting.[67]

Once yarn was spun, if it was not used to produce knitted items the majority was woven into cloth. Once the material was woven the men washed it and bleached it to a bright white before the cloth was polished with a tool made of leather. Most clothes were undecorated other than being pleated, and this was likely carried out when the cloth was wet, allowing the folds to remain in place once it had dried.

Another village-based role for women was that of midwife. Although there was no word in Egyptian for midwife it was necessary for women to aid other women during childbirth, as this was the most dangerous time of their lives. It is thought there was a school of midwifery at the temple of Neith at Sais, where women were trained by temple staff. An inscription at Sais states,

'I have come from the school of medicine at Heliopolis, and have studied at the women's school at Sais where the divine mothers taught me how to cure diseases.'[68] However, most midwives were trained through assisting the village women and therefore the vast majority received no formal training. Midwives were in great demand in any village, as most women had at least five children and many had more. Childbirth was discussed in greater length in chapter four.

A new mother who survived childbirth and was in need of an income could hire out her services as a wet nurse. They were hired by the upper classes to nurse young children. A number of contracts between wet nurses and employers have survived, indicating how common they were. At Deir el-Medina a wet nurse was paid as much as a doctor and there were legal agreements between wet nurses and parents from the later periods of Egyptian history; she was required to work a trial period, provide good-quality milk, not to nurse other children and not to fall pregnant.[69]

Royal wet nurses were held in particularly high esteem and in the New Kingdom high officials often married royal wet nurses to further themselves politically. In their tombs it is carefully recorded that their wives nursed princes. Children of royal wet nurses were considered 'milk siblings' to the king and it is likely that they grew up together with him and the royal circle.[70] Hatshepsut's nurse Sitre was buried near the queen, showing she remained part of her household long after her services were no longer needed. Non-royal nurses are also shown in tomb reliefs and stelae with the family they worked for. It was normal for children to be nursed for three years as a safeguard against pregnancy and a way of ensuring uncontaminated food.[71]

In addition to midwives, at Deir el-Medina there was a woman called the *ta-rekhet*: knowing woman or wise woman. Personal names of these women were never given as they were referred to by their title only, indicating an other-worldly status. She gave advice on apparently impossible situations, and understood the complex realm of the dead and the gods, as well as predicting the future. She was approached by both men and women, although whether she worked from home or a chapel is not recorded. On an ostracon from Deir el-Medina, Kenherkhopshef rebukes a woman Inerwau for not visiting the *ta-rekhet* to discover why her two children died:[72]

Why did you not go to the wise woman on account of the two boys who died in your charge? Ask the wise woman about the death the two boys have incurred. 'Was it their fate? Was it their destiny? You shall question [her] for me about them. You shall [also] look after the life of mine and the life of their mother. As regards whatever god of which one will [speak] to you, you shall afterwards write me his name. [You shall fulfil] the task of one who knows her duty.[73]

Kenherkhopshef was perhaps the father of these two boys, and Inerwau their nurse, and he was concerned about the health of the mother of the boys. It is clear that it was possible to address the wise woman in person or by letter, indicating that she was literate or at least had a scribe willing to read these letters on her behalf.

As medicine or communing with the gods was not everyone's forte, some women entered the entertainment industry: that of musicians and dancers. Unfortunately, like farmers and servants, musicians and dancers are often anonymous, although there are more artistic representations of them in addition to archaeological evidence of the instruments themselves.[74] Dancers were hired to dance at banquets and religious festivals and many processions of Hathor involved elaborate dances. One dance is particularly intriguing, where the dancer holds a mirror in one hand and uses it to reflect her other hand. Mirrors were often used for scrying so this dance may have been related to seeing into the other world. Another dance depicted at Beni Hasan shows the dancers with plaited hair with balls attached to the end of each plait, which were used to weight their hair as they dragged it along the ground. Hair was often used for dancing by flicking it in an erotic manner.

Dancers often appeared naked, wearing either a small loincloth or a beaded hip belt made of small golden cowrie shells, an example of which can be found in the Cairo Museum (JE 30858). Cowrie shells were an erotic image as the shape was considered to resemble a vagina and therefore was an image of fertility. Therefore the emphasis in Egyptian dancing was the hip area of the dancer, as is the case with modern belly dancing. To further emphasise their fertility, dancers often had tattoos of Bes on their thighs, keeping the attention on the lower region of the body. Dancing, however, was clearly segregated from the audience[75] and there are no representations of the dancers dancing with anyone else.

Dancers were closely connected with acrobats in regard to entertainment and there are numerous images of both men and women performing great feats of flexibility with forward and backward flips, crabs and group acrobatic tumbling where back flips result in landing on a fellow's back. Some images show contortionists and in the tomb of Antefoqer (TT60) from the twelfth dynasty there is an image of a man and a women lying on the floor touching their feet to their heads from behind. Some of the tomb scenes are almost like comic strips, such as the tomb of Baqti III from Beni Hassan which has four images of a man in the process of performing a pirouette, with each image showing a different element of the turn. This comic-stip representation is also shown at the temple of Hatshepsut at Karnak, where three images of acrobats demonstrate all elements of a forward flip and a fourth image showing a movement to the side, almost a cartwheel. Some flips were carried out with a partner as depicted in the tomb of Khety at Beni Hasan, where two girls hold each other belly to belly, with one girl's head near the other girl's feet,[76] and in this

C. Beni Hasan showing a partnered tumble, tomb of Khety. (Drawing after Decker, 1992, fig. 110).

way they roll rather like a wheel, which would no doubt have looked incredible at a lamp-lit banquet.

Often dancers and acrobats were accompanied by musicians and a singer. Instruments were played by both men and women although from the Middle Kingdom women tended to dominate this industry. The tambourine was the most popular instrument in street music and was always played by women. A tambourine ensemble was sometime accompanied by a young girl who waved a one-handed pair of clappers or held her hand to her breast concealing a small object in her palm, perhaps a jingle.[77] At banquets and festivals women often played flutes, reed pipes, clappers, harps and tambourines and were sometimes accompanied by blind male harpists. Blind musicians often have heightened senses and some believe this enhances their musical ability. Interestingly, in twenty representations of male harpists where the eyes are visible only four or five are blind or visually impaired, indicating blind harpists were not as commonplace as is often stated.

A rather bizarre twist on the idea of blind musicians can be seen in the Karnak reliefs from the Amarna period, which show a group of musicians wearing blindfolds over their eyes. They are providing musical accompaniment to the offering rituals for the god Aten. As they are in direct communication with the deity the blindfolds could prevent them from seeing the god directly, which some believed caused blindness. Some may have believed that as the blindfold prevented the musicians from being able to see in general, it also prevented them from being seen.[78]

We do not know the name of many ancient Egyptian musicians, as they appear in tombs as an anonymous addition to the banquet scenes. However, in the Middle-Kingdom Theban tomb of the vizier Antefoker there are images of two harpists and a man and a woman who are identified by name; the singer was Didumin and the songstress was Khuwyt. They sang songs to the goddess Hathor and to the vizier himself.[79] Another named musician was Mahu, who was a singer of the noble harp of Amun, from the eighteenth dynasty. Mahu explains how he 'followed the kings' footsteps in foreign lands', indicating he was a royal travelling harpist [80] and followed the king, and perhaps sang and played the harp to entertain him.

Religious musicians primarily played the sistra, which was sacred to Hathor and comprised a bronze arch through which short bronze sticks were threaded mounted on a handle, or the menat necklace, which was a faience-bead necklace that was shaken to provide a rattling sound. The sound of the sistra and the menat had their roots in an old ritual of Hathor, which was to pull up stems of papyrus and shake them before the goddess. The sistra rattle is thought to sound similar to this.[81]

The status of the musician in society is an interesting one, as they were involved in religious processions and therefore could have the same status as the priestesses, and those who played at banquets often wore the same clothes as the party guests, coupled with being named in some tombs. All this indicates they were of the same status as the party revellers themselves.[82] There is no evidence that noble women played instruments in public, but that is not to say that elite women could not play musical instruments and did not play in the privacy of their own home. In the sixth-dynasty tomb of Mereruka his wife sits on the end of their bed playing a harp. In the tomb of the Old Kingdom vizier Merefnebef, four wives are shown playing harps for him. Whether these were wives who had passed on or evidence of polygamy is not entirely clear.[83]

There were many household roles which were carried out by men and women, and household servants and slaves could be either male of female. The question of slavery often comes up in relation to ancient Egypt, but there is no clear definition of the terminology used. There were various terms which may

D. Mereruka is entertained by his wife, Saqqara. (Drawing after Manniche, 1991, fig. 70).

refer to slave status, including dependants, personnel, forced labourers, workers, servants, royal servants and prisoners of war.[84] There seems to be what Meskell refers to as a sliding scale of slavery, ranging from prisoners of war to native Egyptians who were forced to sell themselves into slavery at times of extreme poverty.[85] It is believed that once they had paid their debts through their manual labour then they were freed. Many of the male slaves worked as domestic servants, brewers, cooks and farmers.[86] Slaves who had been captured as prisoners of war were possibly sold door to door and one woman Iryneferet records how she had paid for a Syrian slave girl. The rather random list of items, some of which were borrowed from other people, indicates perhaps she was buying the slave at the door and was simply looking around the house for items to reach the proposed value.[87] Sometimes such female slaves acted as concubines for the master of the house or were purchased in order to bear children for a barren wife, as was the case with the Adoption Papyrus (see chapter four).

This concept of selling yourself or even your children in payment for a debt was not unusual and one of the documents from the Djekhy and Iturekh archive discusses a loan where Hepy, an embalmer, borrowed 1 deben of silver from Djekhy, which he was to pay back within seven months. He used all of his possessions, even his children, as collateral. 'They (the capital sum plus interest) will be on my head regarding the securities you will require from me, whichever one, be it house, male servant, female servant, son, daughter, silver, copper, clothing, oil, emmer, or whatever in this world.'[88] A later document further indicates that people were indeed used to pay back debts, as Iturech leaves a document describing how he purchased a 'son', Hor. The document is a statement from Hor claiming he is happy with the money paid and that he and his children will be 'sons' of Iturech. Hor comments on the transaction,

You (Iturekh) have satisfied my heart with my silver to be your son. I am your son, together with my children who will be born to me, together with all I possess and will acquire. No one on earth will be able to exercise authority over me except you, be it father, mother, brother, sister, master, mistress or any creditor or myself. My children are the children of your children forever.[89]

It is uncertain how old Hor was, although it is suggested that as his name is not signed as one of the witnesses he was possibly a minor. Donker van Heel further suggests the word son was used as being more acceptable at the time than 'slave'.

Slaves are often believed to have been responsible for the manual labour required on the pyramids and other large-scale monuments in Egypt, but this is not the case. While the Nile was flooded from July to October every year there were numerous agriculturists standing idle until the waters receded. These were conscripted to work on large-scale building works by the state for the same wage as a standard worker. A roll call card from Hawara, which names the monument which is probably Amenhotep III's pyramid, includes a list of conscripts required to work on it:

> Director Senusret's son Khety
> Secretary Senet's son Senbef Senbef [...]
> Commander Sat-[...]'s son Senusretankh Senbef [...].[90]

As a government-run scheme, unexplained absences from work were viewed as a criminal offence and those who absconded could be treated as deserters, meaning their families were obliged to fulfil their contractual obligations. Some women and children were conscripted into manual service, which was not slavery in the sense that they were not considered personal property, but they were required to work where they were sent and carry out the task specified. What tasks they performed, if indeed there were specific tasks for these state-owned slaves, is unknown, although it seems that many female foreign captives were sent to work in the linen trade.[91]

There are references in the texts to servants who worked in private houses but lived elsewhere, indicating that not all household servants were slaves. There were varying titles from the Middle Kingdom for a domestic servant, including housemaid, cleaning woman and domestic servant – 'she who is allowed to walk through the house'. In Deir el-Medina, for example, women hired people to come in to help grind the corn for the family's flour. It took between 55 and 80 minutes to grind enough flour for one adult for one day,[92] and considering there could be six adults in a house plus children this chore would dominate the day's work. The work was low paid but would have been frequent. A New Kingdom papyrus from Gurob records how Pihy loaned two of his servants to her son Miny. One servant, Kheryt, was to work for seventeen days, and the other, Henut, for only four days; however, a surprising clause in the contract stated that should the days be too hot then the servants were not to work.[93]

There are many cases of servants and slaves being freed and rising to the top of a career. For example, Hesysunebef started his life as a slave and was adopted by his master to become a member of the team of workmen at Deir el-Medina. He rose to rank of deputy, which was one of the highest ranks in the village, and he named his children after his adoptive parents[94] (for more information about Hesysunebef see chapter four).

Then, as now, the sole purpose for work, whether it be as vizier or house slave, was to earn enough to live. Even in a society with no monetary system the motivation was the same. It is rather interesting that some working conditions have not changed in 5,000 years. For example, those in government employment, such as the workmen at Deir el-Medina, were paid on the twenty-eighth day of each month. These wages were in the form of rations and were essential for the daily sustenance of the workmen and their families. These rations comprised grain, fish, vegetables, oil and clothes. A workman at Deir el-Medina received monthly from the granary 4 sacks (300 litres) of emmer and 1.5 (115 litres) sacks of barley. Captains received 5.5 sacks of emmer and 2 of barley.[95] The workman's ration was enough to feed a family of ten and provided a little extra, which could be exchanged for other goods. Further supplies from the treasury and the supply staff included, during the reign of Ramses III, 8.4 kilograms of fish per month per workman, plus vegetables, fruit, beer and one or two cakes per month.

However, during the reign of Ramses III there were numerous problems with the grain supply at Deir el-Medina, starting in year 17, when a corrupt official Paser was using a short measure to distribute the rations, keeping the excess for himself. Akhpet, the scribe of the vizier, noticed that the grain ration was 5 per cent short.[96] Akhpet remeasured all the rations with an accurate measure and redistributed them.

In year 29 of Ramses III the payment of rations was delayed, resulting in a number of protests from the workmen at Deir el-Medina. From delivery records it appeared that deliveries were made to the workmen every ten days. The records of the strike start on day ten in the second month of winter, and the deliveries show that Sary had delivered the normal quantity of 380 fuel rations but Pashed had only delivered 200 of his 500 fuel rations. This was not the only problem, and the Strike Papyrus, which starts on this date, records that

> on this day the crew passed the five guard posts of the tomb saying, 'We are hungry for 18 days have already elapsed in this month', and they sat down at the rear of the temple of Menkhepere. The scribe of the enclosed tomb, the two foremen, the two deputies and the two proctors came and shouted to them, 'Come inside'.

They swore great oaths saying, 'Please come back, we have matters of pharaoh.' They spent the day in this place and the night in the tomb.[97]

This strike was called as the rations were eighteen days late; however, rather surprisingly strikes rarely started on a work day and instead protests were made at the weekend. In order to make their presence felt they sat down in the road at the rear of the temple of Thutmosis III and ignored all requests to return to the tomb.

On day twelve the problems had still not been resolved and Mentmose the scribe encouraged them to strike again by saying, 'Finish whatever you are doing that we may go out.'

They reached the temple of Usermaatra-Setepenre [Ramses II]. They spent the night quarrelling in its entrance. They entered into its exterior and the scribe Penteweret, the two chiefs of police, the two gatekeepers of the gatehouse of the tomb, the chief of police, Mentmose, declared that he would go to Thebes saying; 'I will fetch the mayor of Thebes. He ... I [Mentmose] said to him.' Those of the tomb are in the temple of Usermaatra-Setepenre. He said to me ...'treasury' ... you ... there is not ... give you [to the place] one is ... They said to them, 'The prospect of hunger and thirst has driven us to this; there is no clothing, there is no ointment, there are no fish, there are no vegetables. Send to the pharaoh, our good lord, about it and send to the vizier, our superior, that we may be supplied with provisions.' The ration of the first month of winter was issued to them on this day.[98]

So on day twelve they were paid for the first month of winter, however the strike continued until day seventeen when the rations were also paid for the second month of winter. By the third month of winter the workmen were once more on strike due to non-payment of rations. One of the workmen was so desperate in his hunger that he made an oath: 'As Amun endures and as the ruler whose wrath is greater than death endures, if I am taken from here today I shall go to sleep only after having made preparations for robbing a tomb'.[99] Whether he needed to persevere with his threat is not recorded but it is interesting that such a threat was made, although the Tomb Robbery Papyri (see chapter seven) indicate that this was not necessarily an unusual act. However, a statement from the vizier on day twenty-eight of the fourth month of winter showed the desperation of the situation: 'It so happens that there is nothing in the granaries – but I shall give you what I have found.'[100]

In the first month of summer the workmen threatened to go to the public marketplace and protest directly to the vizier about the lack of payment, but they were warned by the scribe Amennakhte, 'You go then and I will have you convicted in any court you will go to.'[101] Another two weeks passed and there was another protest, this time at the temple of Baenra-Meryamun (Merenptah), where they were given fifty sacks of emmer to tide them over until the full rations arrived. These problems and subsequent strikes had been taking place for six months at this point and were to continue at regular intervals over the next seventy years. All of the protests took place at a mortuary temple on the West Bank as this was where the granaries were situated from which the rations were distributed. This continuing problem with the payment of rations was a direct result of the failing political system at the time and the decreasing economy.

The Egyptian working life was long, with no official retirement age. Although there were a plethora of jobs available, often the career chosen was dictated by the role held by an individual's parents. It was unusual for someone to break away from family tradition and enter a brand-new industry. This was unfortunate if an individual's interests were not the same as his father's, but without a lot of luck there was little anyone could do to change this situation. People needed to accept their lot in life, work hard and if Maat was smiling on them they would live a happy and comfortable life.

7

LEGAL MATTERS

'Confess nothing and I will get off.'[1]

Ancient Egypt, like any society, ancient or modern, was comprised of law-abiding citizens and criminals. As with every other aspect of ancient Egyptian life, we have records of crimes committed and, in many instances, the punishments meted out for these crimes. However, there was no official codified law until the Third Intermediate Period, and the earliest example of a set of laws comes from the Ptolemaic Papyrus Mattha. However, this reads more like a practitioner's handbook than a code of law reference book.

In the New Kingdom the word *hep* was translated as either 'law' or 'custom', showing there was in fact a fine line between the two. Furthermore, there is only one legal text where the punishment was administered according to the pharaoh's *hep*. This was a case regarding inheritance and the *hep* quoted states, 'Let the property be given to the one who buries.'[2] Whether this could be identified as a law or a guideline is open to debate.

However, the absence of a codified law, as we understand it in the modern world, is not to say the Egyptians were a lawless society;

they were governed by a strict moral code by which everyone was expected to live. This code is outlined in the Instruction texts which, while not law books as such, offered advice on the appropriate way to behave in all situations. These rules are further emphasised in the Book of the Dead in the Negative Confession (chapter 125), which lists all the things which the deceased had not done and comprised a combination of criminal and trivial acts together. Moreover, to the Egyptian mind set it was more important to avoid sin than to pursue a virtuous life.[3]

Criminal acts were separated into two groups: state crimes, which obviously interested the vizier and included tomb robbery and plots of regicide, which resulted in harsh punishments; or civil acts, such as breach of contract or petty theft, which were sorted out within the community and could incur a fine or a beating.[4]

As with most other aspects of daily life in ancient Egypt, much of the information about crime and punishment comes from the records at Deir el-Medina. As Tyldesley rather glibly states, 'The fifty or so families at Deir el-Medina were a remarkably quarrelsome and surprisingly light-fingered lot.'[5] Unfortunately often the ends of papyri are damaged or missing, and while we have the crimes the verdicts have not always been preserved. Papyri records were generally made regarding crimes against the temples or palace and these were kept in the mortuary temples at Thebes. Many notes about legal dealings were additionally made on ostraca and were not official documents but rather personal records of events. Through these records it has been possible to build up a record of standardised crimes and typical punishments.

With no official legal code in the New Kingdom, identifying a crime was not as straightforward as in the modern world, and with no lawyers or detectives to investigate a potential crime there was a lot of reliance on questioning, torture and hearsay. There were three legal avenues open to someone from Deir el-Medina in the New Kingdom: the oracle of Amenhotep I, the vizier's office and the *knbt* (court). These three avenues, however, were not independent of each other and all ultimately were governed by the state and overseen by the same people. The vizier's office was responsible for criminal matters, the oracle was approached for civil concerns and the *knbt* for keeping the peace.

For an injured party often the first port of call was the *knbt sDmiw*, or court of hearers. At Deir el-Medina the *knbt* was excavated in the chapel area and showed sixteen seats, some of which were inscribed with workmen's names, indicating they held regular office here.[6] These sixteen officials were known as the notables or magistrates. The notables of the Great *knbt* of Thebes were the vizier, chief priest of Amun, second priest of Amun, two royal butlers, the steward of the House of the Divine Votaress, a lieutenant of chariotry, a standard bearer of the navy and Prince Pesiur of Thebes.[7] These groups of notables never included the auxiliary staff of the village, like watercarriers, and therefore maintained a certain class level. Their knowledge of most of the people who came to the court, as well as perhaps knowing background information on the disputes, was part of the reason they were chosen for this role. This was a little like a modern jury, although they were not necessarily there to discover the truth, but rather to maintain public order. This could result in bowing to pressure from the general public in regards to punishment. They did not investigate the cases brought to them; instead they listened to the claimants and the accused and formed their judgement based on that.

A trial consisted of the examining body, the criminal, witnesses and the notables. The claimant stated their case to the notables and the accused defended themselves against the accusations. If the case was complicated witnesses may be called to speak, but often the claimant and accused were enough. There was no jury (as an impartial group) or lawyers for either side. The innocent put their trust in the truth.[8] It is unknown if the notables of the court needed to come to a unanimous decision on a case[9], although it seems unlikely, and there was no limit to how long a legal dispute could continue. The case of the police chief Mentmose was active for over eighteen years, which could have been down to the *knbt's* reluctance to pass judgement or the plaintiff's refusal to press charges against the defendant. A case could not really be brought to the *knbt* unless there was a suspect (as in the case of vandalism or theft), as with no investigation team cases without an accused were never solved.

Another *knbt* was situated outside the gate of the temple of Khonsu at Karnak temple, in what appears to be an open square. These examples may indicate that while these courts were perhaps commonplace they were not housed in purpose-built structures but were instead set up in public squares and easily accessible areas. This also suggests that justice was a public event, which no doubt affected the proceedings, with public opinion being made clear as a trial continued. Any oaths or sentences were read out at the temple gates,[10] meaning the general public participated in the enforcement of the sentence.

The *knbt* was overseen by the vizier, who appealed to Maat the goddess of truth and justice. Maat was central to the functioning of the *knbt* and the entire justice system as she governed moral behaviour for king and commoner alike. Should the law of Maat not be upheld then the equilibrium of the cosmos would be unbalanced. The vizier's position here was very powerful as he ultimately decided on the punishment for the crimes brought before him. In the tomb of Rekhmire (TT100) the vizier is seen in his judgment hall with the forty rolls of the law in front of him.[11] However, for very serious cases the *knbt* may be superseded as the king became involved, choosing three or four of the highest officials, including the vizier, to oversee the trial.[12]

Essentially the vizier held the life and death of everyone who appeared before him in his hands, as well as the lives of the condemned's family for generations, and they were often caught taking bribes. A criminal and his family were sometimes sentenced to lifelong labour as state-owned slaves, or the criminal would lose his position and this punishment was also extended to the entire family. Losing a high position from the village of Deir el-Medina was not just a loss of a job and status but also the loss of a government-owned home, forcing the whole family to relocate. One individual who suffered this punishment was the seventeenth-dynasty temple official Teti, who was condemned, for an unspecified crime, to lose his office but also to 'be expelled from the temple of my father Min, and let him be removed from the position in the temple, from son to son, from heir to heir.'[13] This punishment not only destroyed him and his immediate family but also any further generations. Such an unfair or potentially corrupt system could not really be called justice. One litigant appealed to the god Amun to save him from the system. 'Amun-Re, the one who intercedes for the lone man when he is in distress, may he cause the court to be of one voice when they answer concerning the lone man! (So that) the lone man becomes justified and the one who carries gifts is grieved.'[14] This man refers to himself as the lone man, meaning he is one without rich benefactors and connections and cannot pay the bribes required for a positive outcome to his trial.

The vizier was ultimately responsible for questioning suspects and witnesses, although this may well have been delegated. There was no premise such as 'innocent until proven guilty' and Papyrus Leopold II tells how eight men were arrested and questioned on the basis of a rumour that they had been involved in tomb robbery,[15] which was known as 'leg-stretching' in reference to the method of entering the tomb shafts by fitting their feet in slots on the opposite wall.[16] In the case of thefts it was often the vizier and the chief priest who recovered the stolen property.[17]

Questioning was referred to as 'to examine by beating' or 'to examine with the stick'. This was continued until the witness or criminal cried, 'Stop I will tell.' If the statement that followed was not satisfactory then he may have been beaten again.[18] If this was proving unsuccessful then they were questioned with *memyny*, an unclear word which derives from the Egyptian verb 'to twist' and could mean the arms and legs were painfully twisted,[19] perhaps until they snapped. There was a 'place of examination' where anyone being questioned was taken, and sometimes in the texts it was referred to as being 'taken to the riverbank',[20] indicating this was where the examination centre was. Both witnesses and defendants were questioned in the same manner, whether they were guilty or not.[21] Such methods encouraged false statements. One man, when confronted by someone he had accused, withdrew his accusation, saying, 'I said it from fear,' and in another example a man says to a female witness, 'Confess nothing and I will get off,'[22] showing there were flaws in the system.

An alternative to visiting the vizier and the *knbt* was to seek the advice of the oracle of a god. The workmen of Deir el-Medina appealed specifically to the oracle of Amenhotep I, the deified founder of the village. Like many things which were considered normal in ancient Egypt there are no clear records of how the oracle worked, although using a combination of records of the questions presented to the oracle as well as an image in the Theban tomb of the priest Amenmose (TT19)[23] the process can be made clearer.

Approaching the oracle was often carried out via written messages presented to the divine statue of the god, or by facing the statue, asking the question and casting lots with straws or twigs for the answer. During festivals with processions through the streets anyone could approach the bier with the statue and ask a 'yes' or 'no' question. However, the answer was not considered infallible and in one instance the god answered 'no' to a petitioner, who then simply rephrased the question so the only answer could be 'yes'; this was the judgement he accepted.[24] The god answered by encouraging the priests [holding the bier] to move the statue from side to side or up and down.[25] The questions were generally short and straightforward: 'My good lord! Shall we be given rations?', 'As to the cattle that the woman is claiming, does she have a share in them?', 'As to the dreams which one sees, are they good?'[26] One document records how Mery-Re the carpenter made two statues for Ruty. On seeing the statues, Ruty realised they were worth less than he paid. As Ruty and Mery-Re were unable to agree on a solution they went to the oracle to solve the problem. The oracle sided with Ruty and Mery-Re was asked to reimburse him the difference in value.[27]

An ostracon from Deir el-Medina concerns a woman who approached the oracle regarding an inheritance dispute. She approached the god on behalf of herself and her husband. Before he died her father had promised to give her husband a certain amount of grain over six years, but this had not been received in full and she wanted to know how to acquire the remainder of what was owed to them.[28] Whether this was part of a dowry is unclear, as was the response from the god, but it shows that women could also approach the oracle on behalf of men, and this is not the only example of women working on behalf of their husbands.[29] Women were able to approach the oracle and address the god directly without using a male intermediary, although of all the known examples of oracle requests only 5.4 per cent were from women.[30]

Other than the oracle of Amenhotep I at Deir el-Medina, as an ordinary person could not address the statue directly they asked their question to a priest who acted as an intermediary. In New Kingdom, temple-based oracles it was popular to have the voice of the god echo out from the sanctuary, and there was no doubt a priest listening to all the requests from a hidden place and answering on behalf of the god.

It was not only the ordinary people who approached the oracle with questions, and from the Middle Kingdom onwards kings received divine counsel in this way. For example, Hatshepsut consulted the oracle of Amun in order to legitimise her right to rule: 'Very great oracle in the presence of the good god proclaiming for me the kingship of the Two Lands.'[31] The oracle could therefore be approached regarding any problem or question, not just regarding legal matters.

There was no limit to the number of times someone could appeal to the god about the same subject, and in one case the accused ignored the judgment of the oracle of three different gods on no less than five occasions. In the reign of Ramses III, during the annual Opet Festivals, Amenwia, a villager from Deir el-Medina, appealed to the oracle of Amun to find out who had stolen clothes from him. When he read out the names of the villagers, the god nodded when one name was reached: Petjauemdiamun. Petjauemdiamun declared, 'It is false, it is not I who has stolen them.' He then went to two other oracles and was distressed when they answered in the affirmative as to his guilt. He rigorously denied it but eventually he confessed when he was beaten by his long-suffering colleagues.[32] He swore he would return the clothes and should he rescind on this then he would be 'thrown to a crocodile'.[33]

Even sentences passed in a *knbt* could be ignored and there are cases where defendants ignored their verdicts and their punishments, even after being called back to the court multiple times to justify their actions.[34]

Although both the oracle and the *knbt* justice system were open to corruption and misuse, to lie in front of the vizier or the oracle carried a harsh punishment. For example, if a person saw a tomb being robbed and did not report it, they were considered as guilty as the robbers themselves.[35] Perjury was also often considered more serious than the crime. Diodorus (first century BCE) recorded,

The penalty for perjury was death: the reasoning being that the perjurer was guilty of the two greatest sins, being impious towards the gods and breaking the most important pledge known to man. Again if a man walking along the road should happen to see a person being attacked or killed and did not come to his aid, he had to die. If he was genuinely prevented from helping the person he was required to lodge information against the assailants and to testify against their crime; if he failed to do this as the law required, he would be beaten with a fixed number of blows and be deprived of food for three days. Those who brought false accusations against others had to suffer the punishment that would have meted out to the accused had they been found guilty.[36]

In one court case, the foreman Hay, from Deir el-Medina, stood in court accused of 'speaking against the king.' He was accused by four workmen who were severely below his rank in the village and in the court itself. However, he needed to defend himself and stated that when he was supposed to have said the contentious things he was sleeping. The four men quickly retracted their stories and when questioned again they stated they had heard nothing. They were warned, 'If you hide today, only to speak of it tomorrow then may your noses and ears be cut off.'[37] Amputation of ears and noses was a common form of punishment for state crimes. As noses and ears were mostly cartilage, the victim was unlikely to bleed to death[38] and once healed they were able to continue working, probably in the mines or quarries. Although this is often recorded as a punishment, no mummy or skeleton discovered from ancient Egypt has shown evidence of such amputations.

The crime of making false accusations was an important one as it constitutes lying to the gods and to the king and the punishment was harsh. In the New Kingdom one woman and three men were given 100 blows each for making false accusations. Truth and honesty were therefore considered essential and once a criminal was found guilty the vizier was sometimes satisfied with the defendant swearing an oath that they would not commit such a crime again. Sometimes these oaths were acquired under torture, but all follow a similar format.

> He said: as Amun endures and as the Ruler endures, if it be found
>   that there was any man with whose name I have concealed, let
>   his punishment be done to me.
> If it be found that I had anything to do with the thieves may I be
>   put on the stake.[39]
> If ever in the future I go back upon my statement let me be sent to
>   Kush.[40]

Once this oath was made the case was generally considered completed, although there is at least one incident where the oath was not taken at face value. A woman Herya was asked to swear under oath than she had not stolen a copper chisel from the workman Nebnefer. After she swore the oath they continued to question her, and then went to her home where they discovered the copper chisel and a number of other copper objects from a local cult. This elevated the level of the crime from a civil dispute dealt with by the *knbt* to a state crime and the scribe suggests she should be 'taken to the riverbank'.[41] It seems a further trial followed, leading to a harsher punishment. These oaths were considered to be made directly to the gods and the king and therefore should the criminal break them, not carry out any works or pay any fines promised, then they were severely punished.

The phrasing of the oaths also introduced some of the most drastic punishments available, which included being impaled on a stake. The Nauri Decree, from the reign of Sety I (1291–1278 BCE), describes the punishment as being 'caused to fall, he being placed on top of the wood'. If the stake pierced the heart or a major blood vessel the death was quick, but if they aimed to miss the major organs then death was slow and painful. There are no images of executions, although there is a hieroglyphic determinative of a man with a sharp spike through his chest on the Amada stela of Merenptah (1212–1202 BCE). Such an execution may well have been a public event and the Nauri Decree records that temple thieves were 'placed upon the top of the wood next to the temple from which he shall have stolen'.[42] It cannot be known for sure. If this was a public spectacle, nor if it was how popular they were; the absentee records at Deir el-Medina do not mention time off for public executions, which indicates that it was perhaps not a spectator sport.

Another form of execution was burning; in the Middle Kingdom Papyrus Westcar an adulterous woman suffers death at the command of the king who 'placed fire on her' and her ashes were thrown in the river. The man she was adulterous with was given to a magical crocodile and dragged to the bottom of the lake. Both of them were denied a burial, and therefore an afterlife, which was essentially the main punishment. It is possible that those who were burnt had already been killed by some other means and the punishment was the destruction of the body, denying them an afterlife and ensuring punishment continued after death.

The Middle Kingdom stela of Neferhotep describes that the punishment for misuse of the temple at Abydos was being destroyed by fire, and the Tod inscription of Senusret I explains that someone who vandalises a temple was executed by means of being 'placed on the brazier'. Even general theft could result in being 'thrown into the fire', as one man discovered when he was sentenced for stealing three state-owned chisels. Furthermore, by the end of the dynastic age it was an accepted although not the sole punishment for treason and rebellion.

The Middle Kingdom stele of Sehetepibre warns, 'there will be no tomb for he who rebels against His Majesty, and his body shall be thrown in the river',[43] which denied them a proper burial and afterlife in the same manner as burning. The New Kingdom

Ostracon Nash 1[44] describes how, after discovering temple objects in her house, the court accused the woman Herya (mentioned above) of being 'Great False one, worthy of death' and she was 'taken to the riverbank', possibly for execution[45] in this case rather than questioning. She certainly disappeared from the records after this. The vizier wanted to make an example of her so 'there shall be no other woman like her, again to do likewise'.

While it appears that execution was a standard punishment for some crimes, and the vizier was working on behalf of the king in these matters, the king himself was surprisingly coy about the practice. In the Harem Conspiracy Papyri, Ramses III claims that although he was aware of the death penalty he delegated the sentencing;

> I spoke to them strictly saying; 'Take care, in case you should allow an innocent man to be punished by an official who is not his superior'. This I said to them repeatedly. As for all this that has been done, it is they who have done it. May the blame fall on their heads while I am safeguarded, exempted forever, for I am amongst the just kings before Amun-Re.[46]

The Harem Conspiracy was essentially a plan devised by a secondary wife, Tiye, who wanted her son, Pentewere, on the throne in place of Ramses III. She involved a lot of people in the plan, which is perhaps why they were caught; there were six wives of the harem, gateway guards, thirteen courtiers, eleven harem officials, five military men and two priests. Some of the trial judges were then also charged for gross misconduct with some women from the harem. As the people here were charged with conspiracy to kill the king the penalty was death, although the king did not want his soul tarnished by administering the punishment himself.

A less severe, although not necessarily better, punishment was being sent to Kush to work in the mines or quarries. Nebnefer was given three punishments for an unspecified crime: 100 blows, 10 brands and hard labour in the quarries. Normally this sentence was until death, although Nebnefer was sentenced until the vizier decided he had done enough. Those people sentenced to the quarries often died on the journey to Kush before starting their period of enforced hard labour.

> Now one of these days it happened that His Majesty [Ramses II] was thinking about the desert lands where gold could be got, and thinking of plans for digging wells along the routes made difficult because of their lack of water, in accord with a report made as follows: there is much gold in the desert of Akuyati, but the road to it is extremely difficult because of the water shortage. Whenever the gold prospectors went there it was only ever half of them that arrived, for they died of thirst on the way, along with their donkeys.[47]

Hard labour was not always in Kush and included 'stone-cutting in the Theban necropolis, the Place of Truth' and was a sentence for a violent crime: 'Year 6, third month of summer, day 16. Setting A'o-nakhte to hammering (stone) in the Place of Truth (for?) striking the head of Djaydjay, Pa-idehu and Montu-pa-hapy.'[48] This was not just a punishment given to those living at Deir el-Medina, as there is a fragment of a letter which tells of a policeman from another village, called Nakhte-Seti, who was sentenced to forced labour for hitting someone with a stick.

Those who were not sentenced to death, hard labour or a beating may have been sent to prison. There are no extant buildings that were clearly prisons, but records indicate that prisoners were included in the grain rations at Deir el-Medina and the Turin Necropolis diary has a list of names with a grain allocation next to each one. Seven of the sixty-eight names have 'prisoner' written next to them. Six of the names are tomb robbers.[49] Furthermore, there are texts which refer to confinement in the 'Enclosure of the Necropolis' or being 'made to sit in the Enclosure' as a punishment for theft, although whether this was private theft or state theft is uncertain. The short period of confinement – 'spent 40 days sitting' – would perhaps indicate it was a minor crime.

The most compelling evidence is in the form of records referring to the Great Prison, which was an institution with many functions, including a store of legal documents, as well as the location of the court. Those found guilty of a crime could be held in the prison on a temporary basis while they awaited sentencing. It was also a holding area for those who had been conscripted and were awaiting information on the location they were expected to work.

Conscription was not popular with the community; 'The field worker cries out more than the guinea fowl. His voice is louder than that of a raven When he returns home from marshes he is worn out, the corveé has wrecked him.'[50] Due to the harshness of the corveé system people were not ready to volunteer freely, so it was made illegal to refuse to go when called and there were harsh penalties for deserting once on consignment. 'An order was issued to the Great Prison ... to release his [or her] people from the law-court and to execute him [or her] the law relating to one who deliberately absconds for six months.'[51] This text makes it clear that once someone absconds from their site of conscription their family was taken and held hostage in order to exact pressure upon the deserter to return. Ideally the family would be released upon his return, although sometimes they were not and were included in his punishment. The punishment for deserting could be unduly harsh; 'I found the royal servant Sobekemhab, who had run away, and handed him over to the prison for justice ... he will be condemned to death.'[52]

In ancient Egypt women had the same legal rights as men, although they did not necessarily exercise these rights as frequently. Prison lists show that fewer women were in prison than men, although the punishments received were the same.[53] Women could bring an action of law against another person, bear witness to legal documents, be the executor of wills (see chapter nine) and be equal partners in legal contracts.[54] Legal rights were attributed according to class rather than gender, and women owned property and could inherit and participate in business activities. All landed property was handed down from mother to daughter to ensure it remained in the family as paternity could be questioned but maternity could not. On some inscriptions men claimed 'they were son of [mother's name]'[55] rather than their father's name. Women who owned property were able to own and administer the land independently[56] and during the Middle and the New Kingdoms women ran large estates alongside their husbands, although the Ramesside Wilbour Papyrus shows women only held 10.8 per cent of apportioned plots.

Women sometimes owned and participated in business activities and were often depicted selling and buying goods at the market. In the eighteenth-dynasty tomb of Kenamun in Thebes a female merchant is depicted selling cloth and sandals at the market, and in the Tomb of Niankhkhnum and Khnumhotep at Saqqara (fifth dynasty) there is a port scene in which both men and women are trading[57], indicating that women could buy and sell independently of the men of the household.[58] In the twentieth-dynasty Tomb Robbery Papyri the wife of a tomb robber was asked where she got the money to buy slaves, to which she responded, 'I bought them in exchange for produce from my garden.'[59] While we have no way of knowing whether she was telling the truth, her answer was considered believable enough to be considered.

An ostracon[60] from Deir el-Medina lists a large number of things given to an individual woman and it has been suggested that she may have owned a shop or a storage place for things to be sold.[61] Although it is clear that women were able to work and sell items at the market we do not know what percentage of the profits had to be given to her husband. Any property a woman owned when she got married remained hers rather than automatically passing into the hands of her husband, and she could own, lend, inherit and sell any of her property with the same freedom as if she were single. In 249 BCE a woman called Tay-Hetem took advantage of this situation and loaned her husband 3 deben of silver (273 grams) at a rate of interest of 30 per cent to be paid back within three years. This was the usual loan rate.[62]

Upon her husband's death a widow was entitled to inherit one-third of his property with the other two-thirds being divided between his children and siblings. Any property she owned before coming into the marriage and any she accumulated throughout the marriage was not taken into account when her husband's goods were divided. However, a widow was often reliant on her family members to care for her should her husband have been less than wealthy. The Stato Civile Papyrus fragments in Turin show one elderly woman lived in her husband's house but in a later record she had moved in with her son and daughter-in-law, presumably after the death of her husband. Any income a widow received was transferable, and a man records, 'Now, as for the message you had sent about your mother stating she had died. You said "Let the wages that used to be issued to her be given to my sister, who has been a widow here for many years until today." So you said, "Do so, give it to her until I return!"'[63] This indicates that widows were often at the mercy of the charity of others. However, if a husband wanted his wife to inherit more than the standard third of his property he could leave her more in his will or divide it in life. To do this he needed to produce an *imyt-pr*, a land-transfer document. For example, in El-Lahun, Ankhren a minor government official left all his property and servants to one of his brothers, Wah. The document was stored in the records office and Wah made an inventory list of everything the *imyt-pr* included in order to make it clear what he was able to transfer to others as his property.[64] Five years later Wah passed all the property to his wife Teti, which she could distribute as she wished, along with a house from which she could not be evicted.[65] Another Middle Kingdom man did exactly the same thing by leaving his wife fifteen servants in his will when in life he had already given her sixty servants so they would not be distributed after his death to his children[66], ensuring all sevety-five servants were passed onto her.

When a woman died she could distribute her personal property in any way that she wanted and was able to disinherit her children if she deemed it necessary. It was not uncommon for women to write wills in order to ensure their children received their property after death. For example, the female choachyte (funerary priest) Tsenhor (see chapter six) had a contract drawn up in order to name her daughter Ruru as a beneficiary;

> To you (Ruru) belongs half of what I own in the field, the temple, and the city, namely houses, field, slaves, silver, copper, clothing, it grain, emmer, ox, tomb in the mountain, and anything else on earth, as well as half of my share that comes to me in the name of the choachyte of the Valley, Nesmin ... My father.[67]

The inheritance of servants is a contentious issue as it raises the issue of slavery, which is discussed briefly in chapter six. As discussed, people could sell themselves into slavery in order to pay a debt and once the debt was paid they would be free once more. However, as a punishment for a crime a defendant could be sentenced to a loss of liberty. If the crime was severe enough, wives and children could also lose their freedom and be forced into slavery because of the crimes of the husband, although a man could not lose his freedom due to the crimes of his wife. Families were held responsible for the acts of all individuals, and they were not allowed to profit from the illegal gains of a criminal.[68]

One of the most notorious crimes in ancient Egypt was that of tomb robbery and, as there have only been a handful of Egyptian tombs which were not robbed in antiquity, it is the crime that most people today will associate with ancient Egypt. It is no secret that often the tomb robbers were the people who constructed the tomb and therefore knew their location. Paneb, one of the workmen at Deir el-Medina, was accused of tomb robbery and this perhaps consequently led to his dismissal, and possibly even execution. The accusations against him can all be found on Papyrus Salt 124, written by Amennakhte. However, some of the accusations on this papyrus should be taken with caution. Paneb, an orphan, had been adopted by Neferhotep, the chief workman of the village, and was raised as his son, inheriting his job and possessions upon his death. Neferhotep's brother Amennakhte was jealous of this inheritance, which he believed was rightfully his, and was rather bitter towards Paneb. This bitterness manifested itself in Papyrus Salt 124. However, it is thought that there was an element of truth in the accusations, as many involved or were witnessed by other people in the village. The accusations ranged from abusing his position of foremen – 'Charge concerning his ordering the workmen to work on the plaited bed of the Deputy of the Temple of Amun, while their wives wove clothes for him. He made Nebnefer, son of Wadjmose feed of his ox for two whole months.'[69] It is assumed that this work was unpaid, which is why it was included as a charge – to the most serious charges of tomb robbery, which were supported by other sources. Paneb disappears from village records shortly afterwards, with the last known record stating, 'Year six, the fifth month, the killing of the chief.' He was accused (among other things) of removing the covering of the chariot of Sety II as well as a 'charge concerning his ordering the workmen to cut down stones on the top of the tomb of Sety Merenptah. They took them away to his tomb and he erected four columns in his tomb of these stones.'[70] He was also accused of robbing the tomb of Henutmira, a daughter of Sety I, in the Valley of the Queens, stealing a goose which was probably covered in a precious metal. If royal tombs were not enough, he was also accused of robbing four villagers' tombs.[71] Whether he was caught, tried and executed is not known for certain, but his disappearance from the Deir el-Medina records suggests this was the case.

A particularly interesting group of papyri recording further tomb robberies is from year 16 of Ramses IX (1082 BCE). The fullest record of the procedure of the robbery is found on the Abbott Papyrus and describes a four-day period between day 18 and 21 of the third month of inundation. On the 18th day, Pawer'o, the Prince of the West of No and Chief of Mazoi of the Necropolis, reported to the vizier, the notables and the butlers his suspicion of the robbery of two eleventh-dynasty, seven seventeenth-dynasty and one eighteenth-dynasty tomb. On his advice an inspection party went to the necropolis to check the tombs. This party comprised inspectors of the Necropolis, the scribe of the vizier and the scribe of the overseer of Pharaoh's treasury. Their investigation discovered that the tombs Pawer'o suspected of being robbed had not been, but that the tomb of Sobekemsaf, two tombs of the Divine Votaress's and a number of tombs of lesser personages had been violated.

Pawer'o was able to produce a list of names of the thieves, who were later arrested and tried. The next day, on the 19th, the vizier, Khaemwese, and the royal butler, Nesamun, went to examine the tombs in the Valley of the Queens, accompanied by Peikharu, a coppersmith who had been accused of tomb robbery two years earlier. He had been examined by 'beating', which led to the confession of his robbing the tomb of Isis, a queen of Ramses III. However, once he was in the Valley he was unable to locate the tomb of Isis (an apparently newly robbed tomb), only the tombs he had entered two years previously. It is likely he only confessed to stop the torture he was being subjected to while being questioned. On examination of the tomb entrances, all were found to be intact, indicating they had not been violated.

That evening two scribes approached Pesiur, another Prince of Thebes, to report a further five tomb violations.[72] This conversation was overheard by Pawer'o, who wrote to the vizier denouncing the scribes for not following protocol. The scribe of the Necropolis was expected to report any concerns directly to the vizier,[73] rather than informing Pesiur first. Reporting crime itself had a strict hierarchy, with ordinary people reporting to local officials (like these scribes) who then went directly to the vizier.[74] The great court of Thebes was then called on the twenty-first day of the third month of inundation, not to investigate the robberies but to investigate Pesiur and the two scribes. The tombs had been found intact, and the list of thieves provided did not reveal any evidence of robbery, indicating his information was false. Pesiur likely included the name of Peikharu the coppersmith in the list based solely on his being arrested in year 14 for loitering in the Valley.[75]

It appears from the evidence provided that Pawer'o and Pesiur were rivals and that Pawer'o overheard Pesiur's plan to demand an investigation into the tomb robberies and pre-empted him. When it proved to be false information, Pawer'o denounced Pesiur and therefore he was questioned in court regarding this, leaving Pawer'o in the clear.

We are able to put together the intricate details of the tomb robberies as well as the complex nature of the people involved from a number of other papyri. In the Amherst Papyrus on day 19, a prisoner recalls the thefts in the tombs of Sobekemsaf and Nubkhaas. He lists eight men who were in 'the pyramid tomb of this god', which include Hapiwer, Setekhnakht, Hapi'o, Irenamun, Amenemhab, Kamwase and Ahautinufer. The eighth man, Setnakht, escaped.[76] In addition to these eight men responsible for the actual robbing of the tomb, Papyrus BM 10054 tells us of the fisherman Panekhtmope, who ferried six thieves across the river and received payment of three kite of gold (approximately 27 grams). Once the robberies took place, the robbers enlisted the help of Amenpnufer to transport the gold and silver.[77] Pawer'o and the high priest of Amun Amenhotep were responsible for the recovery of the stolen items from the eight thieves.[78]

Stealing from the tombs of royalty and even the temples was not uncommon in the New Kingdom, and Papyrus BM 10054 includes the record of a priest Penwenhab who, accompanied by other priests, went to a place and stole gold foil from a statue of Nefertum belonging to Ramses II, before going to another place associated with Ramses II or Nefertum and stealing four silver objects which were replaced with items made of wood. A goldsmith is called to give evidence to the facts and gives a list of more people who were connected with the crime and received plunder from the thefts.[79]

However, it was not only precious metals that were stolen from tombs and temples; wood was considered a valuable commodity and BM 10053 contains a number of criminal charges of wood theft, including,

> Charge concerning the door-frame of the House of the Divine Ennead which the carpenter Peson and the carpenter Nesamun cut up: and they made it into four boards and he gave them to the troop captain Peminu.

> Charge concerning the door of the Mut shrine of cedar which the scribe Sedi stole and gave to the troop captain Peminu.

> Charge concerning the four boards of cedar belonging to the 'floor of silver' of Usimaatra Setepen ra, the great god which the scribe Sedi gave to the citizeness Teherer, the wife of the divine father Hori.[80]

Any worries the thieves had about the wrath of the gods were clearly superseded by the economic value of the wood they could acquire, cut up and then sell. At the time these robberies were occurring, during the reign of Ramses IX, the Egyptian economy was particularly weak at all levels of society, and the west bank was plagued by bands of Libyan tribes in the western desert, which led to the abandonment of Deir el-Medina to the nearby safety of Medinet Habu.

Not all crimes were against the state in the form of temple theft, tomb robbery or conspiring to assassinate the king. Crimes were obviously carried out against other members of the community and even in the home, as the records of domestic violence suggest. However, this was only considered a crime in particular circumstances. Ostracon Nash 5 describes domestic violence between a woman and her husband;

> My husband ... then he made a beating, he made a beating [again] and I caused the [...] to fetch his mother. He was found guilty and caused [...] and I said to him 'If you are [...] in the presence of the court' and he swore [an oath of the lord] saying 'as Amun endures as [the Ruler] endures'.[81]

Unfortunately the oath that the husband made is lost, meaning we do not know what he had to agree to in order to end the case.

Should a woman be further abused, the Kahun Gynaecological Papyrus has a remedy for the victim of rape: 'Instruction for a woman suffering in her vagina, and her limbs likewise, having been beaten. You shall say concerning her; this has loosened her uterus. You should then prepare for her; oil to be eaten until she is well.'[82]

Paneb, the rather notorious inhabitant of Deir el-Medina, was also accused of rape by Amennakhte, his adopted father's brother. Apparently he stripped the lady Yemyemwah of her clothes and 'threw her on top of the wall and seduced her'. She was the sister of his adopted father and Amennakhte. As with most of Amennakhte's accusations against Paneb, this one also did not result in a court case or punishment, which either indicates they were unfounded or Paneb was able to bribe the officials and remain un-reprimanded.

There is even a possible case of male rape recorded in the Turin Indictment Papyrus. It is a 'charge concerning the violation done by this sailor Panakhtta [... to ...] a field labourer of the estate of Khnum, Lord of Elephantine.[83] What the outcome of this charge was is not recorded. It is thought that in many instances seduction or rape may have led to forced marriages, although this is not supported by written evidence. A more likely consequence of rape was pregnancy, and in the Anatomical Museum in the Cairo School of Medicine there is a young girl less than twenty years old who met a rather violent and untimely death. She lived in the twenty-sixth dynasty and at the time of her murder she was six months pregnant. She was killed by a number of blows, breaking her left forearm, her left shoulder and the left side of her jaw and fracturing her skull.[84] The blows all being on the left-hand side is indicative of a right-handed assailant. It is unknown if she was killed due to her pregnancy but it seems likely, although whether the pregnancy was the result of a rape or a dalliance is unknown.

Adultery, on the other hand, was not a criminal offense, but the officials became involved in order to keep public order and to restrict the vendetta of the wronged husband. The adulterous man could expect to be killed by an enraged husband and this type of revenge was considered acceptable. The husband was expected to be able to pursue his revenge but within the limits of public order. If he pursued his case through the courts he would not get any financial compensation but would receive advice on the best course of action.

One case from Deir el-Medina concerns the workman Merysekhmet, who was discovered having sex with a servant's wife. The servant complains, 'As for me I am a servant of Ameneminet, a man of the necropolis. I carried bundle to the house of Pa-ym and I made his daughter my wife.'⁸⁵ Due to his status when he complained about Merysekhmet he received a beating of 100 blows. A scribe stood up for this servant by stating, 'What is the giving of 100 blows? One carries a bundle while another has illegitimate sex.' Merysekhmet was simply asked to swear an oath that he would not commit the offence again and the case was considered closed.

Vigilante justice was not uncommon in ancient Egypt, and rather than going through the legal channels individuals or groups would often seek out a criminal themselves and administer a beating to them. One Papyrus (BM 10416) describes such a situation surrounding an affair had been going on for eight months. A group of eight people who were supporters of the cuckolded husband were hunting for the woman in the affair in order to beat her up, and the man in the affair had already been beaten up by his betrayed wife's supporters. Another fragmentary letter (P. BM 10418 +10287) adds that 'if we will not find her to beat her we will find Rta her little sister and we will find [...] ist also'. This seems a little extreme for a consensual affair and even the scribe who discusses the mob claimed, 'Really, even I held them back this time, I will not hold them back another time.'⁸⁶

Obviously, as in the modern world, not all legal dealings involved criminal activity and people would visit the *knbt*, vizier or notable in order to countersign a document or witness a contract. For example, a doorkeeper Khaemwaset was selling his ox and signed a document to say he was happy with the price of 50 deben. He had a witness signature from the workman Neferhotep who was watchman on duty that day. Khaemwaset states, 'I will not contest it [the price] in the future.'⁸⁷

Evidence like this demonstrates that the ancient Egyptians were not much different from their modern counterparts. Khaemwaset was essentially providing a receipt for his ox, which protected himself and the buyer from problems in the future. Documents like the Tomb Robbery Papyrus and the papyri recording the Harem Conspiracy are simply records of important cases, perhaps to keep track of the proceedings and punishments, perhaps for future reference should similar cases happen again. This type of record keeping is not very different to the modern records of legal cases. The only real difference is the inconsistency in laws and punishments, and perhaps these records were part of an attempt to standardise such proceedings.

8.

DISEASE AND MEDICINE

'Something has entered his mouth. Death is approaching.'[1]

Accidents, injuries and diseases were as much a part of the lives of ancient Egyptians as they are of ours today. Some of these proved to be fatal. Egyptian doctors were well known throughout the ancient world for their effectiveness and knowledge, and many of their remedies form the basis of modern medicine. Herodotus records that the King of Persia requested a king of the twenty-sixth dynasty send him the most skilful of Egyptian ophthalmologists. The doctor who was sent to Persia however was rather bitter towards the Egyptian king: 'His pretext was as follows. Cyrus had sent to Amasis to ask for the services of the best oculist in Egypt, and the one who was selected, in resentment at being torn from his wife and family and handed over to the Persians.'[2] For revenge this doctor was said to have incited the Persian king to attack Egypt in 525 BCE.[3] This could therefore be propaganda to explain the Persian invasion. Other evidence, however, backs up the use of Egyptian doctors abroad. A New Kingdom doctor, Nebamun, is depicted receiving gifts for medical services administered to a Syrian prince, and Ramses II sent Pariamakhu to the Hittite court to prescribe medication for the king.[4]

Even with world-famous doctors the average life expectancy was low, with women dying at approximately thirty years old and men at approximately thirty-five years old. A study was done in the early nineteenth century on 709 dynastic skulls, which showed the average age at death was thirty-six years old.[5] Another study carried out on the Turin skeletons from Gebelein and Asyut show that at the age of thirty the population was halved and by the age of forty-three the population was reduced to a quarter.[6]

Child mortality was also extremely high, and many children died in the first year of life. Many died at the age of three during the transition from breastfeeding to solid food, but if a child survived this there was a good chance they would survive until adulthood, and possibly into their seventies. However, reaching such a ripe old age was a dangerous journey, with risks from disease, infection and even the doctor's remedies.

However, not everyone died young; for example, Ramses II (1279–1212 BCE) lived until ninety years old and Pepy II (2278–2184 BCE) ruled for ninety-four years and is the longest reigning king in history.[7] Even among the ordinary people some survived into old age. One woman, Iyneferti from Deir el-Medina, was over seventy-five at death[8] and the Chantress of Amun Asru (see below) was in her sixties when she died. Reaching old age was considered something to be proud of and Amenhotep son of Hapu, architect and scribe under Amenhotep III, boasts on one of his statues, 'I reached eighty years, great in favour with the king. I will reach 110 years.'[9]

While in reality the age of death was extremely low, the idealised age was 110 years old and this was often cited in literary tales to show the wisdom of old age. The Westcar Papyrus (or the 'Tales of Wonder') describes the magician Djedi: 'He is a man of 110 years, who eats 500 loaves of bread, half an ox for meat, and drinks 100 jugs of beer to this very day.'[10]

Living to old age was also used as a polite greeting: 'May you complete 110 years upon earth, your limbs being vigorous.'[11] Considering the ailments which afflict the elderly it is not surprising that the introduction to the 'Tale of Woe', on Papyrus Pushkin 127 states, 'May he (Atum) cause you to reach 110 years upon earth, your body whole, growing old with a contented heart, without illness in your limbs, but with continuous gladness and joy in your heart and without the weakness of old age, you having indeed arrested it.'[12]

Unfortunately, as people did not live as long as modern communities, it is difficult to monitor the typical ailments which only afflict the elderly, as one of the main resources for learning about Egyptian disease are mummies. However, evidence for many diseases is also found in the written records.

There are numerous medical papyri listing ailments and the recommended treatments. Some of the papyri focus on a particular branch of medication like the Kahun Gynaecological Papyrus; the Old Kingdom Edwin Smith Papyrus, which is primarily concerned with surgery arranged in order from the head downwards; or the Chester Beatty VI Papyrus, dealing solely with diseases of the anus, rectum and bladder. Other papyri are more general, such as the Ebers Papyrus (1542 BCE), which discusses diseases of the eye, skin, extremities, gynaecology and surgical diseases, and the Hearst Medical Papyrus, which covers everything from a 'tooth fallen out' to bites from humans, pigs and hippopotami.

The medical papyri describe not only the illnesses but also the cures. These remedies were a combination of practical medicine and magic, with incantations considered essential for success. The Egyptians saw no difference between the two practices and combined practical medicine with unguents, oils, dancing, music, incantations and laying hands on the patient. The remedies cited focused on the relief of symptoms rather than dealing with the cause of the illness.[13] It is thought these papyri filled the role of medical text books for students and physicians alike.[14] This would therefore suggest that the doctors were literate, and there is evidence proving some of them were; Heryshefnakht, for example, was a *snnw* (lay physician) and a priest of Sekhmet and it is recorded that his job entailed 'reading the papyrus rolls daily'.[15]

If an ailment was obvious, like an open wound or broken bone, then a purely medicinal remedy was favoured by the doctors, perhaps accompanied by an incantation or prayer. If the ailment was internal and the cause unknown it was considered to be of supernatural origin and therefore it was essential to turn to supernatural means for a cure.

The medical profession had a strict hierarchy of positions, with *snnw* or lay physician being the lowest rank, and the high level *sau* or magic physicians, who were generally priests of Sekhmet. The latter were medically qualified but were seen to cure only those people they felt were being punished by the goddess. However, in general most doctors were priests and their favoured deity determined their speciality:

Sekhmet, the goddess of plagues and epidemics.
Duau, the god of eye diseases.
Taweret and Hathor, goddesses of childbirth.
Horus, the god of deadly stings and bites from crocodiles, snakes and scorpions.
Selqet, the goddess associated with bites and stings from venomous reptiles and insects.

As the gods specialised in different things, so to did the doctors, and Herodotus (fifth century BCE) records, 'The practice of medicine they split up into separate parts, each doctor being responsible for the treatment of only one disease.'[16]

A papyrus on snake bites in the Brooklyn Museum[17] describes the role of the priests of Serqet: 'Beginning the collection of remedies to drive out the poison of all snakes, all scorpions, all tarantulas, and all serpents, which is in the hand of the priests of Serqet, and to drive away all snakes and seal their mouths.'[18]

There were various doctors on location, as it were, including Middle Kingdom doctor Renef-Seneb, who worked in a quarry in Serabit el-Khadim, and Heryshefnakht, who we met earlier, also from the Middle Kingdom, who was based in the alabaster quarries near Tell el-Amarna.[19] Furthermore there were 'estate' doctors who were responsible for the healthcare of the peasant farmers who worked on the large family estates.[20] Within the communities there were village-based physicians and women who acted as midwives, although there was no Egyptian word for midwife, gynaecologist or obstetrician. The only written evidence we have of midwives comes from the literary tale on Papyrus Westcar where Rededjet is aided in her birth by four goddesses. In reality expectant mothers were aided in birth by women who probably learned their craft from their mothers but were no less valid than a temple-trained physician.

Evidence from Deir el-Medina also suggests many villagers self-diagnosed, perhaps using word of mouth, tradition and medical papyri as reference, and sent away for the ingredients required for a cure. The absentee record shows that Paherypedjet took a number of days off work 'to be with' Khonsu or Horemwia, or for the 'preparation of medicine', and it is assumed he was the village doctor or a pharmacist at this time.[21] Not all of his patients survived, and in year 2 (Sety II), month 3 of harvest, days 25–30, he was absent from the tomb to care for Senet-Nofret, who died shortly after.[22] She was clearly an important woman in the village as the whole crew were absent from work in order to attend her funeral.

The stela of the foreman Baki makes reference to Amenmose, who held the title *kherep serquet*, and it is assumed he was the more official village doctor. During the reign of Ramses IX (1126–1108 BCE), there was a physician at the temple of Amun was called Pahatyu, and in the twentieth dynasty Innay was the overseer of physicians at the temple of Ptah at Memphis,[23] indicating the temples had their own team of doctors to deal with the daily ailments of the priests and auxiliary workers. No doubt all doctors were paid well for their services and in the absence of a monetary system the physicians, whether village based or temple based, were paid in kind.

As most remedies in the medical papyri began, 'You shall then prepare for him,' it seems likely that medicines were made as they were needed rather than 'off the shelf' and perhaps Paherypedjet was making medicines according to need in the village.

Peseshet was the only female physician known from Egyptian history and the first recorded female doctor. She lived during the fourth dynasty and was the lady overseer of the lady physicians, specifying physicians rather than midwives. No other female physicians are known until the Ptolemaic Period. Although no other female doctors are recorded, the fact that she was overseer of the lady physicians indicates there were other female doctors for her to oversee.

Mummification enabled Egyptian embalmers and doctors to learn about the internal organs and the workings of the human body. In fact, by the twenty-seventh dynasty, the word *snnw* (physician) also meant embalmer, showing there was perhaps some crossover with the two roles.[24] It was estimated by Rowling in 1989 that over 30,000 mummies have been examined and not one bears the scars of surgical intervention. Evidence therefore suggests that they did not perform surgery on live bodies, other than circumcision (see chapter five) and the removal of tumours such as subcutaneous lipomas, 'which comes and goes under the fingers' and were prescribed 'the knife treatment' followed by treatment of the wounds. Of course, any knife treatments were carried out without anaesthetic.

The Edwin Smith Papyrus describes quite clearly the ancient Egyptian knowledge of the pulse;

It is there that every physician and any priest of Sekhmet places his two hands or his fingers on the head, on the back of the head, on the hands, on the place of the heart on the two arms or on each of the two legs he measures the heart because of its vessels to all his limbs. It speaks from the vessels of all the limbs.[25]

They also knew that the blood supply ran from the heart to all organs in the body: 'It speaks forth in the vessels of every body part.' It was originally thought that the pulse was discovered by the Greeks some 2000 years later. Moreover, the evidence suggests Egyptian doctors were not far from the discovery of circulation.[26]

The Edwin Smith Papyrus describes knowledge of the brain and the connection with paralysis, but they were unaware of the brain's importance in regard to thought processes and emotions. They believed all emotions, feelings and thoughts took place in the heart, and therefore when the body was mummified the heart remained in position, whereas the brain was disposed of.

The medical equipment used was rather primitive and a full set of surgical equipment belonging to Qar, the senior physician of the royal palace, was discovered in his tomb (sixth dynasty). These match the list of medical instruments depicted on the wall of Kom Ombo temple, which dates much later, to the second half of the second century CE, and those recorded on the Edwin Smith Medical Papyrus.

A Rush (used with a knife for cutting treatments)
A fire drill (to burn growths)
Knife/chisel
Cupping glass
Thorn (to burst blisters)

Heated broken glass (for eye treatments)
Swabs, tampons, linen material
Knives, salve spoons, and mortars

The medical procedure itself was very well defined in the Ebers Papyrus and was similar to modern practice. The patient described his symptoms before the doctor conducted a physical examination, which included a study of urine, stools, sputum and blood, and checking the pulse: 'You should put your finger on it, you should examine the belly.'[27] Once the full examination was complete the doctor made a diagnosis, which was one of three decisions: 'An ailment which I will treat', 'An ailment which I will contend', or 'An ailment not to be treated'. Only fourteen out of forty-eight cases on the Ebers Papyrus were considered hopeless. Some of the treatments were open to interpretation and could indicate a certain element of experimentation.

One cure was for the patient to stay 'close to his landing post', presumably meaning get plenty of bed rest. The scribe interprets this as 'the patient should be put onto his regular diet and should receive no medicine'.[28] Is this an ailment the doctor did not treat, or was bed rest and no medication considered a form of treatment?

The prescriptions were described complete with a dosage, which was normally measured as *henu*, which was one-tenth of a *heqat* and worth about 450 ml.[29] However, the measurements were written as 1/8 or 1/16 and could be interpreted as being in relation to the *henu* or as a fraction of the available mixture. This dosage was then applied according to age. 'If it is a big child, he should swallow it like a draught, if he is still in swaddles, it should be rubbed by his nurse in milk and thereafter sucked on four days.'[30] The time of day the treatment was most effective would be specified: 'And the eye is painted therewith in the evening its other half is dried, finely ground, and the eye is painted therewith in the morning.'[31] The duration of the prescription was particularly important; the Ebers Papyrus specifies the number of days, whereas the Edwin Smith describes the patient's condition: 'until he recovers', 'until the period of his injury passes by', or 'until you know that he has reached a decision point'.

Many of the medicines prescribed were logically applied, with medicines taken orally for internal diseases, external applications for pain, ointments for skin diseases, inhalations for respiratory diseases, gargles for mouth disorders, baths and douches for gynaecological problems and enemas for intestinal infections.[32] For example, a remedy for burns on the Ebers Papyrus comprised 'barley bread, oil/fat and salt, mixed into one. Bandage with it often to make him well immediately'.[33] Burns were particularly common as open fires were used not only in the home but also in numerous manufacturing industries. The Ebers Papyrus (482) includes a remedy for burns, which has a detailed day-by-day schedule of application:

Day 1: black mud
Day 2: excrement of small cattle (sheep etc.)
Day 3: resin of acacia, barley dough, carob, oil
Day 4: wax, oil, unwritten papyrus, *wah*-legume
Day 5: carob, red ochre, *khes* part of *ima* tree, copper flakes.[34]

How any of these ingredients would soothe the burn is unknown, other than perhaps the mud on the first day. The other ingredients, especially the excrement, could cause serious infection. Many prescriptions, however, were based on excrement, blood and urine from numerous species, including cats, asses, birds, lizards, crocodiles, flies and humans. For the most part excrement was applied externally, although excrement from lizard, crocodile, pelican and human infant were applied directly to the eyes (Ebers

344-70), and crocodile excrement was inserted into the vagina (see below). Blood of ox, asses, pigs, dogs and goats was also applied directly to the eye to prevent ingrowing eyelashes (Ebers 425) and the Ramesseum Papyrus III also prescribed human urine to be placed in the eyes.[35] Other ingredients were chosen for different reasons. For example, a prescription containing ostrich shell was used to treat a fractured skull based on the skull's similarity to a shattered eggshell.[36] Granite was also finely ground and sprinkled over both eyes, perhaps in the hope that this would enable the characteristics of granite to penetrate into the person, in particular, strength, durability and beauty.[37]

It is hardly surprising that wound infections were rather common and in the Edwin Smith Papyrus there are some detailed descriptions: 'High fever/inflammation comes forth from it; its two lips are red and its mouth is open ... there is great swelling.'[38] Quite often the cure would be a green pigment, either copper or malachite, which may have held some anti-bacterial properties.

The Egyptians' reputation for wearing eye make-up derives from problems with eye infections caused by flies. It is thought that animal fat was originally smeared under the eye in order to prevent sand particles from entering, and ground malachite or galena could have been added[39] to this in order to make it look more appealing. However, as the medical papyri mention eye make-up and in particular malachite in remedies for eye problems, the mineral and not the fat was the important ingredient. Malachite was also recommended on dressings for wounds and tests have shown that it could prevent the growth of some bacteria and therefore may have been effective.[40]

Other remedies simply stated that black eye paint should be applied to the eye, bandaged and left[41] until the infection improved. General eye irritation or inflammation was also treated with black eye make-up or the ground-up tooth of an ass. Although some eye infections were very serious and led to blindness, the only other treatment was honey, ochre and galena, which was also used in cosmetics or an eye-wash made up of cooling agents mixed with ground celery and hemp.[42] The lead in galena may have helped to kill the bacteria carried by disease-carrying flies.[43]

For sufferers of cataracts the cure was a mixture of 'brain of tortoise with honey', which was applied directly to the eye. While this was being applied a prayer was spoken asking gods to remove the 'darkness' from the eye. Here there is a clear juxtaposition of physical treatment for the visible aspect of the disease and religious treatment for the actual cause of blindness. It was generally believed that blindness was caused by a deity for some misdemeanour against them.

Ingredients for medication were chosen from animal, vegetable and mineral groups, although there are many which Egyptologists have been unable to identify. Even when the plant is known it is difficult to identify the part of the plant used or when they should be gathered. However, from those that we can identify some contained properties still considered useful in modern medicine. For example, the Edwin Smith Papyrus describes applying raw meat to a wound on the first day before it was stitched up with needle and thread; meat has an active enzyme which facilitates healing. This was followed on the second day by an application of oil and honey, the latter of which contains antibacterial and anti-inflammatory properties and would have helped to heal wounds quickly. Other drugs containing antibacterial or antiseptic ingredients included frankincense, cinnamon, willow leaves, acacia or fir oil.

The Egyptian doctors were incredibly skilled at stitching wounds and Case 28 on the Edwin Smith Papyrus describes an extreme wound where this was necessary: 'If you examine a man with a gaping wound of his throat, penetrating his pharynx, and if he drinks water he chokes, it coming forth from the mouth of his wound. It is greatly inflamed and he develops fever because of it. You should then draw together that wound with stitching.'[44] Alternative means of securing a gaping wound was to wrap it tightly, perhaps with an adhesive bandage, to hold the wound edges together.

The diseases suffered by the Egyptians were varied, although as the Egyptian environment was dusty, and exacerbated by regular sandstorms, most people suffered from *sand pneumoconiosis*. This is similar to the disease suffered by coal miners and stone masons, and was prevalent among tomb craftsmen. In the lungs of some mummies quartz silica, iron, titanium, granite and anthracite has been discovered,[45] which could be from a combination of quarry work, tomb work or the general environment. It caused shortness of breath and severe coughs. There was no cure other than inhaling honey, cream, carob and date kernels.

Headaches were as common as they are today and there are twelve remedies recorded, one of which was for a severe case of migraine: 'The skull of a catfish, fried in oil. Anoint the head therewith.'[46] The common cold, however, had a religious incantation instead of a practical medicinal application, as the viral cause was not clear to the ancient doctors. The doctor needed to recite, 'Flow out fetid nose! Flow out son of fetid nose. Flow out, you who break the bones, destroy the skull, and make ill the seven holes of the head.'[47]

There were of course ailments that are simply not identified in the medical papyri, although the symptoms are. The most common was infestation by parasitic worms. All mummies studied by the Manchester Mummy Project have shown evidence of at least one parasitic worm, some as many as three, indicating that most people suffered with this. The most common parasite in both ancient and modern Egypt is bilharzia (*schistosomiasis*), caused by the *schistsoma haematobium* worm, released by the water snail. In modern Egypt 12 per cent of the population suffers from this worm.[48] It penetrates intact skin, entering the veins, resulting in anaemia, loss of appetite, urinary infection and loss of resistance to other diseases. Blood in the urine was the most common symptom and there are two columns of remedies on the Ebers Papyrus for this. As many Egyptians worked in stagnant water in the fields and marshes they came in contact with the water snail and bilharzia easily.

Water supplies situated near latrines[49] or stagnant water were easily infected with numerous other worms. Mummy 1770 in the Manchester Museum shows remains of the Guinea worm, contracted through drinking water infected with a small crustacean containing immature forms of the parasite that developed in the stomach. The male was preserved in the calcium of the mummy's abdomen. The female normally settles in the legs, causing ulcers that allowed eggs to be passed out of the body and back into the water supply.[50] However, it is impossible to see the extent of such ulceration as this mummy's legs had been amputated shortly before her death, although this is not thought to be as a result of this infestation.

The body of the weaver Nakht (twentieth dynasty) also had Bilharzia, in addition to Trichnella and Taenia. Trichnella is contracted by eating undercooked pork containing immature forms of the worm. These develop in the intestine and the female deposits up to 1,500 larvae which can travel into every organ of the body. Taenia is caught through consuming undercooked beef or pork. Nakht may have suffered with fever, muscle pain and weakness.

A difficult disease to diagnose in ancient Egypt was cancer, although the Ebers papyrus may include a description of cancer of the uterus, indicating it was not unknown: 'Another for one in whom there is eating of her uterus and ulcers have appeared in her vulva.'[51] As the disease was not really understood there was no viable cure for it. Angina Pectoris (heart attack), another common modern affliction, also appears to be mentioned in the Ebers Papyrus: 'If you examine a man because of suffering in his stomach and he suffers in his arm, his breast, and the side of his stomach. One says concerning him: It is the *wadj* disease. Then you should say concerning it. Something has entered his mouth. Death is approaching.'[52]

A much easier ailment for the doctors to deal with were broken bones, and mummies show breaks to the forearm and leg which had healed completely, indicating they were set correctly in splints, as explained in the Edwin Smith Papyrus, which mentions 'two splints [covered] in linen'.[53]

A study was carried out in 1908 on 6,000 bodies from Nubia, dated from the Pre-Dynastic Period to the fifth century. It was discovered that while breaks of the arm, tibia, fibula and femur were common, there were no examples of fractured patella and breaks below the knee were rare. It has been suggested that this was due to the environment, as people walked around barefoot and did not have to contend with the hazards of stairs, kerbstones and pavements.[54]

In 1908 Elliot Smith discovered in Naga ed-Deir two sets of splints attached to fifth-dynasty mummies. One was attached to the femur of a girl aged fourteen and the other was attached to the forearm of another individual where both the radius and ulna were fractured. The splints were made of wood padded with linen for the young girl and acacia bark, also wrapped in linen, for the second mummy.[55] In both cases a pad of fibre had been used to staunch the blood flow and still retained blood stains, indicating both breaks were compound fractures.[56] Both individuals died shortly after their accidents as there is no sign of healing. The Egyptian method of splinting a bone was to create a tube out of wood wrapped in linen that was then wrapped around the limb, creating a protective shell. This protected the limb from further damage but did nothing to reset the bone. With the broken arm of the second mummy this was enough to set the bone in the correct position, but in the first mummy the broken femur would not have set straight.

Also in 1908, Wood Jones discovered a number of bodies at the site of Dakka (dated from 4000 BCE to the first century CE) which had suffered from blows with a stick to the forearm and clavicle. Many of the fractures had been so well set that the fractures were barely visible.[57] In the workman village near to the Giza pyramids numerous bodies were found with breaks to the forearm and the leg. Most of the fractures had healed completely and indicate they had also been set correctly in splints. Moreover, two skeletons even show complete amputation of a leg and an arm, which show signs of healing, suggesting successful surgeries.

Two skeletons discovered in 2012 and 2013 at El Amarna were wearing copper-alloy toe rings, which are the only such items discovered in Egypt. One of the mummies was male, aged thirty-five to forty years old and had a broken femur which had healed badly and a fractured foot. The ring was discovered on the second toe of the injured foot and is thought to have been worn for medicinal, healing purposes. Unfortunately, the other skeleton wearing a copper toe ring does not appear to have any injuries, which seems to discredit the argument, although this body has not been studied extensively yet and may still uncover evidence to support the theory.

The Edwin Smith Papyrus describes how fractured or broken noses were set by inserting rolls of linen into the nostril like a splint:

> Clean out for him what is in his two nostrils with two swabs of linen, until every worm of blood which coagulates in the interior of his nostrils, comes forth. Now, afterwards, you put two swabs of linen, moistened with oil, placed in his two nostrils. You then place for him two stiff rolls of linen, bandaged on it. You should

treat him afterwards with oil and honey and lint, every day until he is well.[58]

The tomb of Ipuy (TT217) from Deir el-Medina contains a wall scene showing a number of accidents taking place in the workplace, which includes a man suffering with a dislocated shoulder. The arm is being stretched out and manipulated in order to allow the shoulder to fall back into place.

In addition to trauma to the bones, bites and stings were also easy to treat, but only if they could identify what had bitten them. It was the identification of the snake which caused the doctor the most trouble when dealing with snake bites, but it was the first thing the doctor did as the creature ascertained which treatment was most effective. For snake bites, once the species had been identified, the doctor made a prognosis which included 'One does not die because of it', 'He who is bitten by it will not die', 'Death hastens very quickly' or 'If it bites someone he will die immediately'.[59] The treatments often included 'knife treatment' in order to reduce swelling and then packing the wound with natron, [60] or 'very good remedies to be made for those suffering from all snake bites; onion, ground finely in beer. Eat and spit out for one day'.[61] The most common snake bite was that of the horned viper and it was curable, although 'the fever [due to the wound] lasts for nine days'. However, should the person be bitten by a cobra or 'the *apopi* snake, it is entirely red, while its belly is white. There are four teeth in its mouth. If it bites a man, he dies at once.'[62]

Crocodile bites were no doubt common for those who worked in the Nile, such as fishermen, laundrymen or boatmen. The Ebers Papyrus claims, 'If you examine the bite of a crocodile and you find it with the flesh pulled back, while the two sides are separated, then you should first bandage it with fresh meat, as for every wound.'[63]

E. Tomb of Ipuy (TT71): (1) a dislocated shoulder is repositioned; (2) a hammer is dropped on a workman's toe; (3) a doctor applies cosmetics or ointment to a workman's eye. (Drawing after Nunn, 1996, fig. 3.6)

Scorpion stings were greatly feared as it was easy for barefoot workmen to accidently tread on one and the stings were often deadly. The doctors appealed to the gods for help and the victim of a scorpion sting was given sacred water to drink, which had been poured over a healing statue or Horus Cippi.[64]

It is rather bizarre than in addition to the expected bites from crocodiles, scorpions and snakes, human bites were common enough to justify four paragraphs in the Ebers Papyrus: 'Another [remedy] for the bite of mankind. A measure of dough which is in a jar and a leek. Pound and make into one mass, and bandage with it.'[65]

In the absence of sophisticated medication, and the reliance of magic and religion in the treatment of illnesses, the Egyptians were open to trying what we call alternative therapies in the modern world. These treatments included reflexology, heliotherapy and sleep therapy. In the Tomb of Ankhmahor at Saqqara there is an image which many believe depicts reflexology or physiotherapy. There are two men having their hands and feet massaged by a practitioner[66] in order to relieve aches and pains. Another scene in the tomb of Ankhmahor and a similar one in the tomb of Khentika show a patient having his hands rubbed. The therapists in both tombs comment that their actions will make the limbs 'pleasant'.[67] Macy Roth, however, suggests these scenes are not a form of therapy but a form of grooming, with the therapists performing manicures and pedicures as part of a purification ritual.[68] However, in literary texts reflexology is used in order to relax. In Papyrus Westcar the magician Djedi had 'his servant at his head to smear him and another to rub his legs'.[69]

Depression was described as 'fever in the heart', 'dryness of the heart', 'falling of the heart' and 'kneeling of the mind', and is described in the Kahun Papyrus: 'A woman who loves bed, she does not rise, and does not shake it.'[70]

Temple sleep was thought to be a remedy in which entering the sanatorium and falling into a drug-induced sleep would bring a message from the god giving an indication of how the ailment could be cured. It has also been suggested that patients with more extreme illnesses may have undergone more painful treatments while in this drug-induced sleep.[71]

The records have provided the names and titles of more than 100 doctors,[72] many of whom worked within the royal household.[73] Only seven also held the title of dentist. One such man was Hesyre (third dynasty), who had the title of chief of dentists and physicians.[74] He is the earliest known doctor in the world.[75] His tomb was just north of the Step Pyramid of Djoser, and he was clearly a man of high position in Djoser's royal court, and held numerous titles.

An Egyptian dentist dealt purely with the symptoms of dental problems and did not offer much advice in regard to preventative care. The most common ailment for the Egyptians was extreme attrition brought on by collagen in meats, cellulose and silica structures in plants and sand in the flour either from soft grinding implements or the soil in which the grain was grown.[76] In some instances the enamel was completely destroyed, exposing the sensitive inner pulp. Wear of this nature affected both rich and poor members of society.

Pliny (23–79 CE) suggested sand or powdered brick was intentionally added by the Carthaginians when grinding corn to facilitate the grinding process and the same may have been true of Egypt. Evidence of quartz, greywacke, amphibole and mica grains have been discovered in bread samples[77] and all were possibly added to make grinding easier. However, studies carried out in the early 1990s show that grinding emmer or barley wheat to make bread did not require any sand to be added in order to make flour,[78] and there were possibly enough opportunities for sand and dust to enter the bread and flour at all stages of the process, from growing and harvesting the grain, through to grains chipping off the pestle or millstone.[79]

A common ailment, possibly an indirect symptom of tooth attrition, was a dislocated jaw and marked osteoarthritic changes to the jaw.[80] The Edwin Smith Papyrus describes the remedy for this:

> When you examine a man with a lower jaw that is displaced, and you find his mouth open, so that you cannot close his mouth; then you should put your finger on the end of both jaw bones in the inside of his mouth, and put your thumbs under his chin; then you must let them [the displaced joint bone] fall together in their places ... bandage them with the *imr.w* [unknown] and honey every day until he is better.[81]

The most common consequence of such extreme tooth wear and exposed dental pulp were abscesses. Studies by the Manchester Mummy Project showed that in twenty-nine male bodies there were seventy-two abscesses and in twelve females studied there were forty-five abscesses. This clearly was a widespread problem with many people having more than one. Treatment was limited to pain relief or draining, as the Ebers Papyrus informs us: 'a disease that I treat with a knife treatment ... If anything remains in pocket, it recurs.'[82] 'To expel growth of purulence in the gums; sycamore fruit, beans, honey, malachite and yellow ochre are ground and applied to the tooth.' To drain an abscess, the physician cut it and let the pus drain out.[83] Sometimes the doctors were too late and the abscess had started to destroy the jaw bone as it created a path to eject the pus. Mummy studies have shown teeth have fallen out of abscess cavities, as well as cavities caused by periodontal disease, indicating dentists did not perform extractions, even in extreme circumstances.[84] This is based on the absence of forceps of the type found in the Roman Period, as well as conclusive results from examining the holes left in the jaw bones.[85] It is possible, however, that teeth could have been removed by hand should they become loose, or even the old-fashioned method of tying string around a loose tooth and slamming a door.

The only real evidence of extraction can be seen on a mummified head in the Australian Institute of Archaeology dated to the Graeco-Roman Period.[86] The head belongs to a young boy who died at approximately eight years old. The head was examined in order to try to age it, which showed that a number of teeth were missing that may have been removed in order to practice orthodontics. The missing teeth of particular interest were the upper molars, both the primary and the un-erupted pre-molars. The lack of bone where the tooth should be indicates there was once a tooth there and not that it was a congenital abnormality. Examination of the teeth show, had all the teeth been present, the canines would have protruded forward once grown, but the removal of the pre-molars would have enabled them to grow in a more natural position. If these teeth were removed for orthodontic reasons it indicates the Graeco-Roman dentists were familiar with dental growth patterns, and were confident enough to perform the surgery without adequate anaesthetic. It is, however, highly likely that the young boy died as a result of this surgery, probably as the result of infections. Until more examples of this process are identified, such surgery cannot be suggested as the norm at this time.

In cases of extreme tooth pain, the Ebers Papyrus suggests using bitter apple (colocynth), cumin, turpentine (terebinth), cow's milk, earth almonds and evening dew as pain killers. It has even been suggested that in the New Kingdom opium was imported from Western Asia to be used as a pain killer in tall-necked jars.[87] In some cases these cures may have made the infection worse, although cumin is known to have antiseptic and local anaesthetic properties.[88]

The Egyptians, while having extreme attrition, had very few caries (decay) as their diet was low in sugar. However, a change of diet during the Ptolemaic Period to one high in sugar and carbohydrates saw an increase in dental caries in mummies of this period.[89] During the Pre-Dynastic Period, caries were present in about 3 per cent of the population, rising to 7 per cent by the end of the Ramesside Period and as high as 20 per cent in the Ptolemaic Period.[90] As caries are diet related they affected the upper echelons of society rather than the lower levels.[91]

The Egyptians believed caries were formed by the tunnelling of the *fnt*-worm, or tooth worm, and Papyrus Anastasi IV identifies the problem of untreated caries; 'All the muscles of the face dance, catarrh gets into his eyes, the worm gnaws as his teeth.'[92] There is no evidence that dentists performed fillings and therefore caries continued to grow until they reached the inner pulp of the teeth, allowing bacteria to get into the tooth, resulting in further abscesses.

Another common ailment was periodontal disease (gum disease), which is caused by a severe build-up of plaque; this could result in loss of bone structure, and therefore the support for the teeth.[93] With no real knowledge of the benefits of oral hygiene, other than dealing with bad breath, this affected many people.

Important dentistry evidence can be found in the form of two bridges found near Cairo. One was discovered at El-Quatta in the remains of a crushed skull. The bridge was between a central and lateral incisor and a right canine. The central incisor also had a groove on the labial side to accommodate the wire comfortably within the mouth. Calculus on the canine and associated teeth suggests to some that the bridge had been worn for some time. However, due to the alignment of the roots in the bridge, food would have got trapped under them, causing irritation, indicating the bridge had not been worn. Additionally, the gold wire holding the teeth together may not have been strong enough for day-to-day wear caused by chewing. It is suggested that these teeth were dislodged during the mummification process and the bridge made to hold the teeth in place for the wrapping.

The other bridge was discovered in Giza, and comprised a second and third molar connected with a gold wire. Examination of the teeth have identified that they are not from the same mouth as the wear on the third molar is greater than that on the second, which would have erupted first. As with the El-Quatta example, the gold thread was not strong enough to hold teeth in a working mouth.[94]

The ancient Egyptians cleaned their teeth using toothbrushes made of the frayed end of a twig, as the highly polished appearance of the teeth of mummies suggest. They also used cinnamon breath fresheners and chewed on natron to cleanse the mouth. Cloves were used for pain relief, as were beans ground up with willow. Willow forms the basis of modern aspirin and may therefore have been affective in deadening the pain a little.

What is rather surprising is that although most people suffered with extremely painful dental problems the Deir el-Medina absentee records show the workmen did not take days off due to toothache,[95] although nearly 100 days were taken off for illness.[96] Recent studies have uncovered a mummy from Deir el-Medina who suffered from osteomyelitis, a bone inflammation caused by a blood-borne infection. It was clear that he continued to work regardless of the pain and discomfort. Perhaps their pain threshold was higher than modern individuals', the pain was considered normal and something to be ignored or, it has been suggested, there was a great deal of state pressure to remain at work regardless of health.[97] One record states, 'the boss does not order the sick to lift the stone,' indicating sickness was, however, a legitimate reason for absenteeism.[98]

Through the examination of mummies it is possible to identify how unhealthy an average Egyptian was and how many of the ailments mentioned were suffered by one person. The mummy of Asru, a chantress of Amun in the temple of Amun at Karnak (900 BCE), is a wonderful example. Her mother also held the same title and it is assumed she was of noble birth. She was buried in two highly decorated coffins and her body was extremely thin upon discovery, although she had been mummified to a high standard. Her mummy was examined by the Manchester Mummy Project, who discovered she suffered from four parasitic worms: *ecchinoccus* (dog tapeworm), which had caused a twenty-centimetre cyst on her lung, *strongyloides*, *schistosomiasis* and *chrysomyia* in the brain. These four parasites would have caused Asru numerous symptoms.

The *ecchinoccus* worm, probably contracted through contact with a domestic dog, perhaps a pet, was discovered in the lungs and would have caused breathlessness, pleurisy and possibly live worms in her stools. This breathlessness was exacerbated by Asru's sand pneumoconiosis, a common disease associated with the inhalation of the wind-blown sand of a desert environment. This may have added a nasty cough to her symptoms.

Strongyloides, caught through walking barefoot through infected water, caused bowel problems, with blood in stools, chronic diarrhoea, and anaemia. About a quarter of the remedies in the medical papyri are for stomach problems, although they did not address the causes, just the symptoms; 'Another for the purging of the belly and to drive out suffering from the belly of a man. Fruits/seeds of ricinus (castor-oil plant) chewed and swallowed with beer so that everything which is in the belly comes forth.'[99] It has been suggested that this was a cure for either constipation or diarrhoea, which are both plausible.

The *schistosomiasis* discovered in her bladder was contracted through a water snail in stagnant water and can lead to blood in the urine. Eventually her bladder would start to calcify, causing water retention, swelling, pain, exhaustion and sickness. Blood in the urine was a common problem for Egyptians and the Ebers Papyrus has a remedy 'to make normal again the urine of a man who has excessive blood', which includes a drink of beer with tiger nut, *peret-cheny* fruit and *beheh* plant.[100]

The fourth parasite, *chrysomyia*, was discovered in Asru's brain, where it had caused a cyst that no doubt caused headaches at the very least.

In addition to these four parasites, Asru had osteoarthritis in her fingers and there were numerous telltale changes to her joints. She had calcification in the aorta, the bronchi and the lower legs and feet, and a few years before her death she fractured her lumbar vertebrae and the bone had regrown over this area. Increased calcification of the spine in the lower region connected with this old injury would have sent sciatica-like pain down her left leg due to pressure on the nerve endings of the spine.

Her dental health was no better, as many of her back teeth were missing and she had suffered from painful toothache for most of her later life. There was a serious infection in her jaw, with damage to the bone around the roots of her teeth caused by abscesses rotting through the bone itself. Her remaining teeth were extremely worn with the associated sensitivities.

While it is hard to imagine living with the pain of one of these ailments, it is impossible to imagine the pain and discomfort of all of them at one time. It is impossible to identify what Asru died of, although she was in her fifties or sixties, which at the time was considered elderly. Such a variable array of ailments was not unique to Asru, and really does raise the question of the ancient Egyptian tolerance for pain and perhaps lack of concern at blood in urine and stools. While the Egyptian doctors were well known around the world, a large number of their ingredients would have hindered rather than helped the healing process of many ailments and there were no doubt many deaths caused by infection rather than the initial disease. However, once a terminally ill patient had endured the tinkering of a physician he was at least ensured a long, peaceful and prosperous time in the afterlife.

9.

DEATH AND BURIAL

'Old age is the time of death, enwrapping, and
burial.'[1]

As discussed in the previous chapter, by the age of thirty-five an
ancient Egyptian was considered elderly. Women, on the other
hand, were considered old when they were no longer able to bear
children. Rameses II wrote a letter to Hattusili III, the king of the
Hittites, discussing this very subject;

> Concerning what my brother has written to me regarding his sister
> Matanazi; 'May my brother send to me a man to prepare a medicine
> so that she may bear children.' So has my brother written. And so I
> say to my brother; See Matanazi, the sister of my brother, the king,
> your brother knows her. A fifty year old. Never. She's sixty. Look a
> woman of fifty is old, to say nothing of a sixty year old. One can't
> produce medicine to enable her to bear children.[2]

There were three words in the Egyptian language for old: *iau*
and *teni*, which appear to be similar and may bear the same

distinction as between old and elderly in modern English, and the third word, *kehkeh*, refers to the physicality of old age and may mean something like 'hacking cough'.[3] The afflictions of old age are reflected in the discovery of a number of walking sticks at Deir el-Medina, one of which was inscribed, 'Come my stick, so that I might lean on you and follow the beautiful West, that my heart may wander in the Place of Truth.'[4]

Although the concept of old age occurred earlier than in the modern age, the ideas and stereotypes surrounding the elderly is remarkably similar. The opening paragraph of the 'Instruction of Ptahhotep' (fifth dynasty) describes old age;

> Old age is here, high age has arrived,
> Feebleness came, weakness grows,
> Childlike one sleeps all day.
> Eyes are dim, ears are deaf,
> Strength is waning, one is weary,
> The mouth silenced, speaks not
> The heart, void, recalls not the past
> The bones ache throughout.[5]

While Ptahhotep emphasises only the physicality, the wisdom of old age was also greatly revered. In the Westcar Papyrus the magician Djedi is greeted by the Prince Hardedef in reference to his advanced years: 'Your condition is like that of one who lives above age – for old age is the time of death, enwrapping, and burial – one who sleeps till daytime, free of illness without a hacking cough.'[6]

In a community with no state-run care system it was essential for people to have many children in order for someone to provide for and care for them in old age. In a situation where a couple were childless it was not unusual to adopt an orphan or an older individual who then had the responsibility of taking care of their adoptive parents. It is difficult to identify whether there was an official adoption system, as the same terminology was used for adoption of a child or an apprentice. However, the implications were the same. It was the filial duty to be a 'staff of old age', and without children an elderly man or woman could be rendered helpless within the village. In the 'Instruction of Ptahhotep', a fifth-dynasty vizier asks the king, 'May this servant be ordered to make a staff of old age and let his son step in his place.'[7]

The eldest son or 'staff of old age' supported their father throughout his life, and enabled him to essentially retire; as Amenemhat, a high priest of Amun from the reign of Amenhotep II, explains, 'I was a priest and a "staff of old age" with my father while he was living on earth.'[8] Some children played the role well, and one son, Weskhetnemtet, after taking over his father's role, gave him over half his salary for ten months, and on festival days he offered the use of a maidservant, clothes, honey, meat and oil.[9] Another son, the workman Usekhnemte, sent numerous items to his father, including cakes, meat, fat, honey and clothes. The total given to his father was more than half of his own monthly rations. However, not all children were as accommodating. Papyrus Insinger has a passage which indicates should the parent act foolishly then the children are allowed to abandon them. However, this was not the norm, although some children did not carry out their filial duties to the required standard.

Here we turn to the case of Naunakhte, a woman living in Deir el-Medina in the twentieth dynasty. She was first married to the scribe Kenherkhopshef, who was perhaps forty years her senior when he died and left her a widow. They married when she was perhaps only twelve years old and he was in his fifties. It is also thought that he adopted her as a daughter,[10] in order to enable him to leave all his possessions to her when he died rather than the legal third she would receive as a widow. He died when he was eighty-six years old and Naunakhte was in her late twenties.

Her second marriage was to the workman Kha'emnun,[11]

and they had eight children together:[12] four sons who were all workmen, called Maaynakhtef, Kenherkhopshef, Amennakhte and Neferhotep; and four girls, Wosnakhte, Man'enakhte, Henshene and Kha'nub.[13] There is little surviving evidence of the life of Naunakhte, other than her will, which is of particular interest to us here. This document disinherits four of her children, Neferhotep, Man'enakhte, Hen-shene and Kha'nub,[14] for neglecting her in old age, meaning they would only receive their share of two-thirds of their father's wealth and nothing of her third. 'As for any property of the scribe Kenherkhopshef, my husband, and also his landed property and this storeroom of my father and also this *oipe* of emmer which I collected in company with my husband, they shall not share them.'[15] The other four children had obviously provided for her, perhaps giving monthly rations to her. To ensure this document was legally recognised Naunakhte took it to the *knbt* (see chapter seven), in year 3 of Ramses V (1142 BCE). In front of fourteen members of the workforce at Deir el-Medina sitting as judges, she announced her reason for the will was neglect.

> As for me I am a free woman of the land of Pharaoh. I brought up these eight servants of yours, and gave them an outfit of everything as is usually made for those in their station. But see I am grown old, and see they are not looking after me in my turn. Whoever of them has aided me, to him I will give of my property but he who has not given to me, to him I will not give any of my property.[16]

The document was recorded by the scribe Amennakhte, the same scribe who recorded the Turin Strike Papyrus (discussed in chapter six). Naunakhte gave one of her sons, Kenherkhopshef, 'a special reward, a washing bowl of bronze over and above his fellows, 10 sacks of emmer'. It seems that he was a good son and in his own document he promises to take care of his father in old age: 'If I take away the ration of my father my reward shall be taken away.'[17] Her husband Kha'emnun stated at the *knbt*, 'As for the writings that Naunakhte has made, concerning her property, they shall be carried out exactly as prescribed.'[18] This indicates he thoroughly agreed with her reasons for disinheriting her children and was to respect her final wishes. However, situations like this can result in the children contesting the will, and a year later her husband Kha'emnun was back at the *knbt* with his children;

> As far as the writings are concerned which the citizen Naunakhte has made about her things, they are thus exactly, exactly. The workman Neferhotep will not share in them. He will take an oath with the Lord (life prosperity health) saying: 'If I turn back on my word again, he shall receive a hundred blows and be deprived of his things'.[19]

Another example of a contested will was the case of Tgemy, who was married to the workman Huynefer. In her will she names her son Huy as the recipient of all of her goods, as he was the only child who was able to take care of her burial. When Huy died he left part of this inheritance to his son Hay, but Tgemy's other children came forward to claim their share, hoping the first will was forgotten. Their challenge was even brought to the *knbt*, only to be overthrown by the court officials.

One man, Kyky, had no children and therefore had no one to oversee his funeral and mummification, so he donated all his goods to the temple of Mut while he was alive to ensure they cared for his mortuary cult[20] – an ancient case of leaving the money to the 'cat home' or charity.

This duty to care for the elderly became embroiled in the religion, and in the tomb biographies it often states, 'I have protected the widow who had no husband ... I provided for the old one while I gave him my staff, causing the old woman to say "That is good".'[21] These biographies emphasised the good deeds of the deceased to facilitate their entry into the afterlife. Helping widows was also included in many of the Wisdom Texts, which outlined ideal behavioural conduct. One such text, written on an ostracon in the Petrie Museum, emphasised, 'You should not mock an old man or woman when they are decrepit. Beware lest they take action against you before you get old.'[22] However, this advice did not prevent people making fun of the elderly. The Turin Erotic Papyrus depicts a New Kingdom Theban brothel where the clients are balding and likely to be elderly. At the start of the papyrus the man is enthusiastic but as his adventures continue he becomes exhausted, with one scene showing him lying under the bed with a huge, erect penis while the young woman above tries to entice him into her arms. In the next scene he is carried away by two young girls, his huge penis now flaccid.

In the Tomb Robbery Papyri in the British Museum, a man called Shedsukhons shows frustration with his elderly father, who interfered in the division of spoils: 'O doddering old man, evil be his old age; if you are killed and thrown into the water who will look for you?'[23]

There was no official retirement age and people worked for as long as their health allowed. One image in the tomb of Paheri at El Kab shows an elderly man with a receding hairline and a pot belly working in the fields. He boasts to a younger worker, 'If you bring me thousands of bundles, I will still comb them!' The younger colleague was not impressed and shows little respect to the old man, replying, 'Hurry up and don't chatter so much you baldy yokel!'[24]

In a letter from Deir el Bahri from the reign of Hatshepsut, a working old man is annoyed at an elderly labourer: '... regarding the one whom you have given me. Behold, he is an old man and is causing a little trouble for his [son?].'[25]

While the majority of the elderly were at the mercy of the kindness of their children, or, in a worst-case scenario, strangers, a state pension was provided for the workmen at Deir el-Medina and the military. Records at Deir el-Medina showing the amount of grain distributed on a monthly basis mentions a ration going to a few widows and workmen described as 'old'. It is unknown if these people were providing a service or working on the royal tomb; the provisions were less than the average wage, but adequate enough to live on.

Soldiers of working age received land as part of their salary under the proviso that they would be available for work whenever needed. The yield from this land could be maintained as a form of pension once they were too old to fight. In one of the Miscellanies, the life of an Egyptian man is described;

> Man comes forth from the womb of his mother, and he runs to his
>   master;
> The child is in the service of a soldier, the young man is a fighter,
> The old man is made to be a cultivator, the adult man to be a
>   soldier.[26]

This indicates that it was considered normal for an old man, a veteran soldier in particular, to become a farmer upon retirement, as they continued to work the land they had been given as part of their salary.

The king often gave favoured officials an honorary priestly or administrative title once they were too old to work, allowing a salary but with no responsibilities attached. A Theban official, Nebamun (TT90), for example, was given the position of chief of police by Thutmosis IV: 'Now My Majesty has ordered to appoint him to be police chief on the west of the city of Thebes, in the places Tembu and Obau until he will reach the blessed state [of the dead].'[27] The provision of this role until death indicates it was in title only, and was therefore a pension post. Records indicate that a common sinecure was the role of priest in a chapel. For example, Inushefnu, 'who had been a general', was in charge of a chapel of Ramses III in the temple of Min at Akhmin after retirement.

Another man, Dhutemhab, also a former general, was in charge of a chapel to Wepwawet at Asyut. Perhaps these were quiet jobs suited to a man in retirement.

When the time came, one of the most important things a child (eldest son) could do for his parents was to provide them with a decent burial, as well as 'keep their name alive' through voice offerings and prayers. The Egyptians were worried that should these rituals not be carried out adequately they would not enter the afterlife and were destined for oblivion. This led to a fierce patriotism and it was important to be buried in your own town where a traditional burial was guaranteed. In the tale of Sinuhe he asks, 'What matters more than being buried in the land where I was born?'²⁸ So once you were home in your town, according to the Westcar Papyrus, 'Old age is the time of death, enwrapping, and burial.'²⁹

Mummification and the elaborate burial practices have often led to the belief that the Egyptians were obsessed with death, whereas in fact it demonstrates an obsession with life and its continuation. This rested on the belief that after death the deceased continue to live in the afterlife. The afterlife was a replica of Egypt, with a central river and fields of crops in abundance. The dead were buried with all their possessions as they believed there was a need for such items when they were reborn into this eternal paradise. A wonderful example of the belief in a continuance of life is the rather pragmatic addition to the tomb ensemble of shabti figures, which were essentially servant figures. Should the deceased be called upon to carry out any work in the afterlife the shabti figure would jump in and offer to do the work on their behalf.

An interesting document in the British Museum (P. BM 10800) was a receipt for some shabti figures and provides some insight into their role;

> I have received from you the silver for the 365 shabtis and their
> 36 managers, in total 401, my heart being satisfied. They are male

servants and female servants. I have received from you the case
silver for them, the 401 shabtis … So hurry and work to replace the
Osiris beloved by god, the priest Ihafy. Say 'We will do' at any hour
he will ask you to do the daily service. I have received from him the
silver for you.[30]

It is thought that perhaps shabtis, like an average workman, needed
assurance that they would be paid for the work, and receipts like
this were buried with the deceased in order to reassure the shabtis
that they had been paid in advance and ensure they would not
strike due to lack of rations (see chapter seven).

However, the most important item to take to the afterlife, of
course, was the body, as without one it would be impossible to be
reborn at all. This belief eventually led to one of the processes most
synonymous with ancient Egypt – the process of mummification.

Considering the amount of written evidence available from
ancient Egypt, it is unusual that there are no contemporary
records of how the mummification process was carried out. The
earliest written record comes from Herodotus (fifth century BCE),
although earlier tomb images depict some of the funerary rituals.
However, the mummification process was either considered too
mundane or too well known to record. Therefore we have to
use Herodotus in conjunction with the mummies themselves to
understand the process.

For the past century, the earliest evidence of mummification
was from a fourth-dynasty, royal burial. All that remained was a
mummified arm bearing some bracelets of semi-precious stones.
Unfortunately the nineteenth-century archaeologists were more
interested in the jewellery than the arm and therefore discarded
it, leaving only a picture of this early, artificial body preservation.

However, at the time of writing (2014), Jana Jones, from
Macquarie University, Sydney, had carried out a study on fifty
bodies from the Pre-Dynastic Period at Bolton Museum, UK,

producing some interesting evidence. The bodies were from the sites of Mostagedda and Badari and all had a waxy appearance. Studies demonstrated it was a man-made substance of animal fat or oil, pine resin, plant extracts and natural petroleum, which had been heated in antiquity. As this substance was consistent across all the bodies it strongly suggested that the communities of Mostagedda and Badari were practicing artificial mummification two thousand years earlier than previously thought.

Mummification was believed to have been carried out by priests who held a high status within the community. It is assumed the embalmers worked on the west bank of the Nile in a temporary structure called the Pure Place, Place of Purification or House of Perfection,[31] which may also have acted as a showroom allowing the embalmers to display their work for potential customers, although sadly nothing of such structures has been discovered in the archaeological record.

The only evidence we have of the process itself can be found in the numerous embalming caches that have been excavated. Essentially, all the materials used in the mummification process but not buried in the tomb were buried in their own place, which has enabled us to identify some of the items used. These caches include all of the material used in the embalming process: for example, labelled pots and jars containing coloured powders for colouring the mummy; resins for filling, deodorising and sanitising the mummy; linen for stuffing and wrapping; natron for drying the body; wax for covering the body and blocking orifices; various oils for curing and scenting the body and making it supple; terebinth resin to be used as deodorant and perfume; sawdust and chaff for stuffing cavities; lamps; fragments of the funerary feast; and a broom to sweep away the footprints of the last person to leave the tomb. Some caches also contain the embalming table, which was low, due to most of the process being performed in the squatting position, and often stained with natron and oils.

In addition to providing information about the items used in mummification, the embalming caches can also provide information on the funeral itself. For example, Tutankhamun's embalmer's cache was buried outside KV54 in the Valley of the Kings and comprised twelve jars containing floral collars worn by the mourners at his funeral, a gilded cartonnage mask normally placed over small canopic coffins, broken pottery drinking cups, wine jars and two hand brooms. The remains of the funeral feast were also stored away in a jar, which tells us there were eight people present at the feast and they ate mutton, fowl and game bird.

Generally, anything that touched the body was buried with it, as it was considered to hold an element of that person. This meant any hair separated from the body during the mummification process was wrapped and buried, as well as placenta saved from their own birth, which was often mummified and buried alongside them as their 'twin' or *ka*.

Mummification was generally only for the wealthy as it was an expensive process, although there were three pricing options available. The most expensive was designed to create an 'Osiris' of the deceased. The process started when the body was brought to the embalmers and washed. In the New Kingdom they then removed the brain, as it was believed to be superfluous to requirements. All thought processes and emotions were thought to happen in the heart rather than the brain. To remove it, the ethmoid bone at the top of the nose was broken, and the brain was removed in pieces using a hooked instrument. Experiments have shown this method was inefficient for removing the whole organ. An alternative method necessitated pouring juniper oil and turpentine up the nose, dissolving the brain, which was then poured out through the nostrils.

The mouth was cleansed and packed with resin and a paste also made from resin was applied to the face. Next, a cut was made in the left side of the abdomen using a flint knife, enabling the embalmer to remove all internal organs except the heart. As the heart was considered to be the centre of all thought processes and emotions it was believed to be essential for eternal life. The removed organs were preserved, wrapped and placed in canopic jars. These were a set of four jars, each lid formed into a different shape representative of the four sons of Horus. Each son had a specific role in the protection of the organ within. The stomach was placed in the jar with the jackal head (Duamutef), the intestines in the hawk-headed jar (Qebusenuef), the lungs in the jar with the baboon head (Hapy) and the liver in the human-headed jar (Imsety). These were then placed in the tomb, either in their own room if the tomb was big enough, or close to the coffin in smaller tombs.

The body cavity was cleaned with palm wine and an infusion of pounded spices, which prevented it from smelling. The abdomen was then stuffed with bundles of natron wrapped in linen and left to dry. The body as a whole was also packed in natron. Depending on the size of the body the drying process took between thirty-five and forty days. Once the body had dried out the cavity was filled with a mixture of aromatic substances and linen or sawdust to give it shape. The hole in the side was sewn up and the wound hidden with a bronze or leather cover.

A recent experiment carried out at Sheffield University by Joanne Fletcher suggested that in the eighteenth dynasty, instead of covering the body in natron it was submerged in a salt bath, which infused the soft tissues themselves with the salt solution, preserving them from the inside. This solution was made using deionised water, into which natron was dissolved. The internal organs were removed, although the brain was left intact, as the procedure used was not always efficient for total removal. Then the body was placed in the natron solution. After four weeks soaking in the solution and two weeks drying in a temperature-controlled unit designed to emulate the Egyptian climate, a mummy had been formed. This soaking and drying part of the process took forty-two days.[32] Traditionally the wrapping normally took between thirty and thirty-five days giving a total of seventy days for the whole process, but Fletcher's experiment only allowed twenty-eight days for this part of the procedure.

This period of seventy days was significant to the ancient Egyptians as it was believed that when Osiris died (see chapter three) it was seventy days before he was reborn again into the afterlife. This was based on the observation of the star Sirius, closely associated with Osiris, and the approaching inundation. It disappeared for seventy days before reappearing, announcing the New Year and subsequently Osiris' rebirth into the afterlife.

Wrapping was just as important as the preservation of the body, and a priest wearing an Anubis mask oversaw the process. As each limb was wrapped it was essential to recite the appropriate prayers in order to turn the limb into a divine object. There were numerous layers of bandages, with one second-dynasty mummy having sixteen intact layers remaining of what may have been thirty original layers. In the Middle Kingdom, between each layer of bandages was a sheet to provide extra padding. Anything up to 400 square meters of linen could be used to wrap a mummy. Between all of these layers of bandages the priests laid protective amulets, each in a designated place, with a specific set of prayers and incantations attached to them.

To make the body appear more lifelike, pads of linen were placed to emulate breasts, and in the twenty-first dynasty they went so far as to make slits behind the knees, ankles and heels in order to place folded linen pads under the skin, ensuring the body shape was not lost. As the eyeballs were not removed when the body dried they often sank into the head, so false ones were placed beneath the eyelids. These were made of faience, linen or even onions, in the case of the mummy of Ramses IV.

Other modifications were made to the body in order to make them more lifelike, or, in some instances, to provide them in death with what they were missing in life. For example, the mummy of an elderly priestess Nesitet-nebtaris from the twenty-first dynasty had a fracture at the top of the femur that rendered her almost immobile. It seems she spent the latter part of her life bedridden, resulting in pressure sores on her buttocks and back. The embalmers stitched up the worst of the abscess with flax and covered the stitching with resin. Their final act of kindness was to cover her bed sores by grafting gazelle skin over the raw areas,[33] ensuring injury free skin for the afterlife.

Some modifications to the mummies were made for more practical reasons than for those carried out on Nesitet-nebtaris. The twenty-fifth-dynasty mummy of Padiament, for example, had two poles pushed into his neck in order to hold his head in place. These sticks were held fast by resin poured into the throat and mouth. The neck is also padded with extra thick material to stabilise it. As there is no sign of an injury or decapitation it is assumed that the head, which remains heavy even after desiccation, was too heavy for the neck, resulting in it falling off during the mummification process.[34] This does perhaps suggest that the embalmers were not always as careful with the body as they should have been, which is attested to by the mummy of the unknown man in the British Museum (EA22814), whose CT scan has revealed a wooden embalming tool was left in his head. It appears to be a wooden spatula and was lost when the embalmer was removing the brain. As he had lost his tool he was unable to complete the process, or at least he gave up trying, leaving the remainder of the brain in the head.[35]

With such a large amount of linen needed for each body, many of the bandages were recycled household linen. Some bandages bear the names of different people and it is thought these were donated household linens that had been marked up for the laundrymen. Royalty, however, had custom-made bandages and some of Ramses II's were woven from blue and gold thread. The twenty-second-dynasty mummy of Tjayaetimu, the Temple Singer, has a gap in the back of her cartonnage coffin revealing the outer wrappings were of red, brown and blue stripes. This could be her dress or it could be coloured bandages,[36] either one producing an attractive mummy.

In the later periods funerary texts from the Book of the Dead, the most common being chapters one, two and three, were written on the bandages to aid the deceased in the afterlife. Chapter one specifies, 'This spell is to be recited after going to rest in the West, the Tjenenet-shrine being made content with its lord Osiris when going to and fro to the sacred barque of Re; his body on his bier shall be reckoned up, and shall be enduring in the Netherworld, namely that of N.'[37]

Traditionally, seventy days after death the burial took place, and in the Theban tomb of Djehuty (TT110) it states, 'a goodly burial arrives in peace, your seventy days have been fulfilled in your place of embalming.'[38] However, there were instances when the burial process took more or less time. A statue in Cairo (JE 86125), belonging to Ankhefenamun, states, 'He was placed in the Pure Place under the hands of Anubis ... and he completed seventy two days in the House of Perfection.'[39] The fourth-dynasty queen Meresankh III was buried as many as 272 days after her death. Another inscription, belonging to a Ptolemaic high priest of Memphis, the son of Taimhotep discussed in chapter four, states he was buried 200 days after his death. Conversely, in the absentee records of Deir el-Medina, sometimes there was only a matter of a few days between death and burial.

The reasons for such extended delay are unrecorded, although political instability may have been an important factor. The reason for quicker burials, however, is perhaps clearer. Not all bodies were fully embalmed, even those from Deir el-Medina. Some, like Kha and Merit were preserved by submerging them in a salt solution, meaning their brains and internal organs were not removed. Then the bodies were simply wrapped in linen.[40]

Such quicker options of mummification may have been down to cost, and cheaper processes became available in the Middle Kingdom when mummification for non-royals became popular. It did not involve the removal of the internal organs. Instead a mixture of cedar oil and turpentine was injected into the body through the anus, which was stopped up to prevent the liquid escaping. The body was then packed in natron for forty days. After forty days the dissolved organs were drained out through the anus. Some mummies have blocked rectums where the organs have not dissolved fully.

In 1999 Salima Ikram carried out mummification experiments on rabbits, fish and ducks to investigate which technique was most effective. Two of the rabbits were not eviscerated, and one exploded during the first evening. The second one had its torso pierced, but due to bloating and the head exploding was also discarded. Two rabbits were eviscerated and placed in natron to dry out, and successful mummies were created. The fifth rabbit was not eviscerated and instead 168 ml of turpentine was injected into its anus. On the seventh day the liquid was drained out, taking the partially dissolved organs with it, in the same manner as the ancient human mummies. The heart had not dissolved, although it had become detached and was moving around. However, of the five rabbits this process produced the best mummy with the fluffiest fur.[41]

Once the embalmers had drained the organs out of the body as best they could, the body was then washed and prepared for wrapping. The cheapest option meant the body was returned unwrapped to the family. Evidence suggests that once the mummies were returned to the family they were not always buried straight away and remained in the family home for some time until the family tomb was opened, either annually or bi-annually.

If the tomb scenes are to be believed, funerals were big events with a long procession, comprising servants carrying goods to go into the tomb, the coffin drawn on an ox-drawn sled, professional mourners wailing and throwing dirt over themselves and the family walking serenely at the back. The longer the procession of goods and the louder the mourners, the more impressive the funeral was considered. Mourners modelled themselves on the divine mourners Isis and Nephthys, who in mythology cried over the body of Osiris. Public displays of emotion were not favoured by the scribal elite and their families, so, although they were no doubt upset at the death of a relative, they hired professional mourners if they could afford them (see chapter six). However, there are rare scenes of the family women in stages of grief. In the eighteenth-dynasty tomb of Renni at El Kab, his three daughters are shown in the throes of grief. One daughter cries, 'Where are you going my father?' and his wife cries, 'Where should I go, oh my master for eternity.' His wife even sings a public lament: 'I am your sister Meritre, oh great one, do not leave Meritre ... going away, how can you do it to me? I go alone and look I am behind you. You who loved to speak with me, you are [now] silent and you do not speak.'[42]

On the Papyrus of Ani his wife is depicted kneeling by his coffin exposing her breasts in grief. These images of non-professional mourners are rare in tombs, but that is not to say that there were no mourning rituals to be carried out by the general populous. For the most part the records are quiet about these rituals as well, although Diodorus Siculus (I 91.1-2), writing in 60–30 BCE, states,

> Whenever anyone dies among them, all the family and friends cover their heads with mud and go about town making lamentation, until it is the time for the body to be treated. Furthermore, during this time they allow themselves, neither baths, wine or any expensive foods, not do they wear brightly coloured clothing.[43]

This matches earlier evidence too and indicates such practices of non-adornment and not shaving, which were a long-held tradition in Egypt. In the Ptolemaic Period, after a funeral of a fellow funerary priest, his colleagues would drink for two days in the House of Perfection.[44]

A good funeral was essential in ensuring the deceased entered the afterlife. The non-royal population entered the Field of Reeds, the Egyptian equivalent of heaven for eternity, doing whatever they wanted to do with no restrictions of health or wealth. The king, on the other hand, joined the sun god upon his solar barque and travelled the underworld for twelve hours until he was reborn at dawn. This nocturnal environment was hostile, filled with demons and enemies, whose sole purpose was to destroy the solar barque and prevent the sun (and therefore the king) from being reborn in the morning.

An essential element of the burial was a tomb within which to place the body and the funerary goods. In the New Kingdom it was common to have a rock-cut tomb with the burial chamber deep underground. There was a chapel above this subterranean chamber, where the relatives performed the appropriate rituals. It is the tomb chapels of these elite tombs which are elaborately decorated. These images are multifunctional as not only are they aesthetically pleasing but they also held a ritual significance. A false door was a common decorative element in New Kingdom tombs, enabling the *ka* of the deceased to enter and leave the tomb at will. Often these false doors are surrounded with images of servants or relatives bringing food offerings to sustain the *ka* for eternity.

The fishing and fowling scenes (see chapter two) are also vital for the rebirth of the deceased into the afterlife. The scenes show the tomb owner twice, standing on a papyrus skiff in the marshes surrounded by his wife and children: one side of the scene shows him fowling, whereby he scares the birds out of the marshes and throws a curved stick at them; on the other side of the scene the tomb owner is shown fishing. He has a long spear which has skewered two fish, one of which is the fish reputed to have swallowed the penis of Osiris and is considered a fish of great fertility. It was considered taboo to actually eat one of these in life, but in death it was acceptable to catch them as it emphasised the fertility of the deceased tomb owner. The tomb owner was always depicted as a virile young man in the midst of activity, regardless of his age and health at death. The marshes represent the marshes of creation and therefore the beginning of all life, and as he was accompanied by his children and his wife they ensure the deceased was still able to procreate in the afterlife.

Reaching the afterlife was difficult for everyone and relied on the unification of the six elements of the human psyche; if one of them failed the afterlife was unobtainable. The six elements comprised,

The physical body, which was preserved through the process of mummification.

The name, which was repeated in prayers and offerings after death. One of the conspirators in the Harem Conspiracy of Ramses III had his name changed from Mersure (Re-Loves-Him) to Mesedsure (Re-Hates-Him), meaning his true name would be forgotten and he would have no afterlife.[45]

The shadow, which was a spiritual element indicative of the presence and protection of the sun.

The ba was the personality of the deceased and was represented as a bird with a human face. This element only appears after death and can travel away from the body.

The ka was the life force, memory and physical representations of the deceased[46] and was the element that needed to be nourished with food offerings. This is present throughout the deceased's entire life and death was often described as 'joining your ka'.

The akh (spirit) was formed once the ba and ka had reunited. This spirit was powerful and was almost divine in nature.

The unification of these six elements was facilitated by the Opening of the Mouth ceremony, during which the oldest son of the deceased held an adze to the mouth of the mummy, enabling them to speak, hear and smell. This was accompanied by a recitation of chapter twenty-three of the Book of the Dead;

> My mouth is opened by Ptah and what was on my mouth has been loosened by my local god. Thoth comes indeed, filled and equipped with magic, and the bonds of Seth which restricted my mouth have been loosened. Atum has warded them off and cast away the restrictions of Seth ... My mouth is open, my mouth is split open by Shu with that iron harpoon of his with which he split open the mouths of the gods. I am Sekhmet, and I sit beside Her who is in the great wind of the sky; I am Orion the Great who dwells with the Souls of Heliopolis ... As for any magic spell or any words which may be uttered against me, the gods will rise up against it, even the entire Ennead.[47]

There were a number of birthing rituals which were repeated at a funeral in order to aid rebirth, as the two were considered to be intrinsically linked. For example, two instruments used in the funerary rituals were the *peshef kaf* and *ntjrwy* blades, which represent the little finger used by the midwife to clear the mouth of the baby. In the Opening of the Mouth ceremony two jars were included, one full and one empty, called the Breasts of Horus and Isis, in addition to hard and soft food perhaps reflecting breastfeeding and weaning.[48]

On the interior of some Middle Kingdom coffins, images of the pots and jars used in this Opening of the Mouth ritual were depicted in case it was not completed correctly. The *ka* could now enjoy the food and drink offerings and the deceased could hear, see and participate in temple rituals and enjoy everything they did in life. This naturally involved sex and a Middle Kingdom Coffin Text states, 'Concerning every man who knows the formula, he will be able to copulate on this earth at night and by day, and the hearts of women will come to him at any time he desires.'[49] Women, however, were not guaranteed numerous sexual partners in the afterlife and on female coffins the name of her husband was added so he could aid her with rebirth by begetting her and he could also help her form a healthy union in the afterlife with his spiritual self.[50]

After the Opening of the Mouth ceremony had been carried out and the body had spiritually been reanimated, the deceased was now ready to endure the final test before entering the afterlife. This was the Weighing of the Heart ceremony in the Hall of Judgement, where the deceased stood before Osiris, the god of the underworld, to witness his heart being weighed against Maat, the feather of truth. If the heart was heavier it was devoured by the monster Ammit, waiting nearby. Rather than leaving this to chance the deceased recited the Negative Confession, chapter 125 of the Book of the Dead, telling the gods of the underworld the things he/she had not done;

> I have done no falsehood
> I have not robbed
> I have not been rapacious
> I have not stolen
> I have not killed men
> I have not destroyed food supplies[51]

If anything was missed from this list the Egyptians placed an amulet called a heart scarab over the heart, with chapter 30b from the Book of the Dead encouraging the scarab not to betray the sins still present in the heart.

> Do not stand up as a witness against me, do not be opposed to me in
> the tribunal, do not be hostile to me in the presence of the Keeper of

the Balance, for you are my ka which was in my body, the protector who made my members hale. Go forth to the happy place whereto we speed; do not make any name stink to the Entourage who made men.[52]

If the heart weighed the same as the feather of truth, the deceased was reborn and could enter the Field of Reeds for eternity. However, it was essential that offerings of food and drink were continually made and the deceased's name was repeated. If family members were unable to carry out the rituals, or were not wealthy enough to pay for a funerary priest to carry out the rituals on their behalf, the deceased needed to rely on the kindness of passing strangers.[53] Many tombs, therefore, have an inscription encouraging passers-by to recite the inhabitant's name, enabling them to live for eternity; 'Oh, you who live and exist, who like life and hate death, whosoever shall pass by this tomb, as you love life and hate death so you offer to me what is in your hands'.[54] (Middle Kingdom stela from Abydos.)

Sometimes this tradition was combined with a request from the living relative to the deceased to help with some personal problem. As discussed in chapter three, the deceased were thought to transform into an *Akh ikr n re*, or Excellent Spirit of Ra, which gave them powers over the living and the dead. Therefore family members wrote letters to the dead, often on a bowl, which was then filled with food as an offering. Only twenty of these letters have survived into the archaeological record, but they provide tantalising insights into the thought and grief processes of an ancient Egyptian. One letter outlines all the things the man will do for his deceased wife if she cures him of an illness which he has contracted since her death: 'I shall lay down offerings for you when the sun's light has risen and I shall establish an altar for you.'[55]

Another letter (nineteenth dynasty), written on papyrus rather than a bowl, was attached to a painted wooden statue of the addressee, his late wife Ankhiry. The letter itself was written in a rushed manner, indicative of the stress the man was under.

To the able spirit Ankhiry. What evil have I done to you that I should land in this wretched state in which I am? What have I done to you? What you have done is to lay your hands on me, although I have done you no wrong. What have I done to you since I lived with you as your husband, until that day [of your death], that I must hide it? What is there now? What you have attained is that I must bring forward this accusation against you. What have I done to you? I will lodge a complaint against you with the Ennead in the West [the divine law-court in the hereafter], and one shall judge between you and me on account of this letter ... What have I done to you? I made you my wife when I was a young man. I was with you when I held all kinds of offices. I stayed with you, I did not send you away ... 'She has always been with me' I thought ... And see, now you do not even comfort me. I will be judged with you, and one shall discern truth from falsehood.

Look, when I was training the officers of the army of Pharaoh and his chariotry, I let them lie on their bellies before you. I never hid anything from you in all your life. I never let you suffer, but I always behaved to you as a gentleman. You never found that I was rude to you, as when a peasant enters someone else's house. I never behaved so that a man could rebuke me for anything I did to you ...

I am sending this letter to let you know what you are doing. When you began to suffer from the disease you had, I let a head physician come and he treated you and did everything you asked him to do. When I followed Pharaoh, travelling to the south and this condition came to you [that is, you died] I spent no less than eight months without eating and drinking as a man should do. And as soon as I reached Memphis, I asked from Pharaoh leave and went to the place that you were, and I cried intensely, together with my people, before the eyes of my entire neighbourhood. I donated fine linen for wrapping you up, I let many clothes be made, and omitted nothing good to be done for you. And see, I passed three years until now living alone, without entering any house [i.e. remarrying], although it is not fair that someone like me should be made to do so. But I did it for you, you who does not discern good from bad. One shall judge between you and me. And then: the sisters in the house, I have not entered anyone of them.

The last line seems to have been written as an afterthought as it does not flow with the rest of the letter,[56] and yet it could be his guilt at his activities with these sisters that instigated the letter in the first place.

Another important ritual that needed to be repeated to maintain the *ka* was the pouring of libations, in particular water, in order to keep the deceased nourished in the afterlife as well as purifying them. The 'Instructions of Ani' emphasise the importance of this: 'Libate for your father and mother who are resting in the desert valley. When the god's witness your actions, they will say "accepted".'[57] This was something expected of children for their parents and in the absentee record from Deir el-Medina some workmen took up to three days off to libate for their father, brother or son, although never a female relative. Whether this ritual was performed in the home or at the tomb is unknown, although there is evidence that it was performed soon after the death.

All of these expectations of food and libations were part of the elaborate cult of the *ka*, which was the means by which the *ka* was kept alive for eternity and therefore the deceased was able to be reborn successfully into the afterlife. If the cult of the *ka* was not maintained then the deceased died a second and more permanent death.

Despite all these elaborate rituals and processes associated with the afterlife, the ancient Egyptians, like many modern people, did not truly understand what happened after death. They feared rather than welcomed death and in the 'Dialogue of a Man with his Ba' death is described: 'If you think of burial, it is agony, it is the bringing of tears through making a man miserable, it is taking a man from his house, being cast upon the high ground. You shall not come up again to see suns.'[58]

Such uncertain ideas are further expressed in the harpist's songs, which were presented in numerous tombs. An example from the chapel of King Intef tells the living to make merry while alive as it is not possible to take your possessions with you.

> What of their places? Their walls have crumbled and their places are gone as though they had never been. None comes from there, to tell of their state, to tell of their needs to calm our hearts until we go where they have gone.
> Make holiday, do not weary of it!
> Lo, none is allowed to take his gods with him.
> Lo, none who departs comes back again![59]

As the last line states, 'none who departs comes back again', and therefore the best that the Egyptians could hope for was that their names would not be forgotten, for to repeat their name was to make them live again. Perhaps the previous chapters have gone some way to ensure this happens.

NOTES

1. Living with the Ancient Egyptians

1. Houlihan, P., 1996: *The Animal World of the Pharaohs*. London. Thames and Hudson. p. 83.
2. Černy, J., 1973: *A Community of Workmen at Thebes in the Ramesside Period*. Cairo. Bibliotheque D'Etude. p. 325.
3. Graves-Brown, C., 2010: *Dancing for Hathor; Women in Ancient Egypt*. London. Continuum. p. 8.
4. Ibid., p. 51.
5. McDowell, A. G., 1999: *Village Life in Ancient Egypt: Laundry Lists and Love Songs*. Oxford. Oxford University Press. p. 61.
6. Snape, S., 2014: *The Complete Cities of Ancient Egypt*. London. Thames and Hudson. p. 6.
7. Quirke, S., 2005: *Lahun: a Town in Egypt 1800 BC, and the History and its Landscape*. London. Golden House Publications. p. 48.
8. Quirke, 2005, p. 47.
9. Snape, 2014, p. 67.
10. Ibid., p. 64.
11. David, R., 1986: *The Pyramid Builders of Ancient Egypt*. London. Guild Publishing. p. 201.
12. Romer J., 1984: *Ancient Lives: Daily Life in Egypt of the Pharaohs*. New York. Henry Holt and Company. p. 60.
13. Ibid., p. 6.

14. Meskell, L., 2002: *Private Life in New Kingdom Egypt*. Oxford. Princeton University Press. p. 40.

15. Peet, T. E., 1930: *The Great Tomb-Robberies of the Twentieth Egyptian Dynasty: being a critical study, with translations and commentaries, of the papyri in which these are recorded*. Oxford. Clarendon Press. p. 14.

16. Meskell, 2002, p. 53.

17. Ibid., p. 76.

18. Davies, B., 2011: 'Misdemeanours at Deir el-Medina' in *Ancient Egypt Magazine Vol. 11 No. 4 Issue 64*. p. 30.

19. Romer, 1984, p. 16.

20. Paulin-Grothe. E. and T. Schneider, 2001: 'New Workmen's Huts in the Valley of the Kings' in *Egyptian Archaeology No. 19*. p. 4.

21. Romer, 1984, p. 17.

22. Paulin-Grothe and Schneider, 2001, p.5.

23. Booth, C., R. Janssen and J. Janssen, 2009: 'The Market on the Riverbank' in *Ancient Egypt Magazine Vol. 9 No. 5 Issue 53*. pp. 50–1.

24. Snape, 2014, p. 83.

25. Boundary stela. Snape, 2014, p. 156.

26. Reeves, N., 2005: *Egypt's False Pharaoh*. London. Thames and Hudson. p. 120.

27. Meskell, 2002, p. 44.

28. Snape, 2014, p. 87.

29. Petrie, F. W. M., 1889: *Illahun, Kahun and Gurob. Meidum*. Warminster. Aris and Phillips. p. 8.

30. Szpakowska, K., 2008: *Daily Life in Ancient Egypt*. Oxford. Blackwell Publishing. p. 19.

31. Meskell, 2002, p. 30.

32. Ibid., p. 31.

33. Ibid., p. 40.

34. Snape, 2014, p. 80.

35. Meskell, 2002, p. 41.

36. Szpakowska, 2008, p. 26.

37. Graves-Brown, 2010, pp. 119–20.

38. Meskell, 2002, p. 74.

39. Meskell, 2001, p. 119.

40. Snape, 2014, p. 80.

41. Toivari-Viitala, J., 2001: *Women at Deir el-Medina: A study of the Status and Roles of the Female Inhabitants in the Workmen's Community During the Ramesside Period*. Leiden. Nederlands Instituut voor het Nabije Oosten. p. 190.

42. Hobson, M., 2005: 'Dogs in Ancient Egypt' in *Ancient Egypt Magazine Vol. 5 No. 5*. p. 36.

43. Szpakowska, 2008, p. 60.

44. Houlihan, 1996, p. 77.

45. Ibid., p. 78.

46. Janssen, R. and J. Janssen, 1989: *Egyptian Household Animals*. Princes Risborough. Shire Egyptology. p. 11.

47. Houlihan, 1996, p. 81.

48. Van Neer, M., et al. 2014: 'More Evidence for Cat Taming at the Predynastic Elite Cemetery of Hierakonpolis (Upper Egypt)' in *Journal of Archaeological Science Vol. 45*. pp. 103–11.

49. Houlihan, 1996, p. 83.

50. Meskell, 2002, p. 121.

51. Romer, 1984, p. 68.

52. Ibid., p. 70.

53. Tyldesley, J., 1994: *The Daughters of Isis*. London. Viking. p. 148.

54. Wente, E. F. and E. S. Meltzer, 1990: *Letters from Ancient Egypt*. Atlanta. Scholars Press. p. 138.

55. Green, L., 2002–3: 'Feasting with Tutankhamun; Fine dining in the Late-18th Dynasty' in *KMT Vol. 13 No. 4*. p. 63.

56. Samuel, D., 2000: 'Brewing and Baking' in Nicholson, P. and I. Shaw (eds.), *Ancient Egyptian Material and Technology*. Cambridge. Cambridge University Press. p. 565.

57. Murray, M. A., 2000: 'Cereal Production and Processing' in Nicholson, P. and I. Shaw (eds), *Ancient Egyptian Material and Technology*. Cambridge. Cambridge University Press. pp. 505–36.

58. Romer, 1984, p. 61.

59. Guasch Jané, M. R., 2006: 'Ancient Egyptian Wine' in *Ancient Egypt Magazine Vol. 6 No. 6*. p. 21.

60. Bierbrier, M., 1982: *The Tomb Builders of the Pharaohs*. New York. Charles Scribners Sons. p. 29.

61. Ibid., p. 110.

62. Lichtheim, M., 1976: *Ancient Egyptian Literature: Volume II*. Berkeley. University of California Press. p. 137.

63. Graves-Brown, 2010, p. 168.

64. Meskell, 2002, p. 24.

65. Szpakowska, 2008, p. 97.

66. Touzeau, A., et al., 2014: 'Diet of Ancient Egyptians Inferred from Stable Isotope Systematics' in *Journal of Archaeological Science vol. 46*. pp. 114–24.

67. Green, 2002–3, p. 65.

2. Passing the Time

1. Graves-Brown, 2010, p. 168.

2. Green, 2002–3, p. 67.

3. Watterson, B., 1991: *Women in Ancient Egypt*. Gloucestershire. Sutton Publishing. p. 136.

4. Graves-Brown, 2010, p. 168.

5. Szpakowska, 2008, p. 92.

6. Manniche, L., 1991: *Music and Musicians in Ancient Egypt*. London. British Museum Press. p. 15.

7. Ibid., p. 17.

8. Ibid., pp. 17–18.

9. Ibid., 1991, p. 20.

10. Decker, 1992, p. 164.

11. Ibid., p. 166.

12. Ibid., p. 150.

13. (Cairo JE 87742). Decker, W., 1992: *Sports and Games of Ancient Egypt*. London. Yale University Press, p. 92.

14. Graves-Brown, 2010, p. 111.

15. Decker, 1992, p. 91.

16. Ibid., 1987, p. 95.
17. Ibid., pp. 101–2.
18. Booth, C., 2007: 'The Temple of Khonsu at Karnak' in *Ancient Egypt Magazine Vol. 7 Issue 5*. p. 27.
19. Decker, 1992, p. 131.
20. Ibid., p. 135.
21. Szpakowska, 2008, p. 114.
22. Decker, 1992, p. 128.
23. Ibid., p. 124.
24. Polz, D. 1997: 'The Egyptian Painter's Utensils from Dra'Abu el-Naga' in *Egyptian Archaeology No. 10*. pp. 34–5.
25. Houlihan, P., 2001: *Wit and Humour in Ancient Egypt*. London. Rubicon Press. p. 112.
26. Ibid., p. 115.
27. Ibid., p. 66.
28. Janssen, J., 1975: *Commodity Prices from the Ramessid Period: an Economic Study of the Village of Necropolis Workmen at Thebes*. Leiden. Brill. p. 250.
29. Ibid., p. 249.
30. Ibid., p. 250.
31. Vogelsang-Eastwood, G. M., 1999: *Tutankhamun's Wardrobe: Garments from the Tomb of Tutankhamun*. Rotterdam. Barjesteh van Waalwijk van Doorn & Co. p. 22.
32. Ibid., p. 24.
33. Janssen, 1975, p. 260–1.
34. Ibid., p. 251.
35. Vogelsang-Eastwood, 1999, p. 15.
36. Janssen, 1975, p. 250.
37. Vogelsang-Eastwood, 1999, p. 52.
38. Janssen, 1975, pp. 250–1.
39. Vogelsang-Eastwood, 1999, p. 36.
40. Janssen, 1975, pp. 283–4.
41. Veldmeijer, A. and E. Endenburg, 2008: 'Footwear from Qasr Ibrim' in *Egyptian Archaeology No. 33*. p. 20.
42. McDowell, 1999, p. 41.

43. McDowell, 1999, p. 96.
44. Romer, 1984, p. 102.
45. Lichtheim, 1976, p. 182.
46. Tyldesley, 1994, p. 161.
47. Cilli, D., 2006: 'Hathor in Front on Ra; a New Reading' in *Proceedings of the Second International Conference for Young Egyptologists*. Lisbon. Centro de Historia (Faculdade de Letras da Unniversidade de Lisboa). p. 175.
48. Janssen, R., 1996: 'An Ancient Egyptian Erotic Fashion: Fishnet Dresses' in *KMT vol. 6 No. 4*. p. 41.
49. Gardiner-Wilkinson, J., 1854: *The Ancient Egyptians*. London. John Murray. p. 350.
50. Sélincourt, A. (Translator), 1972: *Herodotus*. London. Penguin. p. 158.
51. Booth, C., 2002: *Multi-Cultural or Xenophobic Society: The Study of the Egyptian Attitude to Foreigners through Non-Stereotypical Art*. Oxford. British Archaeological Reports. p. 28.
52. Halioua, B. and B. Ziskind, 2005: *Medicine in the Days of the Pharaohs*. London. Harvard University Press. p. 164.
53. Dayagi-Mendels, M., 1989: *Perfumes and Cosmetics in the Ancient World*. Jerusalem. p. 15.
54. Montserrat, D., 1996: *Sex and Society in Graeco-Roman Egypt*. London. Kegan Paul. p. 70.
55. Sélincourt, 1972, p. 143.
56. Lichtheim, M., 1975: *Ancient Egyptian Literature Vol. I*. Berkeley. University of California Press. p. 233.
57. Dayagi-Mendels, 1989, p. 66.
58. Manniche, L., 1989: *An Ancient Egyptian Herbal*. London. British Museum Press. p. 46.
59. Dayigi-Mendels, 1989, p. 14.
60. Ibid., p. 29.
61. Manniche, L., 1999: *Sacred Luxuries: Fragrance, Aromatherapy and Cosmetics in Ancient Egypt*. London. Opus Publishers Ltd. p. 134.
62. Dayagi-Mendels, 1989, p. 97.

63. Manniche, 1999, p. 63.

64. Tyldesley, 1994, p. 152.

65. Dayagi-Mendels, 1989, p. 36.

66. Lichtheim, 1976, p. 183.

67. Dayagi-Mendels, 1989, p. 44.

68. Humber, C., 2008: 'Ancient Egyptian Eye Paint' in *Ancient Egypt Magazine Vol. 8 No. 6 issue 48.* p. 41.

69. Tyldesley, 1989, p. 159.

70. Stetter, C. 1993: *The Secret Medicine of the Pharaohs: Ancient Egyptian Healing.* Chicago. Edition Q. p. 41.

71. Taylor, J. and D. Antoine, 2014: *Ancient Lives: New Discoveries.* London. British Museum Press. p. 131.

72. Tyldesley, 1994, p. 155.

73. Dayagi-Mendels, 1989, p. 60.

74. Ibid., p. 66.

75. Tyldesley, 1994, p. 156.

76. Nunn, J., 1996: *Ancient Egyptian Medicine.* London. British Museum Press. p. 150.

77. Ibid., p. 149.

78. Ibid.

79. Manniche, 1999, pp. 129–31.

80. Tyldesley, 1994, p. 158.

81. Lichtheim, 1975, p. 186.

82. Ibid., p. 205.

83. Manniche, 1999, p. 129.

84. Lichtheim, 1976, p. 191.

85. Tyldesley, 1994, p. 154.

86. Collier, M. and S. Quirke, 2004: *The UCL Lahun Papyri: Religious, Literary, Legal, Mathematical and Medical.* Oxford. Archaeopress. p. 180.

87. Dayagi-Mendels, 1989, p. 97.

88. Montserrat, 1996, p. 73.

89. Padgham, J., 2014: 'The Cone on the Head and the Ba on Earth' in *Ancient Egypt Magazine, Vol. 14, No. 4.* p. 49.

90. Ibid., p. 53.

91. Tyldesley, 1994, p. 151.
92. Manniche, 1989, p. 44.

3. Household Religion

1. Mertz, B., 1966: Red Land, Black Land. Daily Life in Ancient Egypt. London. Harper Collins. p. 292.
2. Faulkner, R. O., 1998: *The Ancient Egyptian Pyramid Texts*. Oxford. Clarendon Press. p. 198.
3. Ibid., p. 246.
4. Ibid., p. 50.
5. Meyer, M. W., 1999. *The Ancient Mysteries: A Sourcebook of Sacred Texts*. Philadelphia. University of Pennsylvania Press. p. 162.
6. Mojsov, B. 2005: *Osiris: Death and Afterlife of a God*. Oxford. Blackwell. p. 37.
7. Ray, J., 2001: *Reflections of Osiris: Lives from Ancient Egypt*. London. Profile Books. p. 139.
8. Ibid., p. 140.
9. Quirke, S., 1992: *Ancient Egyptian Religion*. London. British Museum Press. p. 57.
10. Moran, W. L., 1992: *The Amarna Letters*. Baltimore. The Johns Hopkins University Press. p. 39.
11. Meskell, 2002, p. 116.
12. Robins, G., 1994–5: 'Women and Children in Peril' in *KMT Vol. 5 No. 4*. p. 31.
13. Kemp, B., 2009: 'A wall painting of Bes Figures from Amarna' in *Egyptian Archaeology No. 34*. p. 19.
14. Meskell, 2002, p. 170.
15. Robins, G., 1993: *Women in Ancient Egypt*. London. British Museum Press. p. 162–3.
16. Harer, B., 2013: 'Obstetrics in Ancient Egypt' in *KMT Vol. 24 No. 2*. p.49
17. Lurker, M., 1974: *The Gods and Symbols of Ancient Egypt*. London. Thames and Hudson. p. 32–3.
18. Robins, 1994–5, p. 29.

19. Shaw, I. and P. Nicholson, 1997: *The British Museum Dictionary of Ancient Egypt*. London. British Museum Press. pp. 53–4.

20. Kemp, B., 2005: *Ancient Egypt: Anatomy of a Civilisation*. London. Routledge. p. 382.

21. Janssen, R. and J. Janssen, 1990: *Growing Up in Ancient Egypt*. London. Rubicon Press. p. 6.

22. Robins, 1994–5, p. 29.

23. David, R., 2002: *Religion and Magic in Ancient Egypt*. London. Penguin. p. 279.

24. David, R., 2014: *Voices of Ancient Egypt: Contemporary Accounts of Daily Life*. Westport. Greenwood Press. p. 94.

25. Pinch, G., 1993: *Votive Offerings to Hathor*. Oxford. Griffith Institute. p. 251.

26. Teeter, E., 2011: *Religion and Ritual in Ancient Egypt*. Cambridge. Cambridge University Press. p. 79.

27. Pinch, 1993, p. 252.

28. Silverman, D. P. (ed.), 1997: *Ancient Egypt*. London. Duncan Baird Publishers. p. 162.

29. Lurker, 1974, p. 80.

30. Quirke, 1992, p. 116.

31. Mertz, 1966, p. 292.

32. Meskell, 2002, p. 81.

33. Faulkner, R.O., 1972: *The Ancient Egyptian Book of the Dead*. London. British Museum Press. p. 137.

34. Meskell, 2002, p. 62.

35. Ibid., pp. 64–5.

36. Adapted from Bierbrier, 1982, p. 32.

37. Graves-Brown, 2010, p. 168.

38. Bryan, B., 2006: 'The Temple of Mut: New Evidence on Hatshepsut's Building Activity' in Roehrigh, C. H., et al. (eds), *Hatshepsut: From Queen to Pharaoh*. New York. Yale University Press. p. 183.

39. Lesko, B., 1999: *The Great Goddesses of Egypt*. Norman. University of Oklahoma Press. p. 115.

40. Janssen, R. and J. Janssen, 1996: *Getting Old in Ancient Egypt*. London. Rubicon Press. p. 52.

41. Meskell, 2002, p. 203.
42. Ibid., p. 55.
43. Ibid., p. 121.
44. Demarée, R. J., 1983: *The 3h ikr n Ra Stelae: On Ancestor Worship in Ancient Egypt.* Leiden. Nederlands Instituut Voor Het Nabije Oosten. p. 282.
45. Janssen and Janssen, 1996, p. 53.
46. David, 2002, p. 275.
47. Meskell, 2002, p. 111.
48. Ibid., p. 171.
49. Ibid., p. 172.
50. Qau tomb 7695.
51. Gardiner, A. and K. Sethe, 1928: *Egyptian Letters to the Dead: Mainly from the Old and Middle Kingdoms.* London. Egypt Exploration Society. pp. 3–5, 17–19.
52. Redford, S., 2008: *The Harem Conspiracy: The Murder of Ramesses III.* Illinois. Northern Illinois University Press. p. 18.
53. Quirke, 1992, pp. 125–6.

4. Love, Sex and Marriage

1. Manniche, L., 1997: *Sexual Life in Ancient Egypt.* London. Kegan Paul Press. pp. 98–9.
2. Ibid., p. 74.
3. Green, L., 2001: 'The Hand of God' Sacred and Profane Sex in Ancient Egypt' in *KMT Vol. 12 No. 4.* p. 56.
4. Manniche, 1997, p. 100.
5. Green, 2001, p. 57.
6. Manniche, 1997, p. 104.
7. Monserrat, 1996, p. 113.
8. Ibid., pp. 113–14.
9. Manniche, 1997, p. 104.
10. Ibid., p. 104.
11. Montserrat, 1996, p. 82.
12. Manniche, 1997, pp. 98–9.

13. Montserrat, 1996, p. 121.
14. Halioua and Ziskind, 2005, p. 175.
15. Manniche, 1987, p. 15.
16. Toivari-Viitala, 2001, p. 151.
17. Graves-Brown, 2010, p. 44.
18. Manniche, 1997, p. 18.
19. Meskell, 2002, p. 102.
20. Romer, 1984, p. 98.
21. Ibid., p. 98.
22. Szpakowska, 2008, note 94, p. 43.
23. Toivari-Viitala, 2001, p. 52.
24. Meskell, 2002, p. 95.
25. Manniche, 1997, p. 28.
26. Toivari-Viitala, 2001, p. 57.
27. Meskell, 2002, p. 98.
28. Toivari-Viitala, 2001, p. 53.
29. Ibid., p. 54.
30. Lichtheim, 1976, p. 143.
31. Meskell, 2002, p. 95.
32. 'Papyrus Harris 500' in Simpson, W. K., 2003: *The Literature of Ancient Egypt: An Anthology of Stories, Instructions, Stelae, Autobiographies, and Poetry: An Anthology of Stories, Instructions and Poetry*. London. Yale University Press. p. 314.
33. Lichtheim, 1976, p. 183.
34. Ibid., p. 184.
35. Toivari-Viitala, 2001, p. 61.
36. Graves-Brown, 2010, p. 132.
37. Ibid., p. 35.
38. Manniche, 1997, pp. 98–9.
39. Lichtheim, 1976, p. 141.
40. Graves-Brown, 2010, p. 59.
41. Meskell, 2002, p. 95.
42. Toivari-Viitala, 2001, p. 19.
43. Ibid., p. 56.
44. Lichtheim, 1980, p. 128.

45. Toivari-Viitala, 2001, p. 65.

46. McDowell, 1999, p. 46.

47. Meskell, 2002, p. 97.

48. Donker Van Heel, K., 2014: *Mrs. Tsenhor a Female Entrepreneur in Ancient Egypt.* Cairo. American University in Cairo Press. p. 65.

49. Toivari-Viitala, 2001, p. 90.

50. Meskell, 2002, p. 101.

51. McDowell, 1999, p. 42.

52. Meskell, 2002, p. 99.

53. Ibid., p. 101.

54. Montserrat, 1996, p. 97.

55. Toivari-Viitala, 2001, p. 61.

56. Donker van Heel, K., 2013: *Djekhy and Son: Doing Business in Ancient Egypt.* Cairo. American University in Cairo Press. p. 47.

57. Montserrat, 1996, p. 100.

58. The oath of P. Turin 1880.

59. Toivari-Viitala, 2001, p. 238.

60. Ibid., p. 87.

61. McDowell, 1999, p. 43.

62. Manniche, 1997, p. 60.

63. Romer, 1984, p. 84.

64. Lichtheim, 1976, pp. 203–11.

65. Meskell, 2002, p. 100.

66. Janssen and Janssen, 1996, p. 91.

67. Parkinson, R., 1995: 'Homosexual Desire and Middle Kingdom Literature' in *Journal of Egyptian Archaeology Vol. 81.* p. 61.

68. Graves-Brown, 2010, p. 103.

69. Allen T.G., 1974: *The Book of the Dead: or, Going Forth by Day: ideas of the ancient Egyptians concerning the hereafter as expressed in their own terms.* Chicago. Oriental Institute of the University of Chicago. p. 98.

70. Toivari-Viitala, 2001, p. 160.

71. Parkinson, 1995, p. 59.

72. Ibid., p. 68.

73. Montserrat, 1996, p. 141.

74. Parkinson, 1995, p. 71.
75. Parkinson, R., 1991: *Voices From Ancient Egypt.* London. British Museum Press. pp. 54–6.
76. Montserrat, 1996, p. 143.
77. Lichtheim, 1976, p. 183.
78. Graves-Brown, 2010, p. 103.
79. Reeder, G., 2008: 'Queer Egyptologies of Niankhkhumn and Khnumhotep' in Graves-Brown, C. (Ed.), *Sex and Gender in Ancient Egypt: Don your Wig for a Joyful Hour.* Swansea. Classical Press of Wales Publications. p. 147.
80. Cherpion, quoted in Reeder, 2008, p. 145.
81. Parkinson, 1995, p. 62.
82. Manniche, 1997, p. 22.
83. Montserrat, 1996, p. 140.
84. Taylor and Antoine, 2014, p. 168.
85. Ostracon Berlin P. Love, Sex10627, twentieth dynasty, Meskell, 2002, p. 65.
86. Robins, 1994, p. 27.
87. Donker van Heel, 2014, p. 81.
88. Montserrat, 1996, p. 84.
89. Robins, 1994, p. 33.
90. Ibid., p. 33.
91. Montserrat, 1996, p. 85.
92. Toivari-Viitala, 2001, p. 146.
93. Szpakowska, 2008, p. 220.
94. Watterson, 1997, p. 85.
95. Szpakowska, 2008, p. 221.
96. Robins, 1994, p. 27.
97. Meskell, 2002, p. 68.
98. Ghalioungui, P., S. H. Khalil and A. R. Ammar, 1963: 'On an Ancient Egyptian Method of Diagnosing Pregnancy and Determining Foetal Sex' in *Medical History Vol. 7 No. 3.* p. 245.
99. Robins, 1994, p. 27.
100. Meskell, 2002, p. 69.
101. Ibid., p. 79.

102. Lichtheim, 1976, p. 138.
103. Meskell, 2002, pp. 81–3.
104. Ibid., p. 69.
105. Watterson, 1997, p. 91.
106. Harer, B., 2013: 'Obstetrics in Ancient Egypt' in *KMT Vol. 24 No. 2*. pp. 47–8.
107. Wegner, J., 2002: 'A Decorated Birth-Brick from South Abydos' in *Egyptian Archaeology No. 21*. p. 3.
108. Ibid., p. 8.
109. Graves-Brown, 2010, p. 64.
110. Szpakowska, 2008, p. 29.
111. Wileman, J., 2005: *Hide and Seek. The Archaeology of Childhood.* Stroud. Tempus. p. 16.
112. Graves-Brown, 2010, p. 62.
113. Meskell, 2002, p. 70.
114. Nunn, 1996, p. 194.
115. Szpakowska, 2008, p. 210.
116. Graves-Brown, 2010, p. 65.
117. Ibid., p. 50.
118. Robins, 1994, p. 29.
119. Wileman, 2005, p. 21.
120. Lichtheim, 1976, p. 169.
121. Graves-Brown, 2010, p. 161.
122. Szpakowska, 2008, p. 213.
123. Montserrat, 1996, p. 86.
124. Nunn, 1996, p. 196.
125. Donker van Heel, 2014, p. 162.

5. Childhood

1. Janssen and Janssen, 1990, p. 76.
2. Toivari-Viitala, 2001, p. 19.
3. Lichtheim, 1976, p. 141.
4. Wileman, 2005, p. 20.
5. Szpakowska, 2008, p. 47.

6. Janssen and Janssen, 1990, p. 50.

7. Ibid., p. 52.

8. Halioua and Ziskind, 2005, p. 158.

9. Wileman, 2005, p. 64.

10. Janssen and Janssen, 1990, p. 51.

11. Meskell, 2002, p. 83.

12. Taylor and Antoine, 2014, pp. 113–129.

13. Janssen and Janssen, 1996, p. 99.

14. Meskell, 2002, p. 84.

15. Szpakowska, 2008, p. 103.

16. Toivari-Viitala, 2001, p. 189.

17. Lichtheim, 1973, p. 185.

18. Lichtheim, 1976, p. 212.

19. McDowell, 1999, p. 129.

20. Fletcher, J., 2000: *Chronicle of a Pharaoh; the Intimate Life of Amenhotep III*. Oxford. Oxford University Press. p. 26.

21. Janssen and Janssen, 1990, p. 76.

22. Ibid., 1990, p. 76.

23. Wileman, 2005, p. 48.

24. Janssen and Janssen, 1990, p. 80.

25. McDowell, 1999, p. 130.

26. Lichtheim, 1973, pp. 185–6.

27. McDowell, 1999, p. 141.

28. Lichtheim, 1976, p. 171.

29. Janssen and Janssen, 1990, p. 75.

30. McDowell, 1999, p. 142.

31. Janssen and Janssen, 1990, p. 48.

32. Ibid., 1990, p. 46.

33. Decker, 1992, p. 111.

34. Ibid., p. 113.

35. Szpakowska, 2008, p. 54.

36. Decker, 1987, p. 68.

37. Ibid., p. 67.

38. Ibid., p. 123.

39. Janssen and Janssen, 1990, p. 64.

40. Houlihan, 1996, p. 105.
41. Janssen and Janssen, 1989, p. 23.
42. Ibid., p. 23.
43. Houlihan, 1996, p. 108.
44. Janssen and Janssen, 1990, p. 42.
45. Robins, 1993, p. 122.
46. Macy Roth, A., 1991: *Egyptian Phyles in the Old Kingdom: The evolution of a System of Social Organisation.* Chicago. Oriental Institute. p. 71.
47. Nunn, 1996, pp. 170–1.
48. Toivari-Viitala, 2001, p. 194.
49. Meskell, 2002, p. 88.
50. Lord, C., 2013: 'To Be or Not to Be; Circumcision in Ancient Egypt' in *Ancient Egypt Magazine Vol. 14 No. 1 Issue 79*. p. 35.

6. Working for a Living

1. Papyrus Sallier. Janssen and Janssen, 1996, p. 99.
2. Meskell, 2002, p. 91.
3. Donker van Heel, 2014, p. 157.
4. Janssen and Janssen, 1989, p. 38.
5. Halioua and Ziskind, 2005, p. 115.
6. Decker, 1992, p. 160.
7. Tyldesley, J., 2004: 'Crime and Punishment in Ancient Egypt' in *Ancient Egypt Magazine Vol. 4 Issue 6*. p. 32.
8. Booth, C., 2005: 'A study of a Ptolemaic head in the Petrie Museum' in *Journal of Egyptian Archaeology Vol. 91* pp. 197–200.
9. Halioua and Ziskind, 2005, p. 123.
10. Manniche, 1997, p. 31.
11. Watterson, 1997, p. 128.
12. Szpakowska, 2008, p. 83.
13. Decker, 1992, p. 76.
14. Ibid., p. 87.
15. Ibid., pp. 62–3.

16. Ibid., p. 64.

17. Wernick, N. 2009: 'Timekeeping in Ancient Egypt' in *Ancient Egypt Magazine Vol. 9 No. 3 Issue 51*. pp. 29–32.

18. Partridge, R., 2002: *Fighting Pharaohs: Weapons and Warfare in Ancient Egypt*. Manchester. Peartree Publishing. p. 81.

19. For more information on these soldiers see Winlock, H., 1945: *Slain Soldiers of Neb-hept-ra*. New York. Metropolitan Museum of Art.

20. Sauneron, S., 2000: *The Priests of Ancient Egypt*. London. Cornell University Press. p. 34.

21. David, 2002, p. 198.

22. Sauneron, 2000, p. 13.

23. David, 2002, p. 200.

24. Sauneron, 2000, p. 42.

25. Ibid., p. 48.

26. Ibid., p. 36.

27. Ibid., p. 58.

28. David, 2002, p. 202.

29. Halioua and Ziskind, 2005, p. 161.

30. Donker Van Heel, 2014, p. 60.

31. Lichtheim, M., 1980: *Ancient Egyptian Literature, Volume III*. London. University of California Press. p. 96.

32. Ibid., pp. 127–138.

33. Ibid., p. 139.

34. David, 2002, p. 203.

35. Donker Van Heel, 2013, p. 70.

36. Ibid., p. 146.

37. Sauneron, 2000, p. 93.

38. Ikram, S., 1995: *Choice Cuts: Meat Production in Ancient Egypt*. Leuven. Peeters: Department Oosterse Studies. p. 110.

39. Payne, P., 2007: 'Re-excavation at the Amarna house of Panehsy' in *Egyptian Archaeology No. 3*. pp. 18–19.

40. David, 2002, p. 199.

41. Graves-Brown, 2010, pp. 25–6.

42. Ibid., p. 135.

43. Donker van Heel, 2014, p. 196.

44. Ibid., pp. 14–15.
45. David, 2002, p. 199.
46. Faulkner, 1998, p. 203.
47. Robins, 1993, p. 164.
48. Graves-Brown, 2010, p. 94.
49. Watterson, 1997, p. 37.
50. Robins, 1993, p. 118.
51. Ibid., p. 116.
52. Graves-Brown, 2010, p. 166.
53. Watterson, 1997, p. 38.
54. Graves-Brown, 2010, p. 139.
55. Robins, 1993, p. 103.
56. Graves-Brown, 2010, p. 81.
57. Szpakowska, 2008, p. 84.
58. Kemp, 1997, p. 8.
59. Sélincourt, 1972, p. 159.
60. Hall, R., 1986: *Egyptian Textiles*. Princes Risborough. Shire Publications Ltd. p. 10.
61. A rove is un-spun but brushed and cleaned wool.
62. Lichtheim, 1973, p. 188.
63. Davies, 1999, p. 84.
64. Kemp, 1997, p. 7.
65. Romer, 1984, p. 61.
66. Booth, C., 2011: 'Knitting Coptic Socks' in *Piecework Magazine Ed. US Issue December*. p. 18–22 and *Sock It!* blog. Found at http://ancientegyptiansock.blogspot.co.uk/
67. For further information on ancient Egyptian knitting see Booth, 2011.
68. Campbell Hurd-Mead, K., 1938: *A History of Women in Medicine: From the Earliest of Times to the Beginning of the Nineteenth Century*. Haddam Press. p. 16.
69. Graves-Brown, 2010, p. 83.
70. Robins, 1993, p. 117.
71. Watterson, 1997, p. 123.
72. Ostracon Letellier. Toivari-Viitala, 2001, p. 229.

73. Janssen and Janssen, 1996, p. 11.
74. Manniche, 1991, p. 9.
75. Szpakowska, 2008, p. 113.
76. Decker, 1992, p. 144.
77. Manniche, 1991, p. 49.
78. Ibid., pp. 99–100.
79. Ibid., pp. 35–6.
80. Ibid., p. 60.
81. Ibid., p. 63.
82. Green, 2002–3, p. 60.
83. Graves-Brown, 2010, p. 58.
84. Tyldesley, J., 2000: *Judgment of the Pharaoh: Crime and Punishment in Ancient Egypt*. London. Phoenix. p. 79.
85. Meskell, 2002, p. 105.
86. Donker van Heel, 2014, p. 114.
87. Ibid., p. 117.
88. Donker Van Heel, 2013, p. 38.
89. Ibid., p. 133.
90. Szpakowska, 2008, p. 111.
91. Donker van Heel, 2014, p. 114.
92. Graves-Brown, 2010, p. 75.
93. Donker van Heel, 2014, p. 119.
94. Meskell, 2002, p. 101.
95. McDowell, 1999, p. 231.
96. Ibid., p. 233.
97. Fransden, P., 1990: 'Editing Reality. The Turin Strike Papyrus' in Israelit-Groll, S. (ed.), *Studies in Egyptology Vol. 1*. Jerusalem, Magnes Press, Hebrew University. p. 168.
98. Fransden, 1990, p. 177.
99. Ibid., p. 186.
100. Translated by Fransden, 1990.
101. Ibid., pp. 189–90.

7. Legal Matters

1. Papyrus BM 10052. Peet, 1930, p. 24.
2. McDowell, 1999, p. 167.
3. Tyldesley, 2000, p. 168.
4. Tyldesley, 2004, pp. 30–1.
5. Tyldesley, 2000, p. 140.
6. Meskell, 2002, p. 110.
7. Peet, 1930, p. 19.
8. Ibid., p. 20.
9. Stocker, M., 2014: 'The Ancient Egyptian Legal system – in Life and in Death' in *Ancient Egypt Magazine Vol. 14 No. 5 Issue 83.* p. 44.
10. Manning, J. G., 2012: 'The Representation of Justice in Ancient Egypt' in *Yale Journal of Law & the Humanities Vol. 24 Issue 1 Article 4.* p. 118.
11. Peet, 1930, p. 16.
12. Ibid., p. 20.
13. Tyldesley, 2000, p. 78.
14. McDowell, 1999, pp. 165–7.
15. Stocker, 2014, p. 43.
16. Romer, 1984, p. 91.
17. Peet, 1930, p. 19.
18. Ibid., pp. 20–1.
19. Tyldesley, 2004, p. 32.
20. McDowell, 1999, p. 193.
21. Peet, 1930, p. 24.
22. Papyrus BM 10052. Peet, 1930, p. 24.
23. Tyldesley, 2000, p. 149.
24. McDowell, 1999, p. 173.
25. David, R., 2002: *Religion and Magic in Ancient Egypt.* London, Penguin. p. 280.
26. Meskell, 2002, p. 111.
27. McDowell, 1999, p. 83.
28. Toivari-Viitala, 2001, p. 68.
29. Toivari-Viitala, 2001, p. 236.

30. Sweeney, D., 2007: 'Gender and Oracular Practice in Deir el-Medina'. Based on a paper given at the workshop 'From Sumer to the Genizah: Diplomatic and Legal Documents in the Ancient World' at the Hebrew University of Jerusalem, 11–13 March, 2007. Found at https://www.academia.edu/810495/_Gender_and_Oracular_Practice_in_Deir_el-Med%C3%AEna_ p.7. [Accessed 26 May 2015.]

31. Tyldesley, 2000, p. 147.

32. Ibid., p. 151.

33. Romer, 1984, p. 103.

34. McDowell, 1999, p. 171.

35. Romer, 1984, p. 65.

36. Tyldesley, 2000, p. 60.

37. Romer, 1984, p. 80.

38. Tyldesley, 2004, p. 32.

39. Papyrus BM 10052.

40. Papyrus BM 10053. Peet, 1930, p. 23.

41. McDowell, 1999, p. 187.

42. Tyldesley, 2000, p. 66.

43. Ibid., p. 71.

44. Ostracon EA 65930.

45. Graves-Brown, 2010, p. 44.

46. Tyldesley, 2000, p. 69.

47. Ibid., p. 80.

48. McDowell, 1999, p. 186.

49. Papyri BM 10053 and BM 10068. Peet, 1930, p. 73.

50. Tyldesley, 2000, p. 41.

51. Ibid., p. 43.

52. Ibid., p. 81.

53. Graves-Brown, 2010, p. 44.

54. Watterson, 1997, p. 28.

55. Ibid., p. 23.

56. Ibid., p. 24.

57. Graves-Brown, 2010, p. 29.

58. Watterson, 1997, p. 26.

59. Graves-Brown, 2010, p. 80.

60. Ostracon GCC 25677.
61. Toivari-Viitala, 2001, p. 233.
62. Watterson, 1997, p. 31.
63. Graves-Brown, 2010, p. 72.
64. Szpakowska, 2008, p. 217.
65. Graves-Brown, 2010, p. 42.
66. Watterson, 1997, p. 32.
67. Donker van Heel, 2014, p. 2.
68. Tyldesley, 2000, p. 77.
69. Bierbrier, 1982, p. 109.
70. Ibid., p. 109.
71. Davies, 2011, p. 32.
72. Peet, 1930, p. 31.
73. Ibid., p. 17.
74. McDowell, 1999, p. 192.
75. Peet, 1930, p. 33.
76. Ibid., p. 47.
77. Ibid., p. 54.
78. Ibid., p. 104.
79. Ibid., p. 54-5.
80. Ibid., p. 119.
81. Ostracon Nash 5. Graves-Brown 2010, p. 40.
82. Nunn, 1996, p. 197.
83. Parkinson, 1995, p. 66.
84. Elliot Smith, 1908, p. 734.
85. Toivari-Viitala, 2001, p. 64.
86. Ibid., p. 219.
87. McDowell, 1999, p. 170.

8. Disease and Medicine

1. Nunn, 1996, p. 87.
2. Sélincourt, 1973, Book III, p. 203.
3. Save-Soderberg, T., 1958: *Pharaohs and Mortals*. London. Robert Hale Limited. p. 203.

4. Nunn, 1996, p. 131.
5. Reeves, C., 1992: *Egyptian Medicine*. Buckinghamshire. Shire Egyptology. p. 19.
6. Toivari-Viitala, 2001, p. 205.
7. Burden, G. M., 2005: 'Ancient Egyptian Medicine' in *Ancient Egypt Magazine Vol. 6 No. 3 Issue 33*. p. 18.
8. Meskell, 2000, p. 92.
9. Janssen and Janssen, 1996, p. 62.
10. Ibid., p. 67.
11. Ibid.
12. Ibid., p. 68.
13. Nunn, 1996, p. 136.
14. Ibid., p. 131.
15. Ibid., p. 128.
16. Sélincourt, 1972, p. 160.
17. 47,218.48 and 47,218.85.
18. Nunn, 1996, p. 135.
19. Ibid., p. 128.
20. Halioua and Ziskind, 2005, p. 120.
21. Nunn, 1996, p. 132.
22. Toivari-Viitala, 2001, p. 214.
23. Amherst Papyrus. Halioua and Ziskind, 2005, p. 162.
24. Nunn, 1996, p. 115.
25. Ibid., p. 113.
26. Stetter, 1993, p. 29.
27. Ebeid, N., 1999: *Egyptian Medicine in the Days of the Pharaohs*. Cairo. General Egyptian Book Organization. p. 58.
28. Stetter, 1993, p. 27.
29. Nunn, 1996, p. 141.
30. Cline, E. and J. Rabalcaba, 2005: *The Ancient Egyptian World*. Oxford. Oxford University Press. p. 73.
31. Ebeid, 1999, p. 253.
32. Tisserand, R., 1988: *Aromatherapy for Everyone*. London. Arkana. p. 19.
33. Nunn, 1996, p. 183.

34. Ibid., p. 182.

35. Ibid., p. 149.

36. Ibid., p. 138.

37. Ibid., p. 148.

38. Ibid., p. 173.

39. Humber, 2008, p. 42.

40. Nunn, 1996, p. 147.

41. Ibid., p. 198.

42. Manniche, 1989, p. 47.

43. Allen, J., 2005: 'The Art of Medicine in Ancient Egypt: an exhibition at the metropolitan Museum of Art' in *KMT Vol. 16 No. 3*. p. 44.

44. Nunn, 1996, p. 172.

45. Halioua and Ziskind, 2005, p. 144.

46. Nunn, 1996, p. 93.

47. David, R. (ed.), 2008: *Egyptian Mummies and Modern Science.* Cambridge. Cambridge University Press. p. 183.

48. Halioua and Ziskind, 2005, p. 116.

49. David, R. and Tapp, E., 1984: *Evidence Embalmed: Modern Medicine and the Mummies of Ancient Egypt.* Manchester. Manchester University Press. p. 95.

50. David and Tapp, 1984, p. 82.

51. Nunn, 1996, p. 81.

52. Ibid., p. 87.

53. Halioua and Ziskind, 2005, p. 132.

54. Wood Jones, F., 1908: 'Some Lessons from Ancient Fractures' in *the BMJ Vol. 2 No. 2486*. p. 456.

55. Nunn, 1996, p. 177.

56. Elliot Smith, G., 1908: 'The Most Ancient Splints' in *British Medical Journal Vol. 1 No. 2465*. p. 733.

57. Nunn, 1996, p. 177.

58. Ibid., p. 175.

59. Ibid., p. 188.

60. Ibid., p. 189.

61. Ibid., p. 144.

62. Ibid., p. 141.

63. Halioua & Ziskind 2005, p. 116.
64. Ibid., p. 137.
65. Nunn, 1996, p. 190.
66. Tisserand, 1988, p. 18.
67. Nunn, 1996, p. 133.
68. Macy-Roth, 1991, p. 68.
69. Nunn, 1996, p. 133.
70. Okasha, A., 2005: 'Mental Health in Egypt' in *Israel Journal of Psychiatry and Related Sciences No. 42.* pp. 116–25.
71. Reeves, 1992, p. 24.
72. Stetter, 1993, p. 65.
73. Nunn, 1996, p. 118.
74. Reeves, 1992, p. 21.
75. Nunn, 1996, p. 124.
76. Forshaw, R., 2009: 'Dental Health and Dentistry in Ancient Egypt' in *Ancient Egypt Magazine Vol. 9 No. 6.* p. 24.
77. David and Tapp, 1984, p. 126.
78. Samuel, D., 1994: 'A New look at Bread and Beer' in *Egyptian Archaeology No. 4.* p. 15.
79. Halioua and Ziskind, 2005, p. 161.
80. David and Tapp, 1984, p. 131.
81. Stetter, 1993, p. 31.
82. Nunn, 1996, p. 76.
83. David and Tapp, 1984, p. 130.
84. Ibid., p. 123.
85. Forshaw, 2009, p. 26.
86. Section taken from Craig, P. and J. Davey, 2001: 'Possible evidence for ancient Egyptian Orthodontics' in *Egyptian Archaeology No. 18* pp. 37–9.
87. Allen, 2005, p. 46.
88. Forshaw, 2009, p. 27.
89. David and Tapp, 1984, p. 105.
90. Halioua and Ziskind, 2005, p. 167.
91. Forshaw, 2009, p. 25.
92. Halioua and Ziskind, 2005, p. 167.

93. Forshaw, 2009, p. 24.
94. Ibid., pp. 481–6.
95. Reeves, 1992, p. 16.
96. Toivari-Viitala, 2001, p. 213.
97. Anne Austin, Stanford University, 2014. Found on http://news.stanford.edu/news/2014/november/healthcare-ancient-egypt-111714.html [accessed 19 November 2014].
98. Halioua and Ziskind, 2005, p. 129.
99. Ebers Papyrus. Nunn, 1996, p. 159.
100. Halioua and Ziskind, 2005, p. 118.

9. Death and Burial

1. Lichtheim, 1976, p. 218.
2. Toivari-Viitala, 2001, p. 207.
3. Janssen and Janssen, 1996, p. 7.
4. Romer, 1984, p. 75.
5. Janssen and Janssen, 1996, p. 5.
6. Lichtheim, 1976, p. 218.
7. Janssen and Janssen, 1996, p. 74.
8. Ibid., p. 76.
9. McDowell, 1999, p. 37.
10. Romer, 1984, p. 74.
11. Černy, 1973, p. 333.
12. Bierbrier, 1982, p. 35.
13. Černy, J., 1945: 'The Will of Naunakhte and the Related Documents' in *Journal of Egyptian Archaeology Vol. 31.* p. 31.
14. Ibid., p. 31.
15. Ibid., p. 32.
16. Bierbrier, 1982, p. 75.
17. Donker van Heel, 2014, p. 192.
18. Černy, 1945, p. 32.
19. Donker van Heel, 2014, p. 190.
20. Meskell, 2002, p. 195.
21. Tomb of Rekhmire, TT100. Janssen and Janssen, 1996, p. 92.

22. Ibid., p. 8.

23. Ibid., p. 9.

24. Ibid., p. 9.

25. Toivari-Viitala, 2001, p. 209.

26. Janssen and Janssen, 1996, p. 99.

27. Ibid., p. 103.

28. Meskell, 2002, p. 189.

29. Lichtheim, 1976, p. 218.

30. Donker van Heel, 2014, p. 168.

31. Ibid., p. 136.

32. TV Documentary, 2011: *Mummifying Alan*. Channel 4. Aired in October 2011. Taxi driver Alan Billis donated his body to be mummified according to this ancient technique.

33. Reeves, 1992, p. 41.

34. Taylor and Antoine, 2014, p. 105.

35. Ibid., p. 56.

36. Ibid., p. 125.

37. Faulkner, 1972, p. 36.

38. Ikram, S. and A. Dodson, 1998: *The Mummy in Ancient Egypt*. London. Thames and Hudson. p. 104.

39. Donker van Heel, 2014, p. 136.

40. Meskell, 2002, p. 183.

41. Ikram, S., 2005: 'Manufacturing Divinity; the Technology of Mummification' in Ikram, S. (ed.), *Divine creatures: Animal Mummies in Ancient Egypt*. Cairo. Cairo University Press. pp. 29–40.

42. Meskell, 2002, p. 190.

43. Ibid., p. 192.

44. Donker van Heel, 2014, p. 137.

45. Tyldesley, 2000, p. 172.

46. Meskell, 2002, p. 179.

47. Faulkner, 1972, p. 52.

48. Graves-Brown, 2010, p. 124.

49. Manniche, 1997, p. 105.

50. Green, 2001, p. 56.

51. Faulkner, 1972, p. 31.

52. Ibid., p. 27.
53. Donker van Heel, 2014, p. 171.
54. Lange, H. and H. Schäfer, 1902: *Grab- und Denksteine des Mittleren Reichs im Museum von Kairo*. Berlin, Reichsdruckerei. p. 3.
55. Robins, 1993, p. 175.
56. Janssen and Janssen, 1996, pp. 57–9.
57. Ibid., p. 50.
58. Meskell, 2002, p. 179; Parkinson, 1997, pp. 151–65.
59. Lichtheim, 1975, p. 196.

INDEX